AF270301

'Like the earthquake that produced the catastrophe at Fukushima, a dire cancer diagnosis produced a series of powerful aftershocks in Michael Handford's life. *Lump in My Throat* proves that an intercultural lens can help patients negotiate and survive the foreign terrain of treatment with a modicum of agency.'

Susan Gubar, author of *Memoir of a Debulked Woman*
and *Reading and Writing Cancer*

'*Lump in My Throat* is a rare and deeply human book. With honesty and grace, Michael Handford draws on his expertise in communication and culture to reflect on facing stage 4 cancer in the shadow of Fukushima. More than a memoir, it is a moving exploration of how language and connection help us endure, make meaning, and hold on to one another in the hardest times. Wise and compassionate, this book shows how communication can sustain life itself.'

James Paul Gee, author of *What Video Games Have
to Teach Us about Learning and Literacy*

'Michael Handford's story of his life before, during, and after cancer masterfully combines a deeply personal perspective with scholarly questioning and explanation. It is simultaneously tragic and funny, assertive and self-deprecating, unsettling and comforting. As a fellow linguist, I am proud that someone from my academic tribe has made such a remarkable contribution to the long-standing tradition of cancer memoirs.'

Distinguished Professor Elena Semino, lead author
of *Metaphor, Cancer and the End of Life*

'Autobiography blends beautifully with theory in this wonderful book, which illuminates the unexpected impact of cancer upon communication – with yourself, your medical team, and your loved ones. I can't recommend this enough to anyone with an interest in health and illness, culture, or communication. For someone with their own diagnosis to navigate, *Lump in My Throat* offers a unique perspective and some useful tools to help think about things a little differently.'

Dr Hannah O'Mahoney, Insight and Engagement
Lead at Tenovus Cancer Care

'This personal memoir of a life-changing event also succeeds in taking us to the everyday of the intercultural and its associated politics. The carefully crafted storytelling is a rare example of a university academic making his specialist knowledge accessible to everyone. Set in Japan, but relevant to how we all need to make sense of others and ourselves.'

Adrian Halliday, author of *Intercultural Communication & Ideology*

'In *Lump in My Throat*, Michael Handford artfully blends emotional content with a fluid, reflective style, simultaneously accomplishing a populist appeal and informing academic scholarship in the study of illness narratives. Uniquely, the *lump* is given a voice, an agency, and a narrator status, emerging as an "I" not "it" – the "communicative other" who speaks directly to the author, and indirectly to the reader.'

Srikant Kumar Sarangi, Editor-in-Chief, *Communication & Medicine*

Lump in My Throat

When faced with a cancer diagnosis, navigating the maze of emotions and decisions can be overwhelming. In this inspiring and deeply personal memoir, Michael Handford – a professor of intercultural communication – shares his experience of a stage-4 throat cancer diagnosis at the age of 42 while living and working in Japan and the UK. Weaving together his professional insights and personal experiences, and through vivid story-telling, Handford examines how communication – whether with doctors, loved ones, or oneself – can shape the cancer experience. He shows that creating meaning and agency in the face of illness can provide a sense of control amidst the chaos. This book is not just about surviving cancer but about reframing it as part of a quest for connection, resilience, and understanding. Poignant, and at times brutally funny, *Lump in My Throat* offers guidance, hope, and tools to navigate the toughest of times with dignity and strength.

MICHAEL HANDFORD is an internationally renowned academic, having held professorships and honorary fellowships at the Universities of Tokyo, Cardiff, and Birmingham. His research explores the relationship between communication and culture, often in professional settings. In 2011–12, he was treated for stage-4 throat cancer in Tokyo and Birmingham. This work interprets his cancer experiences through cultural and communication lenses.

0.1 Enjoying ice cream in Kamakura, early 2011.

MICHAEL HANDFORD

Lump in My Throat

What Cancer Taught Me about Communication

CAMBRIDGE
UNIVERSITY PRESS

CAMBRIDGE
UNIVERSITY PRESS

Shaftesbury Road, Cambridge CB2 8EA, United Kingdom

One Liberty Plaza, 20th Floor, New York, NY 10006, USA

477 Williamstown Road, Port Melbourne, VIC 3207, Australia

314–321, 3rd Floor, Plot 3, Splendor Forum, Jasola District Centre,
New Delhi – 110025, India

Cambridge University Press is part of Cambridge University Press & Assessment,
a department of the University of Cambridge.

We share the University's mission to contribute to society through the pursuit
of education, learning and research at the highest international levels of
excellence.

www.cambridge.org
Information on this title: www.cambridge.org/9781009631396
DOI: 10.1017/9781009631372

© Michael Handford 2026

When citing this work, please include a reference to the
DOI 10.1017/9781009631372

First published 2026

A catalogue record for this publication is available from the British Library

*A Cataloging-in-Publication data record for this book is available from the Library
of Congress*

ISBN 978-1-009-63139-6 Hardback

Cambridge University Press & Assessment has no responsibility for the
persistence or accuracy of URLs for external or third-party internet websites
referred to in this publication and does not guarantee that any content on such
websites is, or will remain, accurate or appropriate.

For EU product safety concerns, contact us at Calle de José Abascal, 56, 1°,
28003 Madrid, Spain, or email eugpsr@cambridge.org.

For Julia and Maya

Contents

CONTENTS

Preface

I had been living in Japan for several years when the earthquakes of 2011 struck: the physical Fukushima earthquake and its aftermath, and the metaphorical earthquake of a stage-4 throat cancer diagnosis six months later. I was a professor of intercultural communication at the University of Tokyo, but before the events of 2011, I had never expected that my academic interests would come to my aid in dealing with such traumatic events. My ivory tower, like other aspects of my world, broke into many pieces, making me unlearn much of what I had assumed. But from the wreckage, and with the support of loved ones, I built a better classroom from where I could relearn this different world.

What were the contents of this unlearning and relearning? As a bat explores the world in the echoes that sounds make, intercultural researchers (sometimes annoyingly) notice cultural identities through their echoes in communication. But in the face of disasters, both the paucity and the necessity of communication become clear. It is through recounting the events of 2011 that I explore the book's main themes of communication and culture. I think awareness of these themes, and how they interact, can help us deal with disasters a little less badly than we might otherwise.

On one level, my experiences could be seen as 'inter-cultural' because, as a British national, I was living in a different national culture when these earthquakes happened. But I emphasise that a cross-national comparison is not the main point of the book. Indeed, one of the central ideas I explore here (and in my academic research) is how we should engage critically with assumptions like 'different nationality=different culture'. In the sorrowful and uncertain months following the Fukushima earthquake, for instance, I'll explain how I felt more a part of society, more at home, than I had at any time, anywhere.

The book is not, therefore, a story of a foreigner's difficult journey in an exotic foreign land, bumping clumsily into cultural obstacles he doesn't understand while obliviously offending the locals. *Every* cancer diagnosis is a difficult series of new events and interactions that require communicating differently. With doctors, yes, but also with loved ones, and even with yourself. This is the case wherever you are. So while seeing cancer through an 'intercultural lens' will not cure your cancer, it may help you navigate the overwhelming new reality of a cancer diagnosis.

Six months after my treatment had finished, I was to spend a year in the UK, and received follow-up care at the University of Birmingham's Queen Elizabeth Hospital. This experience felt equally intercultural as my time at the University of Tokyo Hospital, despite my being born just an hour's drive from Birmingham. Once again, I was initially a novice in that environment, very much an outsider; but once again, this changed over time. I had to communicate with healthcare professionals who had their own jargon, tools, communicative styles, practices, and expectations. And I had to negotiate some degree of agency, some control over my situation. This sometimes caused friction, given that, like all patients, I was in a relatively powerless position. But I was able to become more expert in dealing with these professionals. I was able to learn how to negotiate my needs, which partly involved adopting some of their cultural practices and communicative norms, as well as navigating around certain stereotypes they had of me as a cancer patient.

As a cancer patient, or a carer of a cancer patient, you can often feel powerless. There's the initial overwhelming sense of impotence, a reaction to the diagnosis itself. And for a minority of people who get cancer, it will kill them. I don't know what living the time between unsuccessful treatment and death is like, and I cannot presume to know. But at the most elemental level, there is powerlessness to stop the cancer progressing.

For many cancer patients, there's also the powerlessness you feel, and are arguably positioned to feel, in the various institutions you have to engage with. I'm thinking particularly of hospitals, oncology departments, pharmacies, and so on. You have to follow their procedures; they are certainly less interested in following yours. Sometimes it seems the loyalties of doctors may be more to the practices of the healthcare system and other doctors than it is to you, the patient. And there may be very worthy reasons why that is so, frustrating as it may be. In this book I'll be talking about how my wife Mayu and I managed to negotiate more agency at times, and where at other times we did not. I still regret not being a more disagreeable patient at certain moments.

Much time with cancer is spent apart from the healthcare system, and herein lies other opportunities for greater agency. Exercising informed choices about diet, or exercise, or work, or rest can help provide a greater sense of control in the face of the new reality. I hesitate to say doing this will build more 'resilience', but I do think for many of us, exercising some degree of control following something like a cancer diagnosis is beneficial. If nothing else, it can provide some semblance of meaning in the chaos. And such semblances can, over time, with the support and compassion of others, be nurtured into something approaching resilience.

A word on the way I've organised this book. One of the most challenging things about writing *Lump in My Throat* was figuring out what to do with my academic voice. After all, the intended value, and I think originality, of this book is the application of ideas from communication and intercultural communication studies to the context of cancer. In an earlier draft, one of my friends said the tone, when I was talking about the conceptual stuff, could at times be 'too didactic, hectoring even'. So that had to change. I decided to remove a lot of the explicit conceptual discussions from the main body, and to develop the Notes section at the back of the book. This now contains references and some discussion of the theoretical side, part of the academic undercarriage of the book, as it were. When I was going through cancer treatment and afterwards, my concentration was not the best. For readers who may be feeling the same, the book can therefore be read as a whole, without reading the Notes. But for readers who want to understand more of the why, or to follow up some of the ideas in the book, the Notes section should be useful. Similarly, the Postscript chapter considers some of the implications of my arguments for medical care and is written in a more academic register.

For readers who might prefer not to read a whole book, but instead want to read about specific aspects like diagnosis, most chapters can be read on their own. But as I explain in the Postscript, this book is a narrative, and of a particular kind. Arthur Frank's *The Wounded Storyteller: Body, Illness, and Ethics* describes three types of stories of the sick: one where we get healthy again, or at least hope to; one where the illness throws our life into chaos; and one where the illness might be used for some wider purpose, like helping others. Frank terms this final type a quest narrative. While drawing on all three types of narrative (as many illness stories do), this book is intended to be a quest narrative, one that describes my attempts to move beyond the chaos. For many, a cancer diagnosis descends us into chaos: what we think of as normal is no longer so, and we can feel physically and emotionally petrified, frozen by threat. And that's before we confront the burns, cuts, and toxins of cancer treatment. *Lump in My Throat* is offered as a case study of how certain concepts and tools and practices can help us refind meaning in the face of a cancer diagnosis. With a greater sense of meaning, a greater sense of agency may then emerge.

Introduction

Is cancer a noun, or is it a verb? In other words, is it something we have, or is it something we do? Thirty years ago in his essay titled 'Culture is a Verb', the anthropologist Brian Street asked whether it might be more beneficial to see culture as a verb instead of a noun. What he meant was, seeing culture not in terms of what it is, but instead in terms of what it does, and what we do to recreate it, can help us understand the proper nature of culture, that trickiest of concepts to define.

Culture is being constantly recreated by the actions that people in groups perform. 'It's the way we do things round here' is one definition of culture, with a focus on 'we' (not 'you'), 'do' (not 'have') and 'round here' (not 'over there'). I wonder if we might see cancer in the same way, so rather than seeing it as something people have, it is something that people do. And given that one in two people will get cancer during their lifetime, it's something we all do, some as carers, some as patients. I think seeing cancer in this way increases agency. If cancer is a noun, it's very hard to change it; if cancer is a verb, it's something we do, and we can change our actions to suit our aims. I hope this book will be helpful for those seeking ways of finding the appropriate actions.

Given that this book both draws on and seeks to extend applications of intercultural communication, it's worth briefly clarifying what I mean by it (and there's more in the Notes section). We can contrast two different approaches to intercultural communication, the predominant, mainstream approach, and the critical approach. The mainstream approach sees intercultural competence in terms of knowing a lot about other cultures, especially cultural differences with your own culture. 'In Japan, take your slippers off when you walk on a tatami mat' – that kind of thing. And such behaviours are often tied to values – 'That's because the Japanese are very polite.' The critical approach takes the opposite view. Rather than seeing the focus on cultural differences and the use of stereotypes to explain behaviour as a solution, it sees the mainstream approach as a problem.

Let me give an example from my own experience. When talking to my wonderful Japanese oncologist 'Dr Nishi', I typically saw my identity as a research-engaged patient searching for evidenced answers as most relevant, but he tended to see my British, foreign, identity, and put my behaviour down to that. 'Oh, you like to get dressed out of your pyjamas, that must be because you're British ... Oh, you keep questioning the treatment plan, that's your Britishness I guess.' As a result, I didn't feel my queries were always dealt with meaningfully, and I didn't feel I was being seen as a full person in all my admittedly diminished glory. He was a brilliant oncologist, whose expertise undoubtedly helped save my life, but to my mind he'd bought wholesale into the mainstream intercultural approach. So I learnt to work around his stereotypes, by explicitly framing my concerns in medical terms. Sometimes using the (Japanese) jargon of oncology worked, sometimes bringing in clinical studies helped. But sometimes nothing worked. I also realised that some of the 'You're so British' stuff was intended as a way of building a relationship, banter in dark times, so I would laugh through my critical teeth.

I was applying insights from the critical intercultural approach to help me, a patient, navigate the healthcare system. The critical approach examines how power and stereotypes affect interactions, and is employed in this book, and in my research. The approach is critical in two ways: in the academic sense of seeking to 'look under the carpet' (or 'under the tatami mat' as the Japanese say) by questioning common beliefs about how society works, in this case about communication in society. In so doing, better ways of thinking and acting can be found. But it's also critical of (as in negative towards) the mainstream intercultural approach. With the slippers, or my pyjamas, the focus is on behaviour in terms of national differences, and the mainstream approach explains the behaviour with a well-trodden stereotype. The critical approach argues that focusing on culture at the national level is often a distraction from what is really going on, and largely serves to reinforce stereotypes. By being aware of stereotypes and pushing against them, we can then improve things in society. In healthcare scenarios, for instance, this awareness can lead to better outcomes; lack of awareness has been shown to lead to very bad outcomes.

The difference between the academic mainstream and critical orientations is therefore also about the different stakes. Not knowing you shouldn't wear slippers when walking on a tatami mat is the kind of mistake you can easily make, and which mainstream intercultural experts love to talk about, but you tend to make it only once. You apologise and move on (barefoot). The stakes of stereotyping people from some group can be much higher. In healthcare situations, for instance, differing survival rates for different ethnic groups can be partly explained by the stereotypes about such groups. But even among little children, stereotypes can cause damage and should be called out – though, as I'll describe later, in our experience they may be swept under the school carpet.

Outside of this chapter, as I noted in the Preface, I've tried to make this book light on explicit theory, instead weaving in personal anecdotes and brief mentions of relevant concepts from critical intercultural communication and related fields. One such concept that runs through the book is othering, the way people can perceive someone from a different group as inherently separate and often less than 'us'. It is something we can all be prone to. We reduce the other's individuality by saying they do X because it's their culture or they can't help it, and may exaggerate their perceived threats or negative aspects. We know that sexism or racism are very much othering in action, but it can happen with any type of social category, such as profession, social class, school, and often nationality. And, as I discovered, it can happen when you become a cancer patient.

When you're diagnosed with cancer, you may find yourself experiencing othering in multiple ways. Sometimes it comes from people who lack understanding of your situation. Sometimes it comes from medical institutions. And sometimes – perhaps most disturbingly – it comes from within yourself, as you begin to feel estranged from your own body.

In this book I discuss some instances of othering I've seen, experienced and been guilty of. I do this for two reasons. One because the topics in this book allow for some original reflection on the topic of othering, but more importantly because I argue this concept may help us understand the new, brutal reality of a cancer diagnosis, the emotional chaos accompanying it, and some avenues out of the chaos. And as I'll say towards the end of the book, there are some parallels between racial othering, cancer-related othering, and how we might push back against them. This is the value of a critical intercultural orientation: by shining a light on problems, it can guide us towards solutions, sometimes solutions relevant to one problem (e.g. discrimination) and applied to another (e.g. cancer).

Perhaps surprisingly, being othered can open certain avenues – the less well-signposted ones. You may be motivated to find healthcare providers who see you for who you are; you may build connections with others who share your experiences; and you may find a sense of unexpected freedom by subverting or ignoring the opinions of others. And while I'd say Dr Nishi lightly othered me when he kept attributing my behaviour or requests to my being British, that did partly motivate me to become a particularly engaged type of patient. And that, in turn, also improved my Japanese. As I'll recount in later chapters, my family being racially othered has eventually led to outcomes of which they, we, can be proud.

In 'normal' times, when we're in what Susan Sontag in her book *Illness as Metaphor* refers to as the Kingdom of the Well, I think we can look at communication in at least three ways. There's interpersonal communication (for instance between friends, or loved ones, or strangers we don't perceive as different), intercultural communication (which can also be between doctors and patients), and the emotional and cognitive communication within each of us (including the stories and metaphors we use to see ourselves and the world), called intrapersonal communication.

As I've said, as a patient we might feel like an 'other' sometimes, depending on how we are treated. But my argument is, with a cancer diagnosis, you may feel like an other in all three communicative situations: you may feel distanced from strangers, acquaintances, or even loved ones, and they may struggle to understand you. Sometimes no words seem appropriate. But you can also feel a sense of otherness within, like you are no longer at home in your own body. You have a thing inside you that may kill you, and yet you cannot get away from this most genuine of threats.

As a person with cancer, you may be othered, sometimes by people who may lack empathy for, or are ignorant of, your plight. This may involve blaming you for your cancer, for example, or dismissing you as a person because your ability to communicate has been affected by the treatment, or even dismissing you from your job. Perhaps you are physically marked, following radical surgery to your face or body. You may have less control over your bodily functions, which in public can lead to disgust on the part of strangers. I remember being rather revulsed on a train in Tokyo because a young woman was constantly hacking up green mucus and spitting it slowly into a paper cup. A year later, soon after the radiation treatment had started, I found myself doing the same.

But this is not the only conception of othering that I mean: it is that as someone either with cancer, or if someone we care about has been diagnosed with cancer, we may well see the cancer itself as the ultimate other. What do I mean by that? Cancer is not a person, it's a physical growth, so how can we otherise something that is a non-thinking collection of cells? The thing is, we do. We have an emotional reaction to a cancer diagnosis, one that may never fully leave us, even if our treatment finished years before and we've long returned to our pre-cancer lives. Cancer threatens our very existence, and the trauma of its diagnosis can require many retellings. These retellings are often of our relationship with this other that once almost killed us and may one day return.

Long after it has left the bodies of those who have survived, cancer can linger in our minds. In terms of how this relates to cancer as 'the other', this book will show that having cancer does not necessarily entail seeing it as something horrific; nor does its lingering shadow need to be horrific. I'm not saying you should love cancer (although some people do develop such a relationship with it). But as intercultural communication training can help us reduce the way we perceive people different from us as other, I think it is possible to have a relationship with your cancer that is nuanced and potentially positive, at least in some ways.

Many of the world's religions stress that our over-attachment to this world is a cause of suffering, and that accepting the transitory, impermanent nature of life can allow us to achieve some peace. I'm an atheist, but I wholly believe this to be the case. And something like a cancer diagnosis brings that message crashing home, crashing into our home, breaking down the front door and the walls in the process. But the deep, personal realisation that things like cancer or earthquakes can threaten the permanence of our existence is often followed by another realisation. Life itself is fleeting, transient, despite our sustained strutting and fretting.

We cannot will away cancer: moving beyond seeing cancer as a threatening, malignant, unknowable thing will not remove cancer cells from our bodies. It can, however, help give you more freedom, more agency during your journey or battle or time with cancer. In the preceding sentence you'll notice I frame cancer in three ways: as a journey, a battle, and as something we spend time with. The first two are clearly metaphorical, in that they help us understand our relationship with cancer by seeing it as something we travel with or something we fight against. They are two of the most common ways of describing cancer.

In later chapters I'll be discussing these different metaphors in much more depth, because metaphor sits at the heart of this book. I'll outline the way I made my own cancer metaphor, and how it helped. I'll also discuss some of the recent research on the topic of metaphor-making when you have cancer. The metaphor can define the relationship we have with cancer, and therefore how we think about dealing with this new reality. This is one of the ways we can move beyond seeing cancer as the threatening, potentially disabling other, and instead have more control over our lot. A little metaphor can quieten, even momentarily, the overwhelming mental chaos a cancer diagnosis begets.

CHAPTER 1

Contrasts

Shit, I'm meant to be there in ninety minutes!

What turned out to be the most important hospital appointment in my life, and I'd forgotten about it. It was September 2011, and I was having lunch with my friend David at our favourite Indian restaurant. We were about to go for a coffee afterwards when he casually asked me about my neck. I was to find out much later that he was feigning nonchalance, having become deeply worried about the possibility of something sinister growing in my throat. The coffee would have to wait.

I ran to the station, jumped on the train, then another train, then taxi, making it just in time to the Fujisawa Shimin Hospital. After I'd filled out the pre-examination questionnaire, the doctor, Dr Aoki, had a feel of my neck, asked a few more questions. Producing a large syringe, he extracted some stuff from the gland area just below my left jaw. I also had a scan of some kind. I needed to come back on Monday, he said, but I needn't worry as it was probably nothing.

When I returned on the Monday, his demeanour was different. 'But then it is Monday, nobody likes Mondays', I thought at first. He sat me down and said that more tests needed to be done today, including a biopsy and another scan. 'Biopsy?' Yes, he was fairly certain it was cancer, probably in my tonsils. He sprayed some useless anaesthetic on the back of my throat and extracted a piece of my tonsil, about half a pea in size. It was my first wincing step on the painful path that is neck-cancer treatment. To say it was like someone tearing out a small lump of your throat would be wrong, as there was no 'like' about it.

He said a CT scan could be done the same day if I could wait a couple of hours. I said yes, and decided to make the call to Mayu at her office.

Hello, Japan Nursing Federation.
Hello, can I speak to Mayu Handford please.
Just a moment please.
Hello?
Hi it's me. I'm at the hospital now.
Oh hi, is it OK if I call you back, I'm just in a meeting. Speak to you later.
No Mayu. Stop. I think you better come to the hospital now. The doctor thinks it
  may be cancer.

After the silence it must take for someone to process that, she said she'd leave immediately. Afterwards, her colleague recalled watching her take that call, and noticing how she seemed to involuntarily jerk forward, then wither slightly.

Within the space of two weeks I'd gone from blithely contemplating my future, to being told that it was very likely I had throat cancer. All change. But the week wasn't all bad news.

On the Thursday afternoon I received confirmation my colleagues had unanimously rubber-stamped my promotion, and with that I became, at the time, one of very few foreign tenured professors at the University of Tokyo. Along with being bestowed in recognition of my research, in hindsight I can see that it was also a sign of deep trust. It was acceptance by my Japanese colleagues into a rather hallowed part of Japanese society, and I remain humbled by the fact they chose me.

But on that day, I hadn't waited around for the result, or to celebrate with colleagues. Instead I just needed to go home to see Mayu and the girls. I was being pulled back home, pulled by the utterness of the present. In her poem 'Nostos' Louise Glück wrote, 'We look at the world once, in childhood. The rest is memory.' I think this is true when people are resident in what Susan Sontag terms the Kingdom of the Well. But being transferred to the Kingdom of the Very, Very Sick involves a radical shift in how we see the world. Now I could feel the present throbbing inside me, and much as I longed to grasp it I could not prevent its imminent passing.

Promotion to professor at the tender age of 42, and a stage-4 cancer diagnosis at the tender age of 42, indeed in the same week. 'Where's the humour?' my friend Larry would often say, encouraging us to look on the lighter side of dark moments. At that moment, though, I thought,

'Where's the humour when you're faced with a tumour, Larry?' But he was right, I suspected, from a distance.

That Thursday I got off the train at Fujisawa as usual, and walked up the stairs to the concourse with the hundreds of passengers returning home from central Tokyo. Instead of heading straight towards the exit I veered left towards the station's food court and to Ashi, our favourite cake shop, to pick up the cake Mayu had ordered in expectation of the promotion.

Six months after the Fukushima triple disaster, the lights in the delicatessens were again bright, back to Japan-bright, and the concerns of Fujisawa shoppers had returned to shopping. Strangers no longer smiled or stopped to thank me for being in Japan. Going for a jog in the neighbourhood no longer drew looks of appreciation. Shelves in shops were full again, shoppers were in a rush again, and strangers glanced at me before looking away. Perhaps a child or a certain adult might stare – all signs that the practices of normality were returning. I stood watching the suited businessmen and women and housewives and high-school kids busily building their memories again. They were wrapped in the cacophony of deli-smells: garlic coffee vanilla paprika pork chocolate chilli matcha, and I envied these strangers. It was an envy of their regained certainty of future.

Ashi was tiny, a glass counter with a glistening rainbow of coloured cakes exuding entrancing smells, and five chirpy staff squeezed behind. I caught one of the women's attention and asked for the cake ordered in the name of Handofoudo, the Japanese pronunciation of my surname. They'd written a little message, 'Shuku Kyouju', 'Celebrating your Professorship', on the cake. She displayed it to me with a slight bow of the head, her glance respectfully withdrawing, and the slightest rightways shift in her posture. I smiled with my mouth and paid.

I got home, and as usual the girls ran downstairs shouting 'Daddy! Daddy! Daddy!', giving me a welcome-home kiss, one popped wetly on each cheek. We hadn't told the girls about the painless lump in my neck, the tests, or the appointment tomorrow for the official diagnosis. There was always a small, very small, chance it might be negative. So this was the last night of their permanent Daddy, and they buzzed around me, shining as normal, jolly in their ignorance.

'Where's the cake? Where's the cake?' I gave it to Julia, and little Maya barged in to take half the bag, knocking Julia and the bag against the wall. A hand on each of their intricate shoulders, I felt their strength guiding me upstairs to the living room, where the subtle saltiness of the dinner greeted my nostrils. Mayu had laid out the table and prepared a sumptuous spread of sushi – the large wooden bowl full of vinegared rice, squares of seaweed, dishes of soy sauce and wasabi and ginger, plates of raw tuna, salmon, octopus, bream, egg roll, and those options I stayed away from: salmon roe, sea urchin and fermented soybeans (natto).

Natto, like Marmite: you love it or hate it. I took pride in my daughters' bicultural tastes and many faceted investments that Mayu and I had made to raise them as such. They loved both natto and Marmite, and many other things besides, things that a monocultural existence would have denied them. Their biculturalism meant, and continues to mean, so much more than being able to speak two languages as mother tongues. They could operate in different societies with dexterity and do so with growing self-awareness. They agree that this has meant more challenges in life, probably more sadness even. But whereas most of us have to understand the ways of 'the other' through trial and error, they live with a naturally acquired understanding that 'common sense' is only a local

1.1 Mayu and the girls with my cake.

construct, one of many. And conversely, they know that other ways of doing things may be equally good, if not better. I look at them now as young adults, and delight in the authenticity, and ability to think critically, that their upbringing has enabled.

The little girls reached the top of the stairs, cake still intact. They handed it to Mayu, buzzing around legs. For a long second of silence, Mayu's eyes sought out mine as she held the cake, feelings crackling between our minds. Then, back to parenthood.

After the sushi the girls brought the cake out, a white-chocolate log with the message and some candles, singing 'Happy Professor to you', and encouraging me to blow out the candles. I did so, but was wondering how I'd eat this with no appetite. But Ashi doesn't disappoint, and I couldn't disappoint my girls. Mayu and I shared looks as we ate, with meaning beyond knowing. I felt Larry's rhetorical question come back to mind, in this gap between sudden absurdity and well-trodden normality. In the eating of chocolate cake with my three darlings on a night like this (Figure 1.1).

CHAPTER 2

Diagnosis

The morning after the little promotion party, Mayu and I got the girls off to school, then drove to Fujisawa Shimin Hospital to get the results from the biopsy. 'Shimin', which rhymes with 'brimming', means something like 'Citizens' or 'City Residents', and is the main hospital for the Fujisawa-city area. Like many such hospitals in Japan, its reputation among local residents isn't great. In fact, as a fine demonstration of the darker tones of Japanese humour, the nickname for the hospital is 'Fujisawa Shinin Hospital'. 'Shinin' means corpse – so the translation would be something like Fujisawa Hospital for Corpses. And 'shin' is the word for death, so 'shin' followed by 'in' also sounds like death-ing, or dying. And that's where I was going for my biopsy results, and it was the most likely place I would receive treatment in the event of the now-expected positive diagnosis.

I must say, though, the staff at the hospital were excellent, even if the place itself could do with some brightening up. This was the third time I'd met Dr Aoki about the painless, slightly swollen gland in my neck. He invited us into his office, and confirmed that it was indeed cancer, following the biopsy, blood tests, and the CT scan. The consultation was brief, and he said to come back on the Monday when we could talk about treatment options and so on. He was utterly professional, compassionate yet sufficiently detached. Detached except for the final exchange:

So yes, please come back and we can discuss various options for treatment. Of course,
  we can offer you treatment here. Erm sorry, can I ask why you're smiling?
Oh, it's just the timing. I was promoted to professor yesterday.
Professor of the University of Tokyo?
Yes.
Yesterday?
Yes.

He looked me in the eye for what seemed a long time. Then he got up, took my hand in his and shook it, pursed his lips into something like a grimace, and left the room without another word. The nurse called after him, but he just raised his right hand as if to say 'not now' as he walked away, head down.

He'd written several words on a piece of paper that he'd translated into English, assuming I wouldn't be able to understand them in Japanese. He was wrong. I couldn't understand most of them in English either: metastasis, stage 4, oropharyngeal, human papilloma virus (HPV), squamous carcinoma, TNM. All new words, all bad. Usually I enjoy learning new words, in fact I get a little kick of dopamine from browsing dictionaries, which might explain my choice of work. But I got little in the way of mental highs when checking these words out. Here are the definitions from the National Cancer Institute website dictionary:

Oropharyngeal cancer	Cancer that forms in tissues of the oropharynx (the part of the throat at the back of the mouth, including the soft palate, the base of the tongue, and the tonsils).
Squamous carcinoma of the head and neck	Cancer of the head and neck begins in squamous cells (thin, flat cells that form the surface of the skin, eyes, various internal organs, and ducts of some glands). Squamous cell carcinoma of the head and neck includes cancers of the nasal cavity, sinuses, lips, mouth, salivary glands, throat, and larynx (voice box). Most head and neck cancers are squamous cell carcinomas.
Staging	The extent of a cancer in the body. Staging is usually based on the size of the tumour, whether lymph nodes contained cancer, and whether the cancer has spread from the initial site to other parts of the body. Whereas stage 0 means cancerous cells are present, they have not spread to nearby tissue. This is not cancer, but may become so. Stages 1–3 represent the degree to which the cancer has spread into nearby tissues.
Stage 4	Interestingly, the NCI website doesn't say much about stage 4. But on Cancer.Net, there is the following brief explanation: 'This stage means the cancer has spread to other organs or parts of the body. It may also be called advanced or metastatic cancer.' As Christopher Hitchens said before dying of stage 4 cancer, there is no stage 5.
Metastasis	The spread of cancer cells from the place where they first formed to another part of the body. In metastasis, cancer cells break away from the original (primary) tumour, travel through the blood or lymph system, and form a new tumour in other organs or tissues

in the body. The new, metastatic tumour is the same type of cancer as the primary tumour. For example, if breast cancer spreads to the lung, the cancer cells in the lung are breast cancer cells, not lung cancer cells.

TNM (tumour, lymph node, metastasis)	A system to describe the amount and spread of cancer in a patient's body, using TNM. T describes the size of the tumour and any spread of cancer into nearby tissue; N describes the spread of cancer to nearby lymph nodes; and M describes metastasis (spread of cancer to other parts of the body).
HPV (human papilloma virus)	A type of virus that can cause abnormal tissue growth (for example, warts) and other changes to cells. Infection for a long time with certain types of HPV can cause cervical cancer. HPV may also play a role in some other types of cancer, such as anal, vaginal, vulvar, penile, and oropharyngeal cancers.

The CNI site doesn't mention that HPV is a sexually transmitted virus, albeit one that some estimates say 80 per cent of people get during their lifetime. The vast bulk of those who've caught it never know that they've become infected, and it usually disappears without any physical trace. Lucky you. It can be caught through oral sex, and there is evidence suggesting it can even be caught through open-mouth kissing. Apparently, the increasing popularity in the modern world of oral sex, and various other sexual practices, such as rimming, help account for the increase in the spread of the virus. There are 100 types of the virus, and some of them have been shown to cause cancer. For instance, nearly all cervical cancers are caused by a type of HPV. My type was HPV16, which is a common cause of head and neck cancers.

HPV is a bit of a mixed blessing I came to realise, in terms of the expected outcome after treatment – in other words, the prognosis. No one wants to be told they've had a sexually transmitted infection, even though four out of five people will contract it; when I've spoken to people about HPV, it's funny how many of them don't seem to accept this statistic. I'd say it's because it implies they've had it, or will get it, during their life. Anyway, with HPV-related throat cancers, the survival rates for five years following treatment are quite a lot higher than non-HPV-related throat cancers, the ones that are more directly caused by smoking and drinking. Dr Aoki said he didn't know if I'd had HPV without doing more tests, so couldn't tell if that was a factor. He was also quick to explain, I imagine for Mayu's benefit, that I could have caught HPV when I was much younger. It can lie dormant, and then trigger cancers many years later. It was unusual for someone in their early forties to have throat cancer, but given my history as a previously heavy smoker who drank, it was possible. He also mentioned that for stage 4 oropharyngeal cancer, the odds of surviving more than five years were around 20 per cent.

We needed to come back to the hospital at 1:30 p.m. for some more blood tests, which gave us an hour or so. We headed out onto the main street to find somewhere to eat, and found a dual carriageway with various tatty shops and small offices lining the pavement. The kind of forgettable street you get all over the smaller towns and cities of Japan, cloaked in drabness during the day, and illuminated by tawdry neon signs at night. We didn't know this side of town, the north-side of Fujisawa, and there were few restaurants or cafes. Eventually we found a place that was open, a Mexican-themed steak house. It was dark inside, a restaurant that had clearly seen better days, with faded polaroid photos hanging on and off the walls of long-past events and happier customers. Somebody wandered over, and we ordered something. We knew we had to eat, we had to get through the rest of the day.

But at that point I was having to remind myself to breathe. My mind was in chaos, I was in chaos. I felt like my feet were glued to a road at night, while a huge truck was speeding towards me; but there was another feeling, a sense of shrinking, a fast disappearing from myself, and from the other people in my life. Even from Mayu, who was sat on the opposite side of this scratched, dirty table. I remember placing my hands down on it, to try to get some sense of balance, and my fingers stuck to some old beer stain. I felt revulsion at the stickiness, and then almost started crying for my now dirty hand. I said to Mayu I needed to wash my hands, and she hardly looked up.

There are moments with cancer where language loses its facility to make meaning, where the relationship between words and ideas no longer align. Eventually this facility may return, and we can again make stories of where we are and what's happening to us. But at this moment, as we sat there, it was like our shared story, our home, had been ripped from us. We could only see my probable death, and our inability to do much about it. I felt I'd become detached, displaced from myself, and from those I loved. My body had become alien to me, and I had become alien, other.

There's a frequently heard word in Japanese, *Ganbarou*, which translates as something like 'let's do our best/let's try hard/let's get through this/fight on/we need to endure'. It was a word we uttered a lot in the coming months, until it no longer seemed to fit; you can reach a point with some cancer treatments where the idea of 'doing your best' belongs to a different time and place. But today, we needed to find the will to act, so we said *ganbarou* to each other, many times. I don't remember us saying much else with words.

We had to tell the girls, I had to tell the girls. Some parents choose to not tell their kids about a cancer diagnosis, others do. We'd never been the type of parents to keep much from them really, and even in the best-case scenario (not dying), they'd notice some changes: I'd lose my hair, a lot of weight and my energy, and be in hospital for months. So there was no doubt about what to do. But knowing what to do doesn't mean you can do it. I had a little time in the afternoon before Julia would be back from school, and then I'd walk across the bridge to collect Maya from the nursery. On Fridays Julia's school finished at 3:00 p.m. When she got back I was sitting in her bedroom, looking out of the French windows at the view. It was a glorious autumn day, the summer haze had gone, leaving cloudless cobalt-blue sky views of Mt Fuji, the Hakone Mountains and silver Pacific to its left, and to its right the Japanese Alps.

Hi, Mummy and Daddy, I'm home.
Hi darling, I'm in your room, can you come here?

She didn't reply at first.

OK, did I do something wrong? Is my room too messy?

I chuckled. It was permanently messy.

No, you didn't do anything wrong Julia. Come and sit next to me for a minute, I
have to tell you something.

She sat down next to me on the bed.

I've got some bad news.

She looked up at me, the worry obvious in her eight-year old eyes. The words just wouldn't come out. I coughed, my throat constricted. I rubbed my neck to see if I could get it working. Dry tears hacked out of me.

I've got cancer.

My breath became a little less ragged as I hugged her. She began to cry, and asked,

Are you going to die?

My mind was trying to come to terms with the thought that this might well happen, and the honest answer was 'Probably'. But I couldn't say that to her. 'How do you do this?' I thought. Up until now I had protected my daughters from any pain I could, I was the solid permanent force that fathers want to be. Being a father was the thing I was most proud of, the thing I knew I did better than anything else. At this moment, I felt myself disintegrate. My being was now so temporary, so unbearably light. Nothing had, or could, prepare me for this. The greatest joy of my life had been the love I'd felt for my daughters, and here it was, tearing at me.

I don't think so. I don't think so Julia.

We sat there on the bed, embracing, crying.

In hindsight, I let out too much, putting too much emotion on her little plate. I would like to have been more composed, less ragged. I do feel that Julia's world, Julia's love, developed a fracture, a conditionality that no young child should have to accept. But I also wonder if all cancer patients have at least one conversation that is too much, placing you beyond the bounds of your emotional, communicative self. Looking back at everything I experienced during this time, this conversation was the worst moment. It was not the realisation that I might die. It was the scream in my heart's deepest core that my daughters were very possibly going to grow up without a father who loved them so very much. This realisation made my mind flail uncontrollably, it defeated me.

After a while Mayu came in, and the three of us sat on the bed hugging. Mayu suggested we go upstairs to the living room, and she made a cup of tea. I had to now pick up Maya, and tell her. At least she was so small that she wouldn't realise about the threat to life, and I wasn't going to tell her. I went by myself. It was less than ten minutes' walk from the house; the air and the moment by myself gave me back some equilibrium. As we walked back I told her I was sick, and that I'd have to go to the hospital for a while. 'Can I come and see you in the hospital?' she asked. I picked her up and said she could come and see me anytime she liked, and she could watch TV in my hospital bed if I had one. I told her I'd be losing some weight, which she didn't seem to think was a bad thing. As we passed Fuji Supermarket she asked if we could go in and buy some ice creams to take home.

CHAPTER 3

Home

Thursday 10 March 2011 was the day before the Fukushima earthquake happened, around six months before my cancer experience began. It must have been like any other early spring Tokyo weekday, a day lost in the repetition of normality. In her book *The Year of Magical Thinking* Joan Didion says this is how we make sense of troubles: 'confronted with sudden disaster we all focus on how unremarkable the circumstances were in which the unthinkable occurred'. The context of disaster is given meaning through the practices of the mundane.

I would have left my office at the university at around 4:30 p.m., exiting the campus through the famous Akamon ('Red Gate') towards the subway station (Figure 3.1). This always involved an emotional shift, a slight bracing. I stepped onto the main road, and out of my assured and valued professional identity. I felt at home on campus, and at home at our home, but sometimes so very far from home in the spaces between. It might be a police officer asking to see my ID card for no apparent reason, or the empty seat on the train either side of me (known culturally as 'the *gaijin* seat'), or the long stare of a stranger. Some days, it wouldn't bother me; after all, I chose to live here, and liked living here. But other days, tired days, it would bother me. A researcher on intercultural communication who, at times, found being perceived as different upsetting. There I was, pale, male, approaching stale, with a thin skin.

We all distinguish between being inside and outside a group, whether the group in question is your family, friendship circle, company, nation, or local football team. But in the Japanese language this distinction is captured through a pair of widely used terms: *uchi/soto*. *Uchi* (内) has meanings such as 'inside', or 'home', whereas *soto* (外) can mean 'outside', or

3.1 Woodblock print of the University of Tokyo's Red Gate, by Shiro Kasamatsu.

'foreign'. As is the case everywhere, when people are outside your group you may keep them at a polite distance, but when inside your group you would be more direct, more open, and expect more of them. The distinction is extremely dynamic, being based on the situation. For instance, a peripheral family member might be talked to as *soto*, unless there is a visit from a different family, and then the person may become *uchi* for the period of the visit. Most of the time I was *uchi* at work, accepted as a colleague and a teacher, but in public, strangers may assume I couldn't use chopsticks. Even in my stylish Kansai Yamamoto suit, I looked like an outside person.

The short subway ride would get me to the depths of Tokyo Station. Reaching my next train meant navigating a path through the converging, already burgeoning shoals of commuters. It was a path I now knew intuitively, sensing when to turn a shoulder, or sidestep an oncoming cluster, or briefly decelerate to save time. And most importantly how to react when suddenly confronted with a nervous novice, a visitor from outside the metropolis finding themselves in the right place at the wrong time: avoid eye contact. It wasn't always so. The art of commuting through Tokyo, with all its constraints and options, had to be acquired through practice. As such it was like any cultural practice – you start as a novice, and get better through doing it.

A lot of culture is performed through the body. In lectures, when discussing the culture of everyday life, I'd sometimes enact the following two ways of sitting on a subway, much to the mirth of my students. When I sit down on the London tube, I flop into the seat, often with a sigh, put my bag on the floor, and even splay my little thighs if there's space. I turn my head each way. Then I might puff out my cheeks. When I sit on the Tokyo underground, I carefully decide where is the appropriate space, signalled by slight ridges in the seats. Next I gently, silently descend with my knees together and elbows tight, placing my bag gently on my lap. I make myself into a carefully wrapped package that fits into the box that is that portion of the train seat. I make sure my bag does not slip onto the next seat, but if the strap touches the next passenger then I bow ever so slightly as I carefully bring the offending strap back into position. My students from Osaka would sometimes comment that their hometown was more like London, reminding us all that culture is typically local, and of the diversity within any culture.

Having reached the platform, I'd ride the Tōkaidō Line for forty-seven minutes, a distance of fifty-one kilometres. The first twenty-seven minutes, as far as Yokohama Station, is a blur of greyness at this time of day, being too early for the riot of Tokyo's neon lights. Instead concrete, the reflections of concrete in office windows, and the unorganised unlit shapes of neon signs block the unseen sky. Once past Yokohama, blue from above and green from below begin to reclaim the view. A calming, gradual exhale of colour and space. On the left side there is the odd glimpse of the Pacific, reminding the traveller that 'Tōkaidō' means 'East Sea Road', the same road that was immortalised in the series of woodblock prints by Hiroshige 190 years ago. In early March there may still have been a few pale petals hanging from the occasional grove of plum trees, anticipating the imminent arrival of their illustrious fair-weather cousin, the cherry blossom.

Population density is a thing people strongly associate with Tokyo, and an explanation of many of its stresses. Painful rental costs? Population density. Being bumped into by commuters, pedestrians, and the occasional bicycle, with no guarantee of apology? Population density. A gentle but consistent social pressure to constrain the movement, noise, and placement of your body? Population density. As you move from the centre to the edges of the metropolis these constraints loosen, which helps explain why so many people choose to live so far from work.

Home for us was on one such edge, in the satellite city of Fujisawa, not far from the ancient capital of Kamakura (Figure 3.2). After alighting, a short cycle ride along Sakai River signalled the ending of my commute. Having crossed this concrete-bedded river, lined on each side with small cabin cruisers and delicate-looking yachts, the knots in my shoulders and brow begin to loosen. 'Sakai' means 'Border' and its crossing signalled welcoming territory. Smiling neighbours with easy conversations reminded me I was entering my *uchi*.

Our specific neighbourhood in Fujisawa City is called *Katase* (pronounced ka-ta-say), and is designated as an area of 'local scenic beauty'. This means no tall buildings can be constructed and each new home has to have a specified number of trees on the purchased land. I won't say garden because our metre or two of volcanic soil circling the house hardly counted as that, but it came with four trees. When buying a house

3.2 Visiting the Big Buddha at Kamakura in early spring 2011, a regular cycle ride for us.

in Japan, the size of the land is paid for by the square metre, and taxes are calculated according to the size of the plot. Gardens in the Tokyo metropolitan area are the preserve of the wealthy. But with a metre or two of soil around a house there are plenty of opportunities for digging and planting, watering, and waiting. The delight of getting my hands and the little hands of my daughters dirty. Even as an ineffective gardener, I was learning that getting the soil of a place under your fingernails brings it closer to you. Perhaps like changing nappies makes you a more loving parent.

Fujisawa City is in a region called Shonan. The Shonan area stretches for twenty-five kilometres along the Pacific coast, and in the summer months it teems with daily visitors visiting its beaches. Our house is twenty-five minutes' walk along the winding Sakai River to the local Katase Beach. The fine, dark grey sand is so hot under foot in summer that my tender pale soles cannot cope, causing me to leap and swear, much to my daughters' delight. The beach provides one of the most popular spots for taking photos of one of the world's most photographed mountains (Figure 3.3). Framed by the blue of the sea and the sky, Mt Fuji lies a mere seventy kilometres away from Shonan.

3.3 The Pacific Ocean and Mt Fuji, taken from Katase Beach.

In the neighbourhoods next to the beach there are pretty streets filled with small shops and detached wooden houses of differing designs. There are few pavements, so cars, bicycles, pedestrians, and the famous small green tram (the Eno-den) share these streets. While Shonan may verge on the tacky in places, with overpriced Hawaiian restaurants, random hula-dancing, and more aloha shirts than you'd see at a summertime Japanese Yakuza convention, it is also rich in cultural heritage.

At the top of the beach is the small bridge to Enoshima Island (see Figure 3.4), often compared to Mont St Michel because of its topography, tidal accessibility on foot, and historical role as a place of pilgrimage. As the visitor climbs hundreds of steps leading up to the huge red Torii Gate, and then past several ancient wooden structures along the meandering path through the verdant island, they are met by a chintzy, some might say comical, concrete dragon perched on top of one venerable shrine. But if the visitor keeps walking, they will eventually reach a restaurant literally perched on the back end of the island, where the middling quality of the fried shrimp lunch is greatly embellished by the views of Mt Fuji to the west and the panorama of the Pacific Ocean.

3.4 Woodblock print of 'Fujisawa' by Hiroshige, sixth of the '53 Stations of the Tokaido' series. Beyond the Sakai River you can see Enoshima Island in the distance.

Unlike central-Tokyo kids, with their pallid complexions, the children in the Shonan area are usually deeply tanned in summer. It's not unusual to see bronzed young and old cycling home along the Sakai River without shoes, but with temporary socks of grey sand instead. Under the arm of cyclists you may see a carefully balanced surfboard, navigating the slow traffic and pedestrians in the narrow streets. My younger daughter Maya took to surfing from the age of five, a duck to Shonan's water.

We found our home in Katase in 2008. After yet another Saturday viewing houses in the Shonan area, we'd wanted to return to our rented flat in central Tokyo, exhausted and defeated again. But the estate agent was insistent we see this place. It was late afternoon, and he parked in the ample garage space on what is the ground floor. Entering the house on the first floor, I still recall the rich smell of new wood. And that feeling of knowing; 'protected' is how Mayu said she felt at that moment. On opening the front door, we looked at each other and grinned. First we explored the three bedrooms, flooded with sunshine. Then up to the second floor, with the kitchen, a balcony area, a living room, a sitting room and bathroom. The second floor was even more luminous than the first. We then walked up another set of stairs to the flat roof, in effect

3.5 The evening view from our roof, early 2011

a giant balcony with a wonderful view (Figure 3.5). Little did I imagine that a few years later this roof space would play a transformative role on my road to dealing with cancer.

The house is positioned on top of a small hill, and the large living-room window on the second floor provides a direct view of Mt Fuji. The estate agent, we found out later, had timed our visit so that we would catch the sunset. I had never seen such a sunset, with an uninterrupted sight of the mountain to our West and brilliant red and orange clouds weaved around it. One of our first guests, after climbing the stairs and seeing the view said, 'I know you said you could see Mt Fuji *from* your house, you didn't say it was *in* your house!' The view from the roof provided an even clearer view of Japan's most revered site, as well as views of Enoshima Island, the Pacific stretching to the horizon, the Hakone Mountains where Mayu's parents were (close but not too close), and on the clearest days there were views of the Southern Japanese Alps. My elder daughter Julia christened it 'Orange House' because of its light terracotta colour.

Whereas I worked at the University of Tokyo (locally known as 'Todai'), Mayu worked as a translator at the Japanese Nursing Federation. Our commutes from the Orange House to central Tokyo took about an hour and a half. In contrast my daughters had a wonderfully short commute – the primary school and the nursery were respectively five and ten minutes' walk from home. Katase Primary, which somehow crams in around 1,000 students, was in a singular position. The school has two main buildings, a hall, and a playground. This large playground-cum-sports field ends somewhat unexpectedly where the local cemetery begins. The cemetery has around eight long rows of graves, each row stationed above the next in a gradually rising bank, like a sports stadium for the eternally silent. If it weren't for a high net between the playing field and the cemetery, a good ten-year-old baseball slugger might smack the ball into the fifth or even sixth row of graves.

While this juxtaposing of the young and the dead spooked me a little at first, it didn't seem to bother my wife, kids, or neighbours. Some might even say it reflects Japan's culturally close relationship with dead ancestors. The religious scholar Herman Ooms argued that, 'The dead are not as dead as they are in our [Western] society … It has always made perfect sense in Japan as far back as history goes to treat the dead as more alive than we do.' I saw this on several sports days, as the local residents and teachers would comment on how the deceased would have enjoyed a particular race, or seeing the pure-hearted efforts of the young children. I doubt the school was placed at the base of a cemetery so that the deceased could watch the children play and silently applaud a good slug or a first kiss (again, I'd say it was down to population density), but I came to quietly cherish the odd symmetry.

In the spring of 2011, nine-year old Julia was in her third year at Katase Primary, and our younger daughter Maya, aged five, attended 'Kiddie Nursery'. It was a little further from our house, involving a short walk down the hill, a walk across the bridge over Sakai River, and then a short walk along the main road. It was a pristine and pleasant place, and unlike some forlorn nurseries and kindergartens in Japan, this one featured shiny leather sofas, colourful rooms, delicious, healthy lunches, fun Chinese and English language lessons, eurythmics classes, and jolly staff. Julia had also been there for a year before starting primary school, but Maya had been there since she was two. By the spring of 2011 she was enjoying her third year at Kiddie, and slowly cementing friendships that last to this day. After returning home from Todai, I'd typically stop off at Kiddie to pick Maya up, thus getting to know the staff and her classmates well. Putting her on the back of the bicycle we'd cycle off to get Julia at her after-school club, and the three of us would wander home. Mayu would be back soon after we'd arrived, and we'd cook dinner together.

This was the context of our lives in the spring of 2011. 'All happy families are alike', Tolstoy wrote; I think there is some truth in this, if you look beyond appearances. Just ahead, unseen, were two earthquakes, one physical and one metaphorical, that in the space of two seasons would mean we were no longer like other families. We would find ourselves in the chaos of sudden disasters.

CHAPTER 4

Earthquake

At 2.45pm on Friday 11 March, Mayu was downstairs preparing her next song-list. As well as working full-time as a translator, finishing a degree, and raising two daughters, she did a weekly slot on local radio, called 'Mayu's Golden Music Box'. It was a heady mix of sixties and seventies British and US hits, with some gratuitous social commentary thrown in. It opened to the first bars of Bowie's *Suffragette City*, and with its lack of Hawaiian dance tunes or Japanese pop, it was unlike anything else on Radio Shonan.

What with the academic year starting in April in Japan, this was the last day of the year for schools across the country. Julia had a big *kanji* test that morning, and we'd promised to buy her some boots she wanted if she got 100 per cent. As she'd studied hard, Mayu and I decided to get her the boots anyway. Both of us took the day off work so we could go shopping, have a lazy lunch in town, and be home when Julia got back just before 3pm. We could all then wander over Sakai River to pick up Maya at Kiddie Nursery, Julia no doubt proudly prancing in her new boots, and spend the rest of the day together. This is what we did, the same but different.

Before shopping for the boots we had a lunch that sticks in my memory, being so incongruous with the rest of the day. We went to a large *teishoku* restaurant, one of those that serve a good quality cheap set lunch of rice, miso soup, pickles, deep-fried chicken or pork cutlet, vegetables, and tea, and were the only customers there. Eventually another couple walked in, and sat at the other end of the restaurant. Mayu has remarkably acute senses – as she says, she is talented in all the ways that don't make money. Her eyes lit up as the couple walked into the restaurant. I turned around as nonchalantly as I could, and noticed the man was wearing a rather obvious toupee. There were clear differences in texture, positioning, and colour between the hair on the sides of his head, and the thing perched on top of it. I tried to discourage her from saying anything, what with us being the only others customers and her inability to whisper. We finished our lunch, and I walked up to the till to pay. Mayu, just as she was getting up from the table, noticed I'd left the bill there. She lifted it up above her head and said in her very loud voice, 'Mike, *zura!*' (*zura* being the Japanese for wig). The solitary server and I looked at each other in silence, for that eternity that is shared horror.

Mayu does tend to say what's on her mind in all its senses, not only the Freudian ones. There is a famous, even clichéd proverb in Japanese that roughly translates as 'the nail that sticks out gets hammered down', meaning that the individual who doesn't conform will be coerced to do so by the group. Despite the efforts of many, Mayu valiantly, thankfully, sticks out still; the embodiment of a persistent resistance. I've seen her give two fingers to many an *uchi*, meaning she ends up on the outside.

Our next-door neighbour once said to me, with a certain impressed incredulity, 'Mayu's a very unusual person. I've never seen a mixed-race couple where the Japanese woman stands out so much more than the foreign husband. She's got so much charisma.' I laughed in agreement. She has always had little time for conventions, and there is an edge to her judgements that can be breathtaking. One time, during a disagreement about something artistic, she told me, 'Look, I like things because I know they're good; you like things because you think you should.' But that afternoon, I think she felt too mortified to say anything of such insight, and returned home to the comfort of her song-lists.

While Mayu was organising her tunes, I was sending some emails at our dining table upstairs while enjoying the view of the Pacific and the mountains. Suddenly, I had to hold onto my laptop to stop it falling on the floor, as the oak table took on a life of its own. My seated body was being swayed and jerked beyond my control. The forces from below and the feelings in my chest began to achieve an odd symmetry, an uncanny violence growing without and within. All I could do was try to observe, to keep some balance as the whole room became alive, suddenly a strange and animate space.

As earthquake survivors often report, time takes on a distinct person-ality when the shaking moves beyond the usual. By 'beyond the usual' I mean that it's difficult to stand up. After 30 seconds or so it was clear this was not a usual tremor. The beautiful dark wooden floor under my feet was a moving, animate thing. And the Orange House itself was scream-ing. Not the creaks and groans you might experience from a wooden house during a typhoon; these noises were something more elemental, coming from the heart of our home – as if it were in a struggle with the earthquake itself, to protect itself and to protect us. I looked out the window, and the usually beautiful view itself was alive, with lampposts, homes, and trees all moving in insane asymmetry.

The violence, which had started at 2.46pm, continued for several min-utes. Mayu shouted to me to come downstairs so we could get out of the house. At first I couldn't make it to the stairs. The floor seemed to have morphed into undulating glue. Like a rock-climber I tried to keep as many limbs attached to something as I could, and ever so slowly I made it down-stairs. We embraced, swaying like drunkards on a dancefloor. We opened the front door, still swaying. Standing at the bottom of the steps was Julia, laden with her school bags. She was just about staying upright. We carefully went down the steps to get her, to hold her tight and dry her tears.

Mr and Mrs H were our neighbours, a sprightly elderly couple we'd become friendly with soon after moving to the area. Their house was a couple of minutes' walk from ours, down the hill towards Julia's school. Every morning, after Mr H drove off to the company he still ran, Mrs H would stand in front of her house wishing a good morning to the chil-dren walking to school. As we looked down the hill, we saw her entreating the children coming up the hill. 'Please! Quickly get yourselves home!' Many of these children, between six and twelve years old, were crying, some uncontrollably. As calmly as we could, we repeated what Mrs H had said. I didn't really know what to say, or what was the best thing to do. It wasn't so much panic that I felt, more a kind of absence, like being lost and having absolutely no idea which way you should go. My natural tendency is to make light of things, especially with children. Indeed, as we moved towards Julia, I'd started to dance on the stairs, to try to make her laugh. I failed, and the extreme seriousness of the situation was now dawning on me. 'Get home, get home!' I pleaded, gradually realising that there was no guarantee they would all make it.

For those living near the coast, the greatest threat in the aftermath of an earthquake is often the ensuing tsunami. The water, as in the rivers and the sea, first drains away, and then comes relentlessly back. Although our house was about one kilometre from the sea, I knew from the neighbouring Big Buddha at Kamakura that this means nothing if a big tsunami comes. The Big Buddha sits about the same distance from the coast, and was originally housed in a wooden temple. But in 1498 a tsunami came and washed this away, leaving him open to the elements. Being made of over 120 tonnes of bronze, he stubbornly stayed put, and remains serene and glorious. I remember reading about this tsunami on my first of many visits to see him when I was twenty-four, and being dumbfounded that a wave could travel with such force, so far.

Coming from a place without tsunamis, I used to think that they were all big. My first personal experience with one was back in 1994, before I met Mayu. I was at Shonan Beach, on a daytrip from work in Tokyo, where there was a sudden loud announcement across the Tannoy. My Japanese at the time only allowed me to understand the words 'tsunami coming …' My friends, who had been in Japan longer than me, laughed at my panic-stricken face, as I turned to run. They assured me it would be OK, and encouraged me to join the other swimmers at the end of the surf. 'Watch' they said, as the tsunami, between the regular waves, came in at a height of around thirty centimetres, and eventually dribbled over my toes. I laughed, more in relief than derision. But today was not such a day.

As Mayu and I held Julia in our arms that afternoon, we realised had to make a decision. Maya's nursery was across the river, and although the building was new and sturdy-looking, it was not much above sea-level. It might not withstand a powerful wave. The trip to pick up Maya, which we'd made so many times with such ease, now presented us with a choice, one that I'd never even conceived possible before. To get her we'd need to cross Sakai River, which was rising, and which might flood at any moment. Such floods could wash pedestrians, cars, and even houses away. Or knock a car or other object into pedestrians running through the rising water.

The question was, should we go together, or should one of us go alone? Together or alone. We'd gone back inside the house with Julia, and were staring out of the large living room window as we talked. We could see the sea, the river, and our neighbourhood with Maya's white building glistening as usual in the bright sun.

> *I think we should go soon, you know, hopefully before any big tsunami comes.*
> *But it might come before we get to Kiddie. Before we get to Maya, and then, you know, she'd be erm, alone.*
> *Then just one of us goes to get her?*

We looked at each other in silence, trying to weigh up these absurd but very pressing options. The sound of Julia quietly crying brought me back to the present. I crouched down to look at her.

> *Please don't leave me alone. Please! Please! Please!*

Mayu stroked her hair gentling.

> *Don't worry darling, we won't ever leave you alone. Promise.*

I picked Julia up in my arms.

> *Should I go by myself? I can run faster than you two.*
> *You're not that fast. You can't outrun a big tsunami.*
> *Is your mobile working?*
> *Hold on. No. Shit.*
> *Shall we go down the hill together and have a look at the river? If it looks OK we can sprint across the bridge and then on to Kiddie. If it looks dodgy we can either run back up the hill, or one of us can try to get across.*

This all happened within fifteen minutes of the start of the first quake. From firing off a couple of emails and looking forward to getting the girls home for the start of the holidays, to making decisions I never had even considered making before. We all want to be brave, and do the right thing for our kids. But in this situation, we had to consider ethical dilemmas that only belong in utilitarian philosophy books. What would be the greatest good for the greatest number of my family? Would it be best if we were all killed together? Or, would it be better if just Maya and I were washed away on the return journey home? For the former, a further risk was that Maya might lose her parents and sister while we were making the journey to collect her. So that option risked making her an orphan. For the latter, I might have been washed away on the way there. So that option might mean her losing one parent, and still needing collecting by the other. And the other parent wouldn't know what was happening. Left waiting for a return that would never happen. And all these thoughts were happening in real time, with full awareness that we needed to act at the right time. The right time being when the tsunami was not there. On reflection, I'm amazed by how calm Mayu and I were, somehow managing to be methodical in our reasoning. I think it's because we were together, facing this horror together.

We headed down, and a strong aftershock started. We held onto the rail for those who needed assistance climbing the short but steep hill. I'd used it many times when heaving heavy shopping up the hill, but never before when going down. When we got to the river, it was far higher and fuller than I'd seen it before, and the usual orderly lines of moored small boats were turning messy. Just under the bridge, one capsized boat was bobbing towards us, accompanied by some wooden debris. But the river was still a couple of metres below the level of the road. We stood there, frozen, for several seconds, staring at the growing weirdness below us. Then we ran across the bridge. The three of us held tight hands, me trying to laugh as we ran. I'd heard once that deliberately laughing dispels ghosts, even though I don't believe in them. At that moment it seemed an appropriate thing to do. It caught on with the other two.

As we crossed the road and approached the nursery, I commented that the windows and the front door were open. I should have known that this is basic earthquake procedure, to guarantee potential escape routes. Doors and windows often get warped in strong quakes. As we approached the door, we heard one of the teachers from Kiddie across the Tannoy saying in an inspiringly good-natured tone of voice, 'Come on children, sit under the tables, not on them.' The calm, coaxing delivery of standard earthquake-procedure instructions did wonders for my nerves. Mayu and I laughed, which seemed to help us breathe a bit more easily.

We picked Maya up, who wasn't yet five years old. She said she'd been a bit scared, but not very much. 'A bit? Alright for you!' I thought. But she's always been somewhat underwhelmed by enormity, calm in a crisis. I wondered if having regular earthquake drills from the age of one meant that experiencing a real one wasn't such a surprise. She told us her class had all got under the tables at the first time of being asked. It was some of the younger ones who'd had problems following instructions, we found out later.

We told Maya we were going to race across the river and then up the hill. When we crossed the road we could see that the water was getting higher. Just in the space of a few minutes, a dangled leg would now reach the water. More debris was floating upstream. But it was still the debris of inanimate matter. We sprinted across the river and up the hill, telling Maya it was a race. I was never happier about having two daughters who were quick runners. When we got home, it was by this stage around 3.45pm. And despite the main earthquake and the three considerable aftershocks, the Orange House looked as permanent as ever.

An hour after the earthquake that jolted Japan 11 inches closer to America had started. We began to catch the news online, and tried to call Mayu's parents. As they lived over 1,000 metres above sea level we weren't worried about them, apart from the tremors. It took time to get through, all lines were jammed. When we did connect, they advised us to stay put for the time being.

What happened over the next week or two is a mix of blurred and highly distinct memories. It was also a mix of strong, sometimes overwhelming emotions, and a lethargy induced by waiting and not knowing. By four o'clock that day though, it was becoming clear that a mega-earthquake had happened, followed by a huge tsunami. The epicentre was further north, an area I'd never visited called Fukushima.

I can't remember when we became aware of the damage to the nuclear power stations. But by the next day we, and I mean the bulk of residents living on the Pacific coastline, including Tokyo, Osaka, Kyoto, and Kobe, were in a state of increasing panic. This was partly fuelled by the lack of information coming from the Japanese authorities. The systematic lack of information, or at times misinformation, meant that we were reading about the situation from UK and other overseas news sources. As a case in point, while the overseas media was referring to 'nuclear meltdown' in Fukushima, the Japanese government and media waited two months before admitting it. While much of the news was delayed, and often second-hand, I also became very aware of the tendency in UK news to sensationalise an event or threat, especially when the event is thousands of miles away. So reading the news involved triangulating a plausible reality somewhere between the sparse or anodyne reporting of the Japanese media and the excesses of the UK press. But I was about to discover how the gaps in the domestic reporting could be filled with something about people like me.

CHAPTER 5

Flyjins

I returned to work on the Monday, and surveyed the damage to the university campus. There was surprisingly little: some broken windows in the main auditorium, several branches of the famous Gingko trees strewn around, some pictures off walls, and in my office several books on the floor. The lack of significant damage to my office of seven years was comforting, as I'd expected worse. Also, as the earthquake had struck outside of term-time, the university did not seem that much quieter than usual. After the annual strong typhoons the campus often ended up in a comparable state, and I was sure that within a short time it would look like normal again. 'Clearing up' is something that is well practised in Japanese society, with the natural environment providing regular opportunities.

I spent Tuesday 15 March at home, by which time the Japanese media had finally done something: it had created the memorable neologism 'flyjin'. The Japanese word for foreigner, *gaijin*, is made of the characters *gai* (外) meaning outside (as in *soto*), and *jin* (人) meaning person. So *fly+jin* was a rhyming, bitterly humorous term to describe the phenomenon of foreigners fleeing Japan because of the triple disasters. The term appeared in newspapers and TV, and unsurprisingly those leaving were individuals with the deepest pockets and the puniest roots – the men in finance largely. So the opposite of my foreign friends in Japan, those of us with comparatively shallow pockets and deep roots. And although none of my friends left Japan because of the earthquake, several did end up moving off the main island of Honshu, for instance to Okinawa. But for some residents of Tokyo, there was surprise that any of us were left.

On the subway to Tokyo station the next day, as I began the long commute home, I had the highly unusual experience of a stranger striking up a conversation with me. I'd noticed someone looking at me from the next seat for a long time, and thought little of it. These things do happen sometimes. But then she started up a conversation.

Excuse me, but is Japanese OK?

Yes, maybe.

Oh, can I say I was very surprised to see someone like you on the train, I mean a foreign person, because the TV said all the foreigners were leaving Tokyo.

Ah well, maybe it's best not to believe everything on TV. (smile.)

Huh? Anyway, can I ask, why did you stay? I mean, really, you didn't have to – you must have a home somewhere.

Well actually my home's in Fujisawa, that's where I live.

But no, I mean your real home. You know, your home home.

Erm, Fujisawa is my real home now. I own a house there and have lived there for several years.

No, but I mean why didn't you go back to America? It must be very scary here now.

I'm from Nottingham in England, it can be scary there too. Look, what can I say? Not all foreigners left, some did. I have roots here, family here, a good job here. Here is my home.

Hmm. OK, I see. Hmm.

When I got home, I put on my running clothes and went for a jog down Sakai River to the ocean. The riverbanks, usually lined with small boats and yachts, each in its rightful spot, were now decorated with debris, broken hulls, and unrecognisable rubbish. But I didn't go running to check the river's condition, I wanted to demonstrate, perhaps with a little vanity, that at least one foreigner hadn't flown away. I remember receiving longer-than-usual looks from passers-by, and I couldn't help feeling that they expressed some kind of surprise, followed by appreciation. Did I imagine the occasional slight bow in my direction?

For some years I'd played futsal on the netted roof of a local department store, one of those imaginative solutions to the issue of restricted space so typical of Tokyo. Of the several regular players, I'd become particularly friendly with Arita-san. He was the manager of a care home who'd spend the time between games doing absurd amounts of press-ups. Apart from when alcohol is involved, I think it's fair to say that in Japan physical contact between male friends is not that common. But when the game resumed a few weeks after the earthquake, Arita-san immediately embraced me, saying 'I knew you wouldn't leave!' One of the younger players, who previously would mock my accent for cheap laughs or be overly critical of my misplaced passes, never did those things again.

Over the coming months, other things happened. Strangers would strike up conversations with me more, some clumsy, some enlightening. People would smile at me more, or talk to the girls when we were out together. Seemingly, from people's vulnerability and pain, emerged cultures of kindness. I also found myself becoming more active in the community, doing things like going on rubbish-collection trips along the river and the beach with neighbours. I became more friendly as a result, and felt less fatigued by living as a foreigner. I felt less foreign. The sharp lines between *uchi/soto*, many self-imposed, were blurring.

The day of my first post-earthquake jog, I received the information we'd been dreading. Some senior colleagues with close contacts in the government and bureaucracy were saying how there was a considerable threat of Tokyo and its environs being engulfed by radiation within the next week. They also said that this couldn't be announced to the public because it would lead to mass panic. I told people close to me, but to my horror, many refused to believe it. I was absolutely certain that the colleagues in question were people who did not exaggerate such things. They were applied scientists, individuals for whom data and evidence are sacred. And when they were telling me this, I could sense they were deeply troubled.

Mayu, lover of a good conspiracy theory and long-term critic of the nuclear industry, had no problem believing it. So we had to decide what to do, considering what was best for the four of us. She was able to take some paid leave from her job, and I had no teaching for several weeks. I asked one senior colleague, who knew about the impending threat, for some advice. He said, 'I can't advise you, Mike. This has to be your decision. But whatever you do, it will be accepted.' What he meant was, it would be accepted by him and his colleagues. He too was a father, with children slightly older than mine. I asked him what he would do, and after a long pause he said as an engineer he had to stay and work. He said this with no pride, just a deep stoicism.

The metropolitan area of Tokyo where I lived and worked is the most populous metropolitan area in the world, and holds around 38,000,000 people. So conducting an emergency evacuation with that number of people from an area slightly bigger than Yorkshire would be beyond challenging. And where would we go? Despite the chance of Tokyo being engulfed in radiation, pitifully little information was communicated to the public through official sources. Five years after the disaster, the prime minister at the time, Naoto Kan, admitted that such a reality had been averted by 'a paper-thin margin'.

Although the Japanese media was saying very little about the threat of radiation seeping through Tokyo and its inhabitants, the British Embassy became a source of trusted information for not only UK but also Japanese nationals. The embassy also doubled the number of diplomats in Japan in response to the crisis, and brought in a range of experts. SAGE, the UK government's Scientific Advisory Group for Emergencies, examined worst-case scenarios. One involved a meltdown of all six nuclear reactors, followed by a huge contaminated raincloud blowing its way to Tokyo.

It was announced that British citizens and their dependants could go to the embassy to pick up iodine tablets as a precaution against such a scenario. Iodine works against some effects of radiation by blocking it from being absorbed by the radiation-sensitive thyroid gland. So on the Thursday morning, six days after the quake, the four of us took the train to Tokyo. The trains in Tokyo are usually quiet, and if anything the silence that day seemed more pervasive. The silence was accompanied by an uncanny greyness, with no lights on in trains or stations, or in the buildings we passed. Tokyo felt utterly forlorn, bereft of its usual radiant energy. As the train jolted through crossings, cold drizzle traced fragile lines on the windows, like tears on a cheek. A couple of tremors brought the train to a sudden stop. Heads across the compartment raise as strangers gaze intently into each other's eyes. When the train restarts, our eyes drop again to the floor, or clamp shut.

We reached the British Embassy, a luxurious estate rebuilt in 1929 following the Great Kanto Earthquake of 1923. The girls enjoyed a run around the grounds, while Mayu and I queued for our four iodine tablets. Upon reaching the counter, we called the girls in. The Japanese word for mixed-race children is 'half', as in the awful phrase 'half-caste'. The word always jars, and my daughters have never enjoyed being asked, 'Are you half?' Recently I asked them why, and they said it's because the question made them feel different, it othered them. They see themselves as Japanese, and they felt the implications of this word is that they're not, or least not fully. The word itself means, by implication, 'not whole', and this is how it made them feel. Mayu and I could never really stand in their shoes, but we could give them some tools. Poetry, such as John Agard's 'Half-Caste', was one tool.

> *explain yuself*
> *wha yu mean*
> *when yu say half-caste*
> *yu mean Tchaikovsky*
> *sit down at da piano*
> *and mix a black key*
> *wid a white key*
> *is a half-caste symphony*

It took me a long time to realise that the connotations of the Japanese word 'half' are often not wholly negative, and it is a commonly used term. One stereotype is that mixed-race children (an uncomfortable phrase in itself) are very pretty, *kawaii* in Japanese. And being *kawaii* in Japan is a very prized characteristic for girls. But *kawaii* is a kind of gendered cultural practice: to be *kawaii* you need to look a particular way, act in a particular way, and not look or act in lots of other ways – ways that men can. *Kawaii* constrains. My younger daughter Maya, from the age of two, seemed to sense this. On more than one occasion, I'd be cycling with her seated in the front of the bicycle, when a stranger would utter 'kawaii' as we cycled towards then. She would then grimace and shout 'kawai-kunai!' (I'm not kawaii!), much to the stranger's consternation. The apple never falls far from the tree.

We made it to the front of the silent queue. As we waited for the Japanese staff member at the embassy to examine our passports and give us the tablets, she looked down on the girls standing at our side. She then started talking about 'half' children being so *kawaii*, and how she wanted to marry a foreigner so she could have pretty children. I think Mayu may have said something like, 'It's pretty parents that have pretty kids', hoping to shut her up and deflect attention from the girls' reddening faces.

But looking back, perhaps this conversational gambit was just another clumsy attempt to raise the staff member's, and maybe even our, spirits. We accepted the four pills in a bag, and left. We got back home from the embassy at around lunchtime. As we cooked, we weighed up our options.

What with the radiation threat, and the threat of another tsunami, staying in the Orange House wasn't attractive. We decided to drive to Mayu's parents up in the Hakone Mountains.

We packed up the car with sleeping bags, a tent and some cooking gear, and walked down to Fuji Supermarket to buy food and water, in case the radiation reached Hakone and we had to leave. Apart from water, which was rationed to five litres per family, the shelves at Fuji Supermarket were empty. So was the next place we tried, Itoyokado. But at least we had water. We'd been trying to drink bottled water as much as possible since the news of the nuclear meltdown, for fear of radiation having seeped into the water supply. One Japanese academic I knew described the difference between, say, swimming in irradiated water and drinking irradiated water as akin to walking on hot coals and ingesting hot coals.

Japanese homes typically invest in a set of essentials in case of emergencies like this, and we were no different. I did think it was a bit ludicrous at the time, spending rather a lot of money on a plastic box that for years had doubled up as a stool for Maya to stand on when brushing her teeth. But what did I know, clearly. In the context of natural disasters, I was a cultural novice. We put the box containing hard biscuits, flares, a torch, rope, a water container and other tools of clear current relevance into the car, along with everything else. We drove down the hill, with no idea when we'd be able to come back to our precious home. If the radiation did come, it might not be for years, even decades.

The roads in the neighbourhood, usually gently bustling at this time of day, were silent. We weren't sure if we could get petrol, as there were reports in the media of some garages running out. Although we had to queue for a while at our neighbourhood garage, we were in luck and filled up the tank. Hakone, an hour and a half drive from our home in Fujisawa, was in the opposite direction from Fukushima and the encroaching radiation. And despite the Orange House being eleven metres above sea-level and a kilometre from the sea, we thought it best to get away from the coast. Places in such proximity in Fukushima no longer existed, having been erased by the tsunami. Mayu's parents' house was a thousand metres above sea level. Plus, it was full of food, fine food at that. We could go there, watch for developments, and if necessary keep driving until the petrol ran out.

This was a regular trip, from Katase to Hakone, one we'd make every month or so. But driving along the straight Route 134 with the now peaceful Pacific to my left and the sheer Hakone Mountains straight ahead, I couldn't help feel this was a journey I was taking for the first time. It was hard to fathom that this glistening ocean, flat all the way to the horizon, could have been so different only a few days before, a relentless, grey, churning, seething wall. Part of me still expects huge tsunamis to look vertical, glistening, sublime, the type of waves that surfers break records on. But in reality the damaging ones rarely look like that. Instead they resemble a darkly liquefied relentless conveyor-belt of floating homes, capsized boats, bobbing cars, and corpses.

It is estimated that twenty-five million tonnes of debris were created along the Japanese coast because of the 11 March tsunami. The Great Pyramid of Giza weighs about six million tonnes, so that's the equivalent of around four of them. The sea we drove alongside still held the odd capsized boat or bits of detritus, and some of the road had collapsed onto the beach below. As we drove past one section that had disappeared being bravely examined by a group of engineers, I did a double take. Among them was the professor who, a couple of days earlier, I had talked to about whether we should leave or stay. Seeing him strengthened my resolve not to leave Japan.

CHAPTER 6

In-laws

Despite being of rather variable reliability while she was growing up (all parties agree this), Mayu's parents have always been the best of in-laws (Figure 6.1). I know of many 'international' couples in Japan, typically a *gaijin* man and a Japanese woman, where the couple either keep the relationship secret from her parents, or suffer considerable troubles after announcing it. And sometimes there is never peace between the parents and the couple. My experience was not like this. There's even a family joke that Mayu's father tricked me into marrying her.

By the spring of 1997, we'd been living together for almost two years in Shimokitazawa (or 'Shimokita' to its friends), a part of central Tokyo

6.1 Mayu's parents giving a heartfelt duet at their home in Hakone.

renowned for its local theatres and music venues, second-hand clothes stores, bohemian residents, and numerous small bars and restaurants. By small I mean they may not seat more than eight customers. The ambiance and decor of each place was largely an extension of the owner's invariably unusual personality, and Mayu and I could have given tours of the various flavours of the town. The language school I was hired by to teach anywhere in Tokyo sent me to Shimokita, purely by chance. It is where I worked for four years (1994–1998), where I made my first proper home in Japan, where I met Mayu, where we first lived together, and where our marriage is registered. Shimokita changed my life, and I love it dearly.

We eventually agreed to her father's sustained suggestions that we should move to the outskirts of the metropolis, closer to where they lived. This way, we could save money, and socialise more together. Once we'd agreed to this, he then said, 'Well good, but you'll have to get married now, because it's very conservative round here and the neighbours would gossip if you were living in sin.' This comment came from a man who had so many debt-collectors after him during Mayu's childhood that they used to wrap the telephone in a duvet and tie it up, to muffle its endless ringing. Not exactly a paragon of conservative values.

He was another person who had little interest in conventions (unless it suited him), and claimed, with a kind of performative chagrin, that Mayu's way with the world was his doing. 'I taught her to speak her mind, and never to be subservient to men.' This ranged from a general perspective on gender relations to simple actions like pouring a drink for a man. I've seen senior female academics pour drinks for junior male colleagues at parties, colleagues whom they'd been directing earlier that day in the lab. But not Mayu. This meant that she annoyed many Japanese men she socialised with, and that I had to do a lot of pouring for the two of us.

Mayu and I had been together for about three months when we first took the two-hour journey together up to the mountain hot spring resort of Hakone, where her parents 'Jackie' and Hisako lived (Figure 6.2). Around this time Mayu was looking to escape her career in the music industry. Like many Japanese women of her generation, Mayu had not gone to university after high school, but had instead gone to a two-year college. This was despite having an intimidating IQ, and a natural flair for languages (although a weighty dose of teenage procrastination can't be discounted too). After college she'd worked in the music industry

6.2 Mayu and I on our way from Shimokita to Hakone, summer 1997.

for several years as an assistant producer, but after becoming rather disillusioned with the politics and the values (money, not music), she was thinking about taking her skills elsewhere.

For the next few years she worked for several other companies as a full-time but non-permanent bilingual secretary or administrator. This is the contractual lot of many women in Japan. In fact, according to the sociologist Yoshio Sugimoto in his *Introduction to Japanese Society*, despite the widespread stereotype of the 'typical' Japanese worker being a male with lifetime employment in a large Japanese corporation, statistically speaking the following is the most typical: 'a female, non-unionised and non-permanent employee in a small business without university education'. So there you go Mayu, you were typically Japanese in some ways at least.

I'd been in Japan little over a year, and spoke very rudimentary Japanese at the time of this first trip to Hakone. The evening might have gone badly wrong early on. I tried to compliment Mayu's mother's cooking, but failed spectacularly by deleting the 'n' sound from *o-shinko* ('pickles'), instead announcing that her urine was delicious. Mayu and her parents thought this hilarious, with Jackie-san snorting his beer through his nose.

I warmed to Jackie-san immediately, with his outrageous, full-body humour supported or even held together by streams of expletives – he'd learnt his English as a university student working in a bar for American

GIs. This is also where he'd gained the nickname 'Jackie'. Along with the humour was an enveloping, comforting hospitality, and an honesty of emotion. We arrived at 6pm, and by 8.30pm he went off to bed, drunk and very happy. Hisako-san started the evening by watching me sideways from across the table for the first hour or so, across the plates of entry-level sushi she'd prepared (tuna, salmon, egg roll, and suchlike). She'd then look away when I caught her glance, but three hours later the three of us were singing karaoke and dancing with castanets in their living room, with Jackie sound asleep on his futon. In Japanese society, people often contrast *honne* with *tatemae*, a dynamic that runs through all communication. *Tatemae* means the ability to say something that is socially appropriate in the situation, even if it is not true. As such, it is a means of avoiding conflict. *Honne* is the opposite – the expression of your true feelings. It was immediately clear to me that this was a family that had little time for *tatemae*. I felt very much at home.

Our visits became regular, and the relationship between us all deepened. Over the early years of our marriage, the four of us became a unit, an odd couple of odd couples. Julia appeared five years into our marriage, leaving a lot of time in those early years for going out. Jackie was always the main event, a host who could entertain a room with the prowess of an assured performer spinning plates. I learnt over time that he was about as contradictory a character as I'd ever met. He clearly adored Mayu, and yet criticised her almost out of habit. And while Mayu was adept at pushing back against most attackers, she crumpled when scorned by her parents. Eventually I confronted him, telling him repeatedly she was not stupid, but his saying so made her believe she was. After that conversation, to his credit, he never said it again.

For the time, he seemed to break certain Japanese gender stereotypes quite happily: he'd always do his own washing, would regularly cook meals, and would clean the house and garden with a vigour verging on the disturbed. At the same time, he could use his physical presence or verbal sharpness to threaten wife and daughter, especially after a drink. But both he and Hisako cocooned our relationship in the early days, and no matter how frustrated I might be with Mayu's stubbornness or sharpness, I felt we'd be OK because I knew, from glimpses, that she had inherited the best characteristics of her parents. She just needed time, and care, to let them grow. And she has nurtured the better parts of me,

6.3 Jackie, my father on one of his trips to Japan, me and Yoshi. Jackie is mimicking my father's considerable girth.

while chiselling patiently and sometimes pointedly at the bad. Had I not been welcomed into that family so lovingly by her parents, we might well have broken up. Mayu's parents, and her brother Yoshi, were in that small minority who never thought we would (Figure 6.3).

They were also fiercely loyal, and once cut off connections with a branch of the family because of how we'd been treated. It was the summer of 2000, just before Mayu and I were to move to the UK for my postgraduate studies. Her parents had asked us to attend a barbeque on their behalf, held by some distant relatives. We arrived at their front door with gifts of wine and some food, but instead of the usual effusive welcome you'd expect on arriving at someone's home, we were greeted by a very long silence. The middle-aged couple stared at me, and then Mayu, and then me again. Eventually they stuttered out the customary welcoming words, inviting us in. He curtly told me to take my shoes off, clearly expecting me not to know. She ushered us on to the roof balcony where many other guests were drinking, and then quickly returned to her husband downstairs. Mayu's brother Yoshi, who lived in the same neighbourhood as this family, had been coaxed into doing the barbeque. We said a quick hello and took a moment to appreciate the view.

The other guests didn't greet us with silence, but instead bombarded us with the kinds of comments that we'd already become tired of in our five years together. In normal circumstances we'd physically manoeuvre away from questions like this as swiftly as possible. But we were verily stuck, representing Mayu's family. So there was nothing for it but to smile our best smiles. It began with the loud observation, 'Oh, a *gaijin*! What's a *gaijin* doing here?', followed by a torrent of questions and comments.

Do you like Japan?

Why did you come to Japan?

Can you use chopsticks?

Can you eat sushi?

I've never spoken to a gaijin before. His eyes are kind of green, pretty. He's small though isn't he?

Japanese beer is the best, right?

Do you like Japanese girls?

Of course he does, look he's sleeping with one! Haha!

Hehe. Japanese girls are the best, right?

Do you know what makes a man happy? Having a German car, a British house, and a Japanese wife. Haha.

Mayu, why didn't you marry a nice Japanese guy? You're pretty enough – you didn't need to marry a gaijin.

After about fifteen minutes or so they became a bit bored with our non-committal, tight-jawed answers, and swarmed around the barbeque. Mayu and I took a deep breath, and a few big swigs of our admittedly very good Japanese beer. I asked Mayu if we could leave, but she reminded me the food hadn't arrived yet, and then there were the fireworks. We thought that the worst was now over, whereas in fact we'd just been gently softened up by the support act.

The host appeared and glanced over at Mayu and me sitting at the other end of the roof. He asked in very direct Japanese if we were OK, without waiting for a reply. The absence of formality could signal two things – either we were regarded as being inside his *uchi*, his inner circle, or, he didn't deem us worthy of being addressed in the usual respectful register reserved for guests. He didn't speak to us for another hour or so, but I noticed he did enjoy several large glasses of saké from a very large, cheap-looking bottle. When he did talk to us, he was clearly in a *honne* mindset, the dark kind.

He was clearly the king of his castle. A labourer in his younger days who'd become a self-made businessman in the demolition industry. In his driveway stood five large gleaming diggers, all emblazoned with his name. He ordered his adult children around with the minimum of words or tenderness, and they obeyed. They'd gobble up any joke he tossed out like hungry pets. As I found out later, he was their father and their boss, their provider and judge.

After some time, he beckoned Mayu and me over. He poured us a beer, and asked what I did as a job. I told him, and said that we were going to the UK soon as I was going to do a Master's.

Oh, so you're an egghead!

Mayu, you're going with him? Leaving your family?

Well yes, he is my husband after all.

He didn't laugh, instead replying with a slight sneer. The saké was sweating out of him in the summer evening heat, as his face bubbled into a sharp shade of red. He stared at us, unsmiling, for a long time.

Your poor parents, I feel really sorry for them.

Sorry, what?

Well, pretty girl like you embarrassing your family by marrying a gaijin. My sister did the same with an American thirty years ago. I never spoke to her again, nor did my parents.

Your poor sister.

What! You don't know nothing, stupid young girl. Where's your respect for your elders? Do you know what 'immoral' means? Well you should. That's what you are. You! Disgusting. It's like a dog and a cat fucking, you two. Anyway it doesn't matter – couples like you usually divorce in no time anyway.

Hot angry tears were welling up in Mayu's eyes, borne of the frustration of our situation. I wanted to damage this man, but could do nothing. We were representing the family of Jackie-san and Hisako-san. This awful man's children were now quietly baying for more, egging him on. I did my best to say something to defend us, but they all laughed. We got up and left.

We felt sullied for a long time after and even now, twenty-five years later, that evening stands out as the most hurtful abuse that we've received as a mixed-race couple. A bitter lesson in what it means to be demeaned, bring to mind the etymology of the term, to be de-meaned. But there has been some consolation in the righteous anger of Mayu's parents, and their continued refusal to speak to that part of the family.

There's also consolation that he got the wrong couple. Sullied impotence was probably the strongest emotion that both of us felt that night, as we walked silently back home along the rail tracks running through the town. But over the next days and weeks we made powerful resolutions, ones that have steeled us since. We would never let anyone speak to us like that again, regardless of who they were. We would take them down with our words. And if we had kids, we would not only do our best to protect them from such people, but more importantly teach them how to push back, and push back hard. As Confucius didn't quite say – give a girl a fish, feed her for a day; teach a girl to fish, feed her for a lifetime.

CHAPTER 7

Hakone

Mayu drove steadily along the highway on that Thursday afternoon, now six days after the earthquake and tsunami. Upon leaving the highway, which runs parallel to and just above the sea, we started the snaking drive through the Hakone Mountains, climbing 700 metres in half an hour. This was a route we knew so well, but we were ever-cognisant of the possibility of another quake, which made the route seem somehow alien; the verdant valley to our right and sheer mountainsides to our left were now threatening, their inertness no longer taken for granted. But at least the drive was quick – there being surprisingly little traffic. We arrived safely at Mayu's parents' place as the sun began to set. All our gear we left in the car except for the bare minimum, just what we needed for the night. This was in case we had to make a sudden departure.

We also arrived with a considerable amount of stress, which Jackie and Hisako worked away at alleviating over the following days. That first night, we talked to them about what they would do if the radiation reached Hakone, but they did not seem inclined to flee. 'At our age the radiation might do us good', I remember him saying. He also told us that the house was the safest in Hakone, being relatively recently built to a very high spec. He is also a man who revels in hyperbole, claiming to be the first guy to wear jeans in Japan, and to drink Coca-Cola. But I appreciated his confidence, knowing it was for our benefit.

Like many of his generation he suffered greatly as a child during and after the war years, compounded by the death of his mother while he was only six years old, and being left with an alcoholic father, older sister, and a baby brother. Hunger was a constant towards and after the end of the war, meaning he and his sister would look for anything edible in the wooded mountains of the area. Neighbours shared their breastmilk with the baby brother, who eventually graduated from one of Japan's top universities and had a very successful career in the hotel industry. Jackie-san claims he deliberately left university early to financially support the bright young brother, but we suspect the attractions of Tokyo may have also played a larger role. I saw this younger brother recently, aged 85. He was proudly telling me that his golf handicap had gone down since the last time I'd seen him, as he enjoyed a cigarette and a glass of afternoon beer.

During the war, German soldiers who couldn't return home were stationed in Hakone and built a large pond in Jackie-san's village as a gift for the residents. By the end of the war, the German soldiers had nearly all returned to Europe by ship, but some of their belongings remained. While searching for food during the cold winter months of 1946, Jackie would sometimes break into the basement of the local ryokan to steal food where the German soldiers had been based, and came across a cleaned and pressed German soldier's uniform. The 13-year-old Jackie-san put it on and went off to school through the snow, wrapped up warm in the heavy officer's coat. His teacher, looking up at the tall, handsome young student, complimented him on his style. It made a change from the usual threadbare clothes he wore, unlike most of the children who could afford the school uniform. For some weeks he enjoyed strutting around the playground until the occupying American soldiers visited the area. Unsurprisingly, they didn't appreciate his sense of dress, nor I imagine the defiance in the boy's eyes. He claimed he also gave the Americans a Nazi salute. Reenacting this for us, he'd contort his face into an angry ball and spit out the forbidden words.

He retold this story while we enjoyed a long dinner of deep-fried king prawn and vegetable tempura, including my favourite spring plant, *shungiku*, picked from the local mountains. All served with Hisako's wonderful pickles and assorted *sashimi*. One of many stories he told us that night and the following nights. I was reminded of Jackie and Hisako's ability to wrap the young, recently married Mike and Mayu in a protective bubble. The problems we faced never seemed quite so serious when we were with them. Once again, the threats posed by the current situation and the accumulated stress started to recede thanks to their love.

Mayu's father gets extremely excited by heavy snow. Perhaps it's because of childhood memories in the winter mountains of Hakone, a respite from the tribulations of everyday life. While often quite indolent, when snow falls he is a frantic collection of limbs, clearing pathways, making snowmen, and rolling around. At evening-time he likes to turn all the lights off, get the candles out, and enjoy their reflections on the whiteness while urinating in beery patterns. From morning to night, an exercise in over-excited joy. Somewhat peculiarly, earthquakes seem to bring out a similar side of him. It's best summed up by the onomatopoeic expression *waku-waku suru*, a level of giddy excitement far from the norm.

There's a famous expression, 'Cultures don't communicate, people do.' I believe this, but at the same time, some people are really interesting from a cultural point of view. For me, it's those individuals who seem to disprove some of the questionable but rarely questioned things you read about cultures. For instance, whole countries or continents have been categorised as either collectivist or individualistic. Japan is often described as a highly collectivist culture, which in part means that there is little space for individuality. This isn't my experience of Japan. I've encountered countless fascinating characters there, some decidedly odd, many of whom bump against or simply ignore conservative norms. Which is surely the case wherever you go: all societies exist within the tension of those who follow conservative norms and those who push against them. Jackie-san is one such pusher, and an example of how to make your own line in the snow.

One theme of this book is the notion of what it is to be an other, for instance being treated as *soto* and not *uchi*, being an out-group member, someone not included. I think otherness is something that becomes very apparent in certain contexts, such as a cancer diagnosis. You can feel like an other when dealing with doctors, but also people you are close to; you can even feel a sense of otherness from your self, because the cancer has displaced you from your normal life.

Power can help in understanding what it is to be an other in any situation, as usually the othered person has less of it, whether it is in normal times or times of cancer. But there is also a possible freedom that emerges from recognising and accepting yourself as an other, because the conventions of the in-group don't really apply to you. Like many of the most interesting people, Jackie-san seems to be one such person who has embraced his otherness in society. And although he's ended up with nicknames from his neighbours like *Hakone gaijin*, he also has a circle of friends that include company presidents, famous actors, singers, and criminals. But more importantly, he has an independence of thought that often involves ridiculing the comment 'but that's the way we've always done it' and doing things a different way.

On that first evening in Hakone, and for many afterward, Japanese homes and businesses were being asked to conserve electricity. This meant turning all air conditioners off, and lights when not absolutely needed. There were also many intermittent power cuts, sometimes after an after-shock, sometimes not. Once we'd finished dinner, Jackie-san turned the lights off and disappeared. Ten minutes later he reappeared with a col-lection of candles on a long wooden board, which roughly resembled a cake. He walked steadily into the room, carrying the flickering board in two hands, loudly singing, 'Happy Birthday to you!'. Naturally, it was nobody's birthday. 'Look!' he proudly stated, showing how he'd ham-mered nails into the bottom of the plank to impale the larger candles, and used super-glue for the smaller fairy lights (Figure 7.1). 'We've got the safest house, the best candles, lots of food and beer, we'll be abso-lutely fine! Hahahaha!'

7.1 Jackie organising his candles.

He then reappeared with the ugliest candle I've ever had the misfortune of seeing, a wedding present from the hotel in which we had been married 14 years earlier. It is about a metre high, with garish gold numbers embossed down the shaft, and a huge, plastic flower hanging off it. The idea is you light it each year, to celebrate your anniversary. It had never been lit before, I'd tried to forget it existed, but that night we burnt through several years of our marriage. When I asked Jackie how many years he gave us, he exclaimed, 'You'll be finished after 25!'

Hisako put some music on, and our daughters danced around the candles as she sang. She had been a semi-professional singer before marriage in some of Tokyo's less respectable venues, and I was repeatedly astounded by her voice. The earthquake and the nuclear meltdown seemed very far away that night.

At the end of the week, with no sign of the radiation cloud approaching Tokyo, we drove back to Fujisawa with our unused tents and sleeping bags and water. Back they went into the garage, and Maya's 'stool' was returned to the bathroom, thankfully unopened. I never disrespected the 'stool' again.

CHAPTER 8

Aftermath

Cherry-blossom season, or *hanami* (花見, literally meaning 'flower viewing'), came and went in Tokyo in early April, although this year there weren't the raucous, joyous parties that usually accompany this event. My first *hanami* in Japan was in 1994, having arrived in my new home a couple of months earlier. I remember being really struck by the abandon people showed in the evenings under the pink trees. Parties might start early in the day even on weekdays, often with the new employees of companies, possibly in the first week on the job, being assigned the task of taking a big blue plastic sheet to the local park and trying to get a prime slot under the trees, and marking it out. Many would then stand there for hours until their colleagues turned up for the fun, like earnest sentries in standard garb of new black suits, shiny new shoes, and white shirts. As they stood there alone with their thoughts, I'm sure many would wonder how their relative success at obtaining a prime piece of park real estate for the day might affect their long-term career prospects.

Over time, I began to notice the many different groups within Japan society. Indeed, being a migrant is partly a journey of gradually noticing the massive variety within one's host nation, the differences within the group, as it were. It's like a camera lens slowly coming into focus. Although *hanami* is an event for all ages, it often seemed that the three common groups of cherry-blossom revellers were firstly office workers arriving directly from work, then university students, and then somewhat grizzled groups of older men not in suits. With the first group, the ties of the salarymen would often move from the neck to around the forehead as the evening's festivities progressed and speech became slurred. Groups of students would often sit around with friends passed out on the plastic mat, and the grizzled gents who would not normally be exactly welcoming became friendly generous hosts for the evening, offering food and drink as I'd walk by smiling. Many a fine evening I've had in Japan, many of the best memories (and blurred memories), at this time of year. True, conversations could be rather predictable, often going something like this:

Hello! Come over and have a drink!
It's OK, thanks.
No no, it's hanami so you must.
OK, thanks.
Here you go. Cheers!
Cheers!
So are you American?
No, I'm English.
Ah, English. Great. Much better, haha. Your Japanese is very good.
No, not really. I need to study more.
It's fine, here, have some kara-age chicken. How long have you been in Japan? Wow,
  you use chopsticks very well! Look – his chopsticks are better than yours! Ha ha ha!

Normally I'd try to extricate myself from such conversations as quickly and politely as possible, having experienced them many times over the years, but the power of the flower always works its magic at this time of year. As Christmas seems to soften the edges of strangers towards each other in the UK, so does cherry-blossom season in Japan. But 2011 was a subdued spring with little revelry. The parks and cherry-lined avenues were quiet, bereft of the usual laughter and chatter. A poem from the ninth century, by Tomonori Kino, seemed to capture the incongruity of the setting and the prevailing mood in all our hearts.

On a spring day with soft rays of sun
Flower petals fall restlessly
There is no peace in my heart

The events of 11 March 2011 immediately changed Japan. But unlike the people from Fukushima, who had lost so much, many of the changes faced in our area were not hard to bear. One of the most visible differences was the darkness. Because all the nuclear power stations, which pre-11 March accounted for around 30 per cent of Japan's energy needs, had been closed down indefinitely, energy-saving policies were introduced nationwide. Looking at one of those global maps showing how bright places are at night, Japan is easy to spot because the Tokyo metropolitan area shines oh so very brightly. But following the quake, streetlights were kept to an absolute minimum, homes were encouraged to keep electricity to essential use only, and shops were told to turn their lights off at night. The view from our home was panoramic, as I've mentioned, and this meant we couldn't but notice the difference once night-time came. Whereas the normal view was a scattering of electric lights reaching to the ocean and up the mountains, now the stars took prominence, along with the occasional moving flickers of small fishing boats in the dark calm of Shonan Bay.

Another difference, as spring moved to summer, was the reduction of air-conditioning in public places and on trains. For those who haven't lived in Tokyo, it's difficult to convey the ferocity of summer in the day and through the night. It's not just the heat, though temperatures in the high thirties are not unusual; nor is it just the humidity, which is comparable to cities like Bangkok or Singapore. These two factors are enough to make a place a challenge for someone raised in the UK Midlands. But the thing that really sapped me was the heat-island effect. As the sun goes down, and you would expect the air temperature to cool, the incomprehensible amounts of concrete in the Tokyo area begin to release the heat they've absorbed in the day. During daytime the concrete is like a hotplate, but walking in a natural sauna meant it wasn't as noticeable. But the evenings can actually feel like the weather is getting worse. It's befuddling and inescapable. Beer offers a temporary solace, but it's akin to the Venus-fly trap: I'd sweat more, and it's a sticky sugary sweat that desires more beer; then I'd wake to another sweltering morning with the parched tongue and the accompanying internal cacophony. Water is a much kinder friend.

The ubiquitous air-conditioning in Tokyo's buildings and trains offers a respite from the heat. But it's a sharp uncomforting chill, with the gusts of air often 15 degrees colder than the outside air. On entering the building or train I'd temporarily freeze, then visibly shudder. The unavoidable sweat on my clothes meant I'd retract in panic at the shock of the cold. It was for these reasons that one of the unexpected, pleasant surprises of the post-earthquake Tokyo was a softer air temperature on entering trains and buildings. I remember many residents commented on the benefits of the change in trains and offices, and wondered whether the excessive air-conditioning of previous years might be avoided once a full recovery was under way. Disasters are a disaster but also create the space for us to reflect on more measured solutions to our problems.

While 11 March may have led to a slightly more responsible approach to the problem of uncomfortable weather, it created a range of other problems, some of which continue to this day. Threats that can't be seen are particularly unnerving, and as the months progressed, we were constantly concerned with where radiation might be, and how much there might be. My university installed a Geiger counter on campus, near my office, so I could check daily whether we were still in the 'safe' range for ionizing radiation as I passed it on my way home. Mercifully, the amount in the Tokyo area never reached dangerous levels. We were also concerned about the unknown levels in the sea, and although we still visited Fujisawa Beach, Mayu was adamant that the girls should not swim there. In her usual belt-and-braces approach, this meant for the following five years.

Radiation became a foe and a brutal friend of mine in 2011. As a result I came to understand its different personalities, particularly that of ionizing radiation. Ionizing radiation is the type of radiation used in cancer treatment, but in the spring of 2011 I wasn't yet intimately aware of that. Ionizing radiation in relatively low doses can cause cancer because it damages the DNA in our cells, causing them to grow aggressively. In higher amounts it stops the cells growing, which can result in organ failure.

Such health issues may take time to develop, and it was recognition of this that inspired one of the many poignant stories of the disaster. A group of retired engineers and other professionals volunteered to aid with the clean-up instead of young people. The instigator, Yamada Yasuteru, an engineering graduate of the University of Tokyo, justified the idea as logical: 'I am seventy-two and on average I probably have thirteen to fifteen years left to live. Even if I were exposed to radiation, cancer could take twenty or thirty years or longer to develop. Therefore us older ones have less chance of getting cancer.'

It is tempting to make cultural hay from such a remarkable story, and to ask whether there isn't something essentially, uniquely Japanese in such behaviour. As I'll discuss later, the notion of *gaman*, or endurance, often with connotations of selflessness, is often said to be a supremely Japanese characteristic, and surely this action is a prototypical example. And doesn't such behaviour have shades of the kamikaze pilots of the Second World War? On the second point, Yamada-san said absolutely not: 'The kamikaze were something strange, no risk management there. They were going to die. We are going to come back.' And on the first point, there are other similar stories of selflessness in response to similar disasters. For instance, immediately after the Chernobyl disaster, three divers, termed 'the suicide squad' famously sacrificed themselves to avert a far greater disaster. Knowing that they had no chance of survival, might we not ask whether these were more quintessentially 'Japanese' than Yamada-san and his team?

I'm reminded that, when considering behaviour in terms of culture, our minds often look for differences that capture the 'essence' of a nation or a group, and then use this essence to explain the perceived differences. Such circular reasoning is emotionally comforting, akin to a tranquilizer of the mind. But if we are willing to look a bit more carefully, to think a little more slowly, we may find examples of shared patterns, of shared values, and of fluidity in feelings, that chip away at this assumed predominance of inherent difference. As I suggested at the beginning of this chapter, the gift of being a long-term migrant in a country can be the birth of such a perspective. The stereotypical scales gradually, if somewhat unevenly and at times unwillingly, fall from your eyes.

When looking at groups with a reasonably large population, there tend to be more differences within the same group than between different groups. In other words, there tend to be fewer differences and more similarities between groups. I think this is one of the most insightful things that I came to learn, really learn, at this time. The 'cultural industry' that monetises and politicises cultural differences (from management consultants to media outlets to politicians) would recoil from such a statement, but then they would, wouldn't they?

I was also learning about people's ability to see light, even create light in the gloom, during times of trouble. Indeed, some studies following 11 March found that the relationship between social trust and happiness could become stronger as a result of the disaster. Specifically, for those with higher levels of social trust, reflected in good interpersonal networks and community participation, higher degrees of happiness were found. These findings also chimed with my own experiences following the triple disaster, as I felt myself more at home in Japan than at any other time. I was no longer just floating on the surface of society.

CHAPTER 9

Internationalisation

Another change that happened later in the spring of 2011, one not related to Fukushima, concerned my work. At the time of the disaster I was an associate professor, and was getting on with my teaching and research on professional and intercultural communication. I'd come relatively late to academia, having had too much fun with young Mayu in Shimokita, which meant I was playing catch-up in terms of published research. I'd been writing or editing six books, all of which were now completed or close to completion. I'd told myself it was necessary to suffer a while if I was to establish myself as an internationally recognised academic in my field. I'd been juggling these projects for three years with my regular teaching and university administrative duties, and the stress was getting to me. But through the process of writing, I was learning a lot about communication, and particularly the approaches to intercultural communication I discuss in the Introduction.

At the beginning of May I was approached by the Dean of the College, who was offering me a professorship with responsibility for internationalisation. And internationalisation involves a lot of intercultural work. A full professorship with tenure, meaning I'd be (at that time) only the second non-Japanese to hold such a position within the Faculty, at Japan's most prestigious university, working on a topic close to my heart. When I was offered the promotion, I said no.

I don't know if it's true, but I was told afterwards I was the first person to turn down a professorship at Todai. I have to say, though, I always appreciated my luck in having obtained a job there in the first place. It's an outstanding university – for instance its affiliated staff and students have won 16 Nobel Prizes, across all the categories from Literature to Physics. Within Japan, it's like Oxford and Cambridge rolled into one, in a society where outward prestige carries considerable weight and hierarchies are explicitly marked in language.

Working at Todai was like wearing a magic suit, one that offered protection for me and my family. As is the case in many places no doubt, mixed-race families may, at times, feel othered in Japanese society. But being associated with the Todai brand stymied some of the condescension. I didn't introduce myself by saying things like, 'Hi I'm Mike. Oh and did you know, I work at the University of Tokyo?' but people do ask, and it's the kind of information that travels. So the girls' teachers knew of my job before I'd met them, and I'm sure this helped disabuse them of some negative stereotypes they may have had about mixed-race or bilingual kids ('they may be cute but they ain't that bright').

When the dean provisionally offered me the professorship (dependent on colleagues voting me in), he told me that the changes to the college's internationalisation would take a long time to put in place. I'd therefore be expected to stay in place for at least fifteen years. These envisaged changes, according to the dean, would involve revolutionising the way the college and eventually the university approached internationalisation.

The ultimate aim was to position the institute as completely internationally engaged, part of which would mean attracting outstanding researchers and students from overseas – and keeping them. Language is a potential barrier, as the pool of non-Japanese academics who speak Japanese is very small. English would have to be deeply integrated as a language of the university, meaning it would become a bilingual place. And many discussions around internationalisation in Japanese universities begin and end with the use of English. But to become an international university would also involve changing the culture of the place, becoming more like the leading universities of Hong Kong or Singapore.

Changing a culture would involve getting people to question assumptions, and it would be unsettling. As an example, I commented in class one day that both of the universities I'd attended in the UK (LSE and Nottingham) had had non-British heads, and while that doesn't mean the universities were 'internationalised', it was one option Todai might consider one day. A Japanese student was so upset at this suggestion that he stormed out of the room. I asked him why he was leaving, and he said, 'If you have to ask, you don't understand Japan!' A week later, the student came back in a calmer state of mind. He said that, while he wasn't convinced, he could see the reasoning of what I suggested. I respected him for coming back, and for the process he'd gone through to reach this conclusion. Many people would just stay upset, but he managed to move beyond the emotion to a more considered place. But how many such episodes would be necessary for changes in thinking to occur, and was I the right person to ask such questions?

Japan's demographics cannot be ignored when considering Japanese higher education. Japan has a shrinking population, with many old people who live a very long time. It is predicted that by 2050 the number of eighteen-year-olds will have halved, which has clear implications for the higher education sector: shrink or internationalise. While Todai, given its prominence in Japanese society, would probably be the last place to close its doors, it cannot ignore this reality.

Clearly there is a strong economic case for increasing immigration, with many commentators arguing it is critical for Japan's long-term economic survival. Otherwise, tax revenues will struggle to support the elderly and those in need. But in a society where the central, dominant narrative is one of Japanese uniqueness, there is uneven appetite for more opening of borders. The sociologist Harumi Befu sheds a particular light on this complex issue:

> For the Japanese, their own uniqueness and that of the Japanese culture feature prominently in their conscious thinking. When they characterize their ethnic identity and origin, they are most likely to do this by emphasizing the uniqueness of Japanese culture or some features of it ... The notion that foreigners could fully comprehend Japanese culture and therefore act and behave like any Japanese threatens their ethnic and national integrity.

In other words, it's not just a problem of Japanese uniqueness being diluted by bringing in foreigners with their different views and practices. Even if these foreigners managed to fully assimilate, this in itself is a problem for national identity, because it threatens the very notion on which it is constructed. So from such a perspective, boosting long-term immigration is not attractive, whether it be of Todai academics or factory workers.

I believe in the value of immigration, perhaps not only because I was an immigrant and I am the father of dual citizens, but also because I am the son of a migrant. My mother moved from Ireland to England when she was seventeen to become a nurse, then a midwife, in the UK National Health Service. My father's mother, too, had made the same journey when a young woman, and never left. I'm aware of the risk of conflict, also – my father was a sergeant who fought in Northern Ireland and my mother an Irish nationalist. They'd married a year before the Troubles started, initially bonding over their shared love of Irish history. But two tours in Northern Ireland in the early 1970s, combined with ludicrous amounts of cheap army alcohol, made for a spectacularly belligerent break-up. So while I was keenly aware that cultural identities can clash, I was also not convinced it was my right to argue for immigration in Japan, being non-Japanese. Many Japanese citizens do, however, believe more openness is worth fighting for, and continue to do so.

Mayu and I talked the job offer through at length. A professorship was hugely tempting, for all the usual reasons, and the aim of the role was one I thought important, despite the misgivings about my suitability. But I could not in good grace commit to staying in Tokyo for another fifteen years. I couldn't commit to that anywhere. And, as I'll explain later, we were giving serious consideration to leaving Japan one day, mainly for the girls' education and future. To accept the promotion and then leave not long after would have felt dishonourable.

So I said no. After a shocked silence of some weeks, I was invited to have another meeting with the dean, and after a good discussion of the reasons why I'd refused the offer, we agreed I'd do the role for a minimum three years. As luck would have it, about a month after agreeing I was approached about an attractive post in the UK, but as I'd promised to stay for the three years, I said no.

The Todai job involved grappling with a range of things, from petty tensions between academics ('Why is academia so vicious?' the adage goes, 'Because the stakes are so low'), to genuine issues. Todai used to be the *Imperial* University of Tokyo, and it remains a central pillar and breeding ground of the Japanese elite establishment. Within the university and more widely there are conservative groups who do not want to see certain changes and prefer the status quo, and more progressive elements who argue for the benefits of such changes. At Todai, internationalisation was an issue around which these opposing groups engaged.

Unlike many UK universities, which very much rely on the income from international students, Todai was, in 2011, very well supported by the Japanese government, and student fees at national universities remain relatively low. So the arguments around international students at Todai do not focus mainly on the economic benefits, although for many other Japanese universities the economic aspect is crucial. Because Todai can survive financially as a top domestic university, attracting the best Japanese students and academics, not everyone feels the inclination to welcome or engage with 'the other'. What I mean is, some colleagues at Todai had more atavistic responses to the possibility of Japan's leading university being 'flooded' with foreigners, with many incomers coming from neighbouring countries with which Japan has sometimes prickly relationships.

One shocking conversation I had with someone in a senior management role in a different Japanese university brought this home. This was a professor who was heavily involved in internationalisation and had a considerable worldwide research reputation. During a joint visit to the UK, he invited me to lunch as he wanted my advice on expanding an international research and education network. I'd suggested including a leading university from country X in the network, as there were currently none.

We were having lunch in Oxford, and I'd luckily found a reasonably good restaurant, always a challenge in the UK when you don't know the city you're in. I also knew that the professor in question was famous for travelling with a suitcase half-full of Japanese snacks, because he was not partial to 'foreign food'. So it was with some relief when, after the main course, he said:

> *Thanks Mike, that was a good recommendation. Shall we have a tea?*
>
> *'Sure. I'll have a coffee, I think.*
>
> *Coffee, but you're English! You don't drink coffee, do you. I thought the English only drink tea.*
>
> *Oh, you know, I'm bilingual. I drink both.*
>
> *Huh?*
>
> *Erm, I like to have a coffee after a meal sometimes. Anyway, I wanted to ask what you thought about inviting a university from X to join the network.*
>
> *Well, I think that we have enough contact with them.*
>
> *Yes, but a lot of your partners think you should invite someone from there, to make it more representative. Personally, I agree, as I think you know.*

I said that, knowing full well he knew my views on this. I'd already provoked a whole range of excuses from him for not inviting university from there in previous meetings, such as 'their research isn't good enough', or 'It's too close to Japan, so it's not needed' to 'Our politics are different, so they may not like the network', or 'We might want to talk about educating their students, so it would be too sensitive'. None of these justifications seemed persuasive, and I was intrigued to find out what reason would be given this time. At this point in the conversation he switched into Japanese, and I could hardly believe what I heard. I suspect it is the real reason.

> *Look, the thing is, they're like cockroaches. You let one in, and a hundred will flood through your door.*

I was stunned. I felt the anger brewing inside me, but I didn't know how to react. I stared at him for about twenty seconds, considering whether I should just walk out and leave him at the table. He seemed oblivious, unaware he'd said anything that might be problematic. Indeed, I wonder if he expected me to be flattered, being taken deeper into an *uchi*-relationship by sharing such a statement.

> *Well with that kind of prejudice, it's not surprising relations between the two countries are so bad.*

He looked up, smiled at my rather limp response, and ordered tea for the two of us.

CHAPTER 10

Planning

The period of late spring through summer 2011 was one of increasing happiness for us as a family. As the months progressed, it was becoming clear that we had made it through the threats of the Fukushima disaster relatively unscathed. The aftershocks became less frequent and profound, the readings from the on-campus Geiger counter remained below a dangerous level, and gradually life in the Tokyo metropolitan area became less febrile. The girls were doing fine, both healthy and happy. Julia was still at Katase Primary school, now in Year 4. In Japanese schools the same class stays together through the six years of primary school, and her friendships were becoming deeper with each year. Maya entered her final year at Kiddie Nursery, turning six in May, and winning all the races she took part in in sports events. As a baby she hardly moved, preferring lying on her back to standing up when kicking a ball, so this athleticism was a surprise. Fukushima had become an event in the past for the girls, and unlike so many children from that area, beyond the trauma of the day itself they had suffered very little.

In late April my dear friend David and his family returned to Tokyo, after having spent three years in England. David and I had originally met in 1995, when we both taught English as a foreign language for the same Japanese private language school, which had branches all over the country. At that time, I had been invited to observe training for new teachers at the branch in Ochanomizu, as I'd recently been promoted. David was the head teacher I'd be observing at this branch, and we immediately warmed to each other. After my returning to Japan in 2005 we'd started having weekly lunches together, as well as the occasional family get-together in Fujisawa. I was so pleased that he had now himself returned to Japan, as well as respecting him for taking the opposite journey to so many foreign residents post-Fukushima. Our long lunches near Todai resumed, typically at a small Indian restaurant opposite Todai's famous Red Gate. David would wait under the gate, and I'd rush out of my Thursday lecture at 1pm to meet him. He started doing a couple of classes at Todai, as well, one in creative writing and the other on the twenty-first-century novel.

As the nuclear threat receded into the past with each month, Mayu and I could wholeheartedly engage in one of our favourite hobbies: planning moves. We'd moved a lot in our years together, and by the time we moved into the Orange House this was our tenth home together in twelve years. We now had a big decision to make: do we stay in Japan for the long term, or do we begin to plan for a move either to the UK or somewhere else. Much as our lives were very comfortable, Mayu and I had concerns about the girls being adults in a country that had such a dreadful record in terms of gender equality. While education for women is relatively equal (despite the occasional scandal over entry for women to elite universities), it's in the political and economic spheres where the inequality is most severe.

While the girls were at school, these structural barriers wouldn't be too apparent. There is the everyday sexism that girls, women, and sexual minorities face, but at least they had a forthright, no-nonsense role-model in their mother, and the balancing perspective that being bicultural provides. But it was the prospect of life after full-time education that concerned us. We were also under the impression that the UK was a more ethnically inclusive society than Japan. But I'll return to that assumption later in the book.

In 2009 Mayu had embarked on a part-time degree in English Literature with Nihon University, which allowed her to count the previous two years at college as the first two years of her degree. This meant she 'only' had to complete the equivalent of two further years' full-time education. Her modules had almost all been completed, with distinctions across the board, and come spring 2011 she was in the process of deciding her dissertation topic.

Armed with a BA, she could choose a postgraduate degree. This would help bring the permanence to her career that she wanted. Having worked with the Japanese Nursing Foundation for a couple of years as a translator (on rolling contracts), she'd had a veritable fire lit under her.

The staff there were all women, and many of them had MAs in various subjects. They were working for nurses' rights, and nursing in Japan is largely a female profession. For the first time, right from the interview, Mayu felt genuinely valued for her previous work experience, and often came home with stories of how her colleagues, which included some very senior nurses, were fighting the good fight. They were supportive of her studies, and encouraged her to do a Master's degree.

As I was approaching seven years at Todai, I could apply for a sabbatical. That meant a year, with the family, pretty much anywhere we liked – Istanbul, Bangkok, San Francisco, Sydney, Rome, Rio de Janeiro, Cairo or Paris. We chose Birmingham, England. A major factor in the choice of Birmingham over *any other place in the world* was Mayu's continuing education. As the UK is one of the few places to offer one-year MAs, and given that our future might involve moving back to the UK, we grudgingly decided that a year in San Francisco was not to be. The University of Birmingham had a new MA titled, 'Critical Discourse, Culture and Communication', which Mayu thought was intriguing, so she decided to apply and was accepted. I'd also been invited to be an Honorary Research Fellow at the University of Birmingham, meaning we could have lunches on campus or go for a swim together.

Our plans were firming up. The sabbatical could start in spring or summer 2012, so it gave us plenty of time to get everything in place: apply for the MA, establish myself in my new role in internationalisation, find schools for the girls in Birmingham, find a home, see how the girls reacted to living in the UK, see how we reacted to living in the UK, come back to Japan and then decide what to do. Mayu and I felt almost giddy at the prospect of our futures, the choices that were opening up to us, and the degree of control we had.

Since the time Julia was a baby, we'd made it a goal to go back to 'the other country' once a year together. Between 2000 and 2005 we lived in Nottingham, where I was studying for my MA and PhD and working. Julia was born in 2002, so we travelled to Japan each Christmas for the first few years of her life. Once we'd moved back to Japan, when Mayu was pregnant with Maya, we tried to spend every summer in the UK. This way, the girls' bilingualism and biculturalism could embed, and we could all maintain our roots in both places. It meant we never had any spare money, but it was a small price to pay. I had generous friends with

10.1 Julia and Maya at my mother's house in Ireland, with their wonderful Irish cousins.

comfortable houses in beautiful locations, as well as my parents' homes, meaning we rarely had to stay in hotels.

Watching the girls adjust to life in the UK and Ireland (Figure 10.1) each summer was like watching a dancer relearn steps they hadn't practised for a while. A professor of interpreting and translation, himself a parent to bilingual children, once said to me that being a bilingual was 'a bit like being schizophrenic': you have two distinct personalities, meaning that you not only communicate but even physically move in different ways, depending on the language. I've watched several bilingual speakers on the phone, and they'll bow when speaking Japanese, but not in English. At first my daughters' English responses to questions from relatives and friends were ponderous, and following questions from strangers they would look at me for support before replying. Whereas in Japan a few days earlier they'd been in a state of cultural 'flow', not needing to consider what they should do or say, now they would briefly hesitate before doing or saying something. But within a couple of weeks their normal 'English-speaking' selves were re-emerging, giggling, and chatting, running, and eating lots.

CHAPTER 11

Consulting

Once back in Japan, I had some extra work to do. For some years I'd worked as a communication consultant at a few Japanese multinationals. This allowed me to put into practice some of my research on professional and intercultural communication, while earning extra money for our annual trips to the UK. My friend Hiro Tanaka, a professor at another Japanese university, and I had written a book on workplace communication strategies, focusing on Japanese businesses dealing with overseas partners, clients, and so on. Hiro had decades of experience in the area, both as a researcher and as a consultant, and I had less experience in both, but thankfully enough to be perceived as credible. By the time our book was published in 2009 we'd already been working together for about four years.

Our book had found its way into the hands of the chairman of one of the big Japanese vehicle manufacturers. He was very taken with the main thrust: communication is at heart a collaborative exercise, with colleagues being able to support each other as a team through the practice and adoption of certain communicative strategies. For instance, 'co-construction', the way colleagues can cooperate to communicate a message, and reinterpret what they hear to confirm the intended meaning. This is particularly important for people using a second language, for instance in international negotiations. A higher-level skill is 'strategically summarising', where somebody summarises the discussion so far but does so in a way that aligns with their side's aims. In the book we also discuss how communication is also about the identities we see ourselves and others having.

When I first met the chairman, he explained that his company's staff needed to develop their ability to communicate internationally. He said the older managers were beyond redemption, with too many fixed attitudes, so it was best to train the younger ones. 'These older middle managers, they're so insular, and they can't see more than a year or two into the future. They're like fossils, ha ha! But I can't get rid of them, only the good ones ever leave, ha ha ha! So we need to train the young ones, there's still hope with them. And we need to be planning for what may happen in ten or twenty years! The Japanese market is shrinking, we need to focus on the international market. That's the reason why we need to change our staff's way of thinking, their way of working!' This chairman reminded me of Jackie-san, what with his quick, persuasive judgements and seeming delight in being indiscreet.

Sessions were initially run with the fast-tracked trainee managers who were in their late twenties and early thirties. Later we were allowed to train the older colleagues, many of whom were not fossils. It was challenging work, because some of what we were recommending went against the traditional communicative practices typical of many Japanese organisations, and even wider society. For example, the idea of co-construction sounds attractive in theory, but when you have a senior manager in the meeting who cannot speak English very well being 'supported' by younger colleagues, it could be quite threatening to the manager's sense of 'face'. In other words, as the senior person having a junior colleague interpreting or potentially reinterpreting his (very occasionally her) words might not be well received.

I learnt a lot during the training about the challenges of implementing 'good' ideas. At the end of the day (to use a very clichéd business phrase) in professional contexts, relationships seem to trump everything else. So erring on the side of caution seemed the safest course of action for these young executives. The biggest threat to their future career would be to upset a powerful senior colleague, so we discussed the strategic, targeted use of these ideas.

The training in August and September 2011 would be a culmination of around eight months with the same two groups. We'd moved beyond the use of linguistic strategies, and were exploring the role of culture, stereotypes, and so on. Some years before, we'd found that typically, in this company and the others we worked with, the trainees had a bundle of stereotypes about themselves and others, as we all do. Their stereotypes focused on them as Japanese, and about their non-Japanese clients, partners, and suppliers. It was all very *uchi/soto* (in-group/out-group), with *uchi* being Japanese, and *soto* being the rest of the world. For example: Japanese are more polite than other nationalities, Japanese are shy, Japanese work the hardest; foreigners are lazy, foreigners talk too much, foreigners can't understand Japanese ways of doing things. Much of this is arguably based in the 'uniqueness of Japan' orientation I discussed in Chapter 9.

Unsurprisingly, relationships with overseas clients and partners were not great, which was arguably affecting the bottom line of the company. We'd reported back to the chairman, and he'd asked us to see whether we might break down some of these stereotypes and help the staff to be more inclusive in their thinking and behaviour. This was now the third year we'd been running such training in this company.

Hiro and I had designed several sessions to explore this thorny and culturally embedded issue, with feedback loops built in so the trainees could let us know how things were going, what was working and what wasn't. The first, big step was to deconstruct the main premises, which we identified as: 'nationality is the most important identity we have, essential to who we are'; 'our national identity is fixed, homogeneous, and dictates our behaviour'; and 'being Japanese means we are inherently different from other nationalities'. The next step was to explore how we all have identities beyond the national, and how they may be more relevant in different contexts.

The key concept we introduced is what's termed 'Discourse with a big "D"', in contrast to discourse with a small 'd'. The term 'discourse' (with a small 'd') typically means any stretch of language, for instance a poster saying 'Don't walk on the grass', or a poem, or a transcript of a recorded conversation. When people think about communication, they often focus on **d**iscourse. But to have meaning, we also need to consider the 'who' that is talking/writing/texting etc, what they are doing, where they are doing it, and who and what they are doing it with, what they're wearing, what they are using, what their values and feeling are, and so on. For instance, the words 'I sentence you to five years in prison' need to be said by a judge (a 'who'), in a court (a 'where'), dressed appropriately, with certain values, knowledge, and skills, and so on, to have the power to actually sentence someone. If the same person (the judge) says the same words to her child at home because they haven't tidied their room, they have very different meaning. So **D**iscourse means particular types of people, doing particular types of things, having certain values and beliefs, dressing in particular ways, using types of tools and technologies (in a very broad sense), and being recognised and recognisable by others as being part of that Discourse. An utterance used in one Discourse can have different meanings and effects in a different Discourse. The Discourse of being a judge is clearly very different from the Discourse of a parent, even though it can be the same person, saying the same words. And that's before we dig down further into other identities: the way race, gender, age, class, marital status, and so on intersect, means that the Discourse of being a parent is not the same for everyone.

In the company training, we showed some examples of Discourses I'd noticed in Japanese society. These included Elvis impersonators who gather and dance together every Sunday in a park in Tokyo; students from the construction management laboratory at my university; retired couples at a ballroom dancing club; surfers at Shonan Beach. We then encouraged the trainees to think of different Discourses they were members of, and how this affected communication: how do you talk differently to your weekly choir members and your departmental colleagues? What values are important to each group, and how does this affect the communication? What was the process of becoming a member of the Discourse, and what kind of conventions are important? What happens if someone doesn't follow the conventions? Who are the 'gatekeepers' in the Discourse, deciding who can become a member (or not), and what is appropriate/inappropriate behaviour?

Figure 11.1 shows a range of different Discourses (a) a sculptor, (b) a hiker, (c) an alternative rock fan, and (d) a competitive powerlifter. Each involve the use of different tools, ways of dressing, values, ways of communicating verbally or non-verbally, all of which mean the person can be recognised as belonging to each Discourse.

The point of introducing this concept was manifold: it shows that we all have many different identities; at different moments in our lives, these different identities become relevant; and when members of different Discourses communicate with each other, care needs to be taken as there may be differences in terms of values, tools, practices, and so on. And when we have difference, people tend to make judgements of the other side. We could also appreciate the high degree of diversity within any

11.1 (a) The Discourse of being a sculptor; (b) The Discourse of being hikers; (c) The Discourse of being an alternative rock fan; (d) The Discourse of being a competitive powerlifter.

Discourse, and the role power plays. By eliciting and considering these points, the levels of ethnocentrism, evaluating other cultures from the perspective of our own, seemed to diminish over time.

We also tackled national identity head on: by discussing the variety of Discourses within Japanese society, awareness was raised about the diversity within this apparently homogeneous group. Also, while being Japanese, or Thai, or whatever may be seen (by some) as a Discourse, in many contexts the national is not the most relevant one. This is especially true at work. We shared evidence that differing organisational or professional identities may cause more conflict than national differences. For instance, when salespeople and technical staff communicate, problems can and do arise, some with very serious consequences for the organisation. It is easy for the perceived differences to quickly become issues of trust. We showed studies of humour, and how it can function to bring Japanese and US employees closer.

We also explored the way stereotypes about other Discourses may be self-fulfilling, and how certain communication strategies can help address related issues. We examined how Discourse is a useful way to consider culture, so that intercultural communication can be seen as inter-Discourse communication. This helped to break down the equating of different culture with different nationality. We also practised developing a friendly relationship with a client by finding common ground and shared interests. And we discussed the importance of small talk, for instance about cultural differences around food or weather, as a way of building bridges between different nationalities. We all agreed that if a sense of trust and fairness could be engendered between different professional Discourses, the relationship would be on solid ground.

There were many parallels with my internationalisation work in Todai (see Chapter 9), and working in these different types of organisation allowed for some useful cross-fertilization. Both also provided repeated opportunities for me to realise I didn't understand as much as I initially thought I did about organisational cultures in Japan. But international sales were improving, and the feedback coming through from overseas clients and suppliers was positive. 'Like a different person!', was one such comment we received from a European supplier about one of our trainees. He'd shifted over six months from being highly defensive, ethnocentric and non-communicative, to actively engaging in social occasions, and seeking common ground when he did. The change in attitude seemed to enable a better working relationship, and improved goodwill and sales. We wrapped up the training and it was clear that all parties were very pleased with the results, not least the chairman and the trainees. Hiro and I had a drink at a nearby café to celebrate the invitation to run another year's training.

In late August, David, his daughter and cousin from the UK also came to spend a few days with us in Fujisawa. David has written about some of the most gruesome crimes committed in the UK in the past century but is afraid of the seaside. And sparklers. On the first day, after much haranguing from his daughter, he was persuaded to walk down to Shonan Beach. Like me, he's very pale, so I took my little orange beach tent and we hid from the harsh sun, while the four girls ran around on the sand, and into the sea when David wasn't looking. We then headed back home, and in the evening got some sparklers out. David made sure the kids stood in line at an appropriate distance from each other with their sparklers, at a safe distance. Mayu and I were giggling away as he also prepared a large bucket of water in case of any incident.

Once the kids had gone to bed we had a few drinks in our living room, looking out across the lights of Fujisawa and Shonan Bay and listening to the melodies of Kevin Ayres.

David, do you think Mike's neck looks swollen here?, Mayu asked.
Er, yeah, it is a bit.
It's weird though, I don't have a cold or anything, and this gland seems a bit large,
    I said, feeling around the left side of my neck.
Yeah, my friend got upset with me the other day when I mentioned it. She's usually
    really calm, but she was quite pissed off, Mayu added.
Huh? Why was she upset?
Dunno, I think it's because he hasn't been to the doctor about it. I think her dad died
    of cancer because he'd left it too late apparently.
Yeah, best to get it checked out, just to be sure like.
Yeah, I guess. Huh, imagine if it's cancer! There's no way it is, I feel great.
You don't look it though mate. You look awful,' David said with a grin.
Piss off.

After I'd said goodbye to David and the kids at Fujisawa Station a couple of days later, I popped into a local ENT clinic as it was just a couple of minutes' walk from the station. Japan doesn't have the same GP-surgery system as the UK; instead, there are many small specialist clinics, and then the larger hospitals to which you are referred if necessary. I knew the ENT specialist from having taken the girls to see him a couple of times before. He was one of those rather grumpy but clearly proficient medics. No small talk, just totally clear diagnoses. He felt my neck, uttering a lot of 'Hmm, what's this, hmm, what's this, hmm' as he did. He said he couldn't be sure with the equipment he had in his clinic and recommended another clinic that had ultrasound, and where a more exact examination could be made. It was only five minutes' walk away, so after a quick phone call I wandered up there. The doctor saw me immediately, put the gel on my neck and examined the glands like they were a set of small foetuses. She was also confused, as one of the foetuses wasn't right – there was some kind of lump in there. She assured me it was probably nothing, perhaps some kind of infection, and said I needed to go to Fujisawa Citizen's Hospital to have more tests. An appointment was booked for the following week, and thinking little of it, I returned home via Ashi cake shop to get some family favourites.

CHAPTER 12

Absurdity

Hand in hand with my
Cancer, I watch the white geese
Persevering through
The grey rain. But is it mere
Stubbornness to struggle on?

From Sakai River bank

Japanese is full of words that sound the same, or in linguistics parlance, it is a language that has a high proportion of homonyms. This has several consequences, one being that Japanese can be a confusing language to learn, and another that it's a very easy language in which to make puns. In fact, even for learners of Japanese who haven't reached a high level of fluency, creating puns is not that hard. The problem is, it's what three- and four-year-old Japanese kids do for fun. So while you may think you're being creative and funny, in fact you sound like a four-year-old in a forty-two-year-old's body. The value of things often resides in their rarity, in language as well as elsewhere. Rhyming is so common in Japanese language that it holds little worth, compared to English where rhymes require craft. And so it is with puns.

I'm like the four-year-old who can't help himself. The word for cancer is *gan*, but *gan* also means 'wild geese' (as in a famous novel by Mori Ogai), and 'shore' or 'the bank of a river'. The same syllable also forms part of the words *ganbaru* ('to fight on', or 'persevere'), and *ganko* ('stubborn'). Apart from the wild geese, all these homonyms became relevant at various times during the treatment. And while the above may be a meagre poem in English, the Japanese version is truly awful; it brings to mind the Japanese onomatopoeia *gan-gan*, the sound of being repeatedly hit on the head.

Immediately following my diagnosis at Fujisawa Hospital in September 2011, Mayu's whole focus became my recovery, and this led to many changes. She told me much later that, after returning home with the news and when I'd gone for a walk by myself along Sakai River, she wrapped herself, cocoon-like, in the long curtains in our living room. And she wept like she had never wept before. But when the tears would come no more, she had a realisation that she could help cure my cancer. She said it struck her like an epiphany, with a kind of physical force. To do this, she would have to devote all her attention to the task, and she therefore took a leave of absence from work, and from DJ-ing, to swiftly educate both of us in health and cancer. We started reading everything that seemed relevant, from cancer self-help books to clinical trials on my type of tumour.

The key, we decided, was the boosting of my immune system. It had been ineffective in preventing the cancer in the first place and would need to up its game if I was to survive. The first change involved the transformation of our kitchen into a targeted zone of health. Out went the cocktail shaker and in came a powerful juicer; out went the chocolates, and in came the spirulina; out went the meat, in came the tofu (well, the tofu was there already); goodbye white, hello brown – pasta, rice, bread. As Melanie sang back in the seventies: 'I don't eat white flour, white sugar makes you rot; white can be beautiful, but mostly it's not.' Because Mayu is such a fine cook, the food was not just healthy but delicious, and I felt myself feeling fitter and leaner as the days progressed.

One thing that gave me less pleasure was a daily foot massage. Rather than seeing myself as a coward, as Mayu argues, I'd say I have a strong 'flight from pain reflex'. This is especially so when dealing with pain to my feet. As anyone who's experienced Japanese reflexology will know, it – or at least the version Mayu prefers – is excruciating. It is most definitely not a foot rub – it involves grinding into the soles of each foot with a thin wooden stick to find tender spots. Each part of the foot represents specific internal and external parts of the body, and if a part is sore, this means there is a problem with that part of the body. The neck area, for instance, is the inner part of the big toe. Mine was extremely tender. It therefore demanded a hammering with the Stick of Pain. The hammering continues till the pain subsides (or the victim can deceive the masseur that this is the case).

Mayu had been an amateur ~~sadist~~ reflexologist for twenty years before the cancer came – some of her instruments of torture are shown in Figure 12.1. Now I had no excuse for dodging the stick. As part of my preparation before hospitalisation, and until I was too weak during radiation treatment, I'd have to endure these sessions. Part of the problem was, I do believe that reflexology is effective in addressing health issues. Mayu knew I thought this. So squirming, pleading, swearing, made no difference to her grim purpose. Even crying genuine tears of pain couldn't deter her. She was going to cure me with the stick, even if it reduced me to a crumpled, writhing mass. And Maurice – my friend and yoga teacher who was present many times in these early stages – was no help. He would actually choose to regularly visit 'Dr Foot', a chain of hard-core reflexology salons found across Japan. He was a convert of the 'more pain the better' approach, so his usual compassion didn't extend to my imploring calls. Or probably his compassion was so great that he could ignore the begging, as an exorcist can ignore the words of the possessed and tormented soul. 'Your pain will set you free.' I have no proof it worked, but as Mayu reminds me, I'm still here.

12.1 Some of Mayu's instruments.

So does reflexology actually help in any way? It's accepted nowadays that it can reduce stress, increase well-being, and is (ironically) helpful in pain relief. I know this from personal experience – not just the relief once the session is over, but also in the general feeling of calmness. In terms of how effective it is in boosting the immune system or helping cure disease, 'there is little or no scientific evidence', according to Cancer Research UK, with supporting studies being small in scale or not well designed. And as with acupuncture, there is also a lot of scepticism towards reflexology because of contemporary scientific conceptions of how the body works. How on earth can vigorously massaging certain parts of your foot, for instance, help alleviate migraine headaches? Or how can sticking needles in parts of your ears reinvigorate salivary glands? And yet the clinical evidence shows that it can.

Isaac Newton apparently used to keep a horseshoe on his door, for good luck. When one of his neighbours asked him if he believed in such things, he answered, 'No, but I'm told it works anyway.' Like many cancer patients, this was like my attitude towards a lot of potential remedies. Some may have some evidence supporting them, others not. We decided immediately that the important thing is to not do anything that might endanger my chances of survival. I'm pretty sure that even the more absurd 'remedies' I chose, like sleeping with certain leaves strapped to my neck, didn't do any harm, and you can get a lot of healing benefits from the placebo effect.

Cancer is an absurd disease. Cancerous cells are those that do not stop growing, where cell division occurs inexorably. Like Mickey Mouse's brooms in *Fantasia*. In Siddhartha Mukherjee's imperious ode to cancer, *The Emperor of All Maladies*, he says this unfettered cell division allows cancer cells 'to grow, to flourish, to adapt, to recover, and to repair – to live at the cost of our living. Cancer cells grow faster, adapt better. They are more perfect versions of ourselves …' Cancer tries to kill us, and thus itself, through its perfection of our own cells. That is a considerable absurdity. Then there is the absurdity of the treatment, in my case the poison of chemotherapy and the burning of radiation. Mayu told me of the following joke in Japanese, popular in cancer-circles: 'Doctor, did you cure the patient's cancer?' 'Oh yes, the cancer is all gone. Sadly the patient died, but we got the cancer.'

These are the general absurdities, shared by all cancer-carriers, but there are the specific ones. And each specific one, like every unhappy family, is special in its own way. Some of my absurdities included the timing of the diagnosis and promotion at work, and the lack of any previous cancer sufferers in my family. There was also the state of my health. My body mass index (BMI) was excellent, my resting heart-rate was around forty-five beats per minute (BPM), I played football every week with guys in their twenties and didn't (regularly) feel embarrassed, and my *inteli-scaeru* (intelligent bathroom scales) told me my metabolic age was around thirty-two, ten years younger than my actual age. A week after the diagnosis, I received the results from my annual health check (funded by my employer, a common practice in Japan), and the results on all counts were great.

During those early days I was unsteady, brittle, impotent. And it was always in the evening that the chaos enveloped me. After sitting down for dinner with Mayu and the girls and finding out about their days, the thunder of my emotions became too much. The unfilled space of a fatherless future, and of Mayu walking alone, sleeping alone, crying alone erupted in my mind. Sometimes, suddenly finding myself almost unable to speak, I would excuse myself, put on my favourite shoes (which were now looking threadbare) and head for a walk along Sakai River alone. This was something I'd never done before, and the first couple of nights I did it the girls and Mayu looked sad, rejected even. But by the third night they just let me go. Sometimes I would glance back at our house as I wandered down the bank of the river, and see a figure looking out from the large living-room window.

In the introduction I mention how, when we enter the Kingdom of the Sick, our sense of self, and what we might term intrapersonal communication, changes. When we are well, our body is almost like an absence, because we usually don't even notice it as we go about our daily lives. But with the cancer diagnosis, I was now far from home in my own body, and was wholly aware of it. This was a new sense of otherness, a radical otherness from myself, an otherness within. The philosopher Fredrik Svenaeus considers this sense of otherness during serious illness, saying it can be understood as 'a foreignness that permeates the ill life when the lived body takes on alien qualities'; it is very much being not-at-home (Freud termed this *unheimlichkeit*, not-homelike-ness) in your mental world, and in your body. But we cannot escape from our body, we cannot leave it behind. I think this new reality of emotional chaos desires eventual healing, the chaos having an intrinsic thirst for eventual escape from itself. But the chaos also needs time to be heard, to be walked with, lived with.

Once I was out in the warm early-autumn evening, this sense of otherness slightly receded. It was as if being outdoors created space for the feelings to find equilibrium, but not disappear. And the action of walking gave me a slight semblance of agency; at least I was doing something. Along the riverbanks a few small yachts and pretty cabin cruisers were now moored again. The twists and gentle waves of the river made a changing screen for the nearby electric lights. The red, orange, and green from nearby traffic lights made long, blurred bright paths on the dark water, accompanied by the reflected white lights of doorways along the river. These doorway lights were reappearing as electricity usage increased again. It was now almost seven months after the Fukushima earthquake, and normality was returning to the lives of neighbours.

People were reclaiming their futures again across Japan, whereas I found myself unable to decide if it would be a waste of money to buy a new pair of shoes.

CHAPTER 13

Prognosis

Dr Aoki from Fujisawa Hospital had said I should get a second opinion, even though he was confident the biopsy results from Fujisawa Shimin Hospital were correct. I therefore went to Todai Health Centre the following Monday to arrange an appointment with the University of Tokyo Hospital. I'd been to the health centre several times, for the annual health check that all staff receive, and also any time I had a sore throat or flu symptoms. It was free to students and staff, and always had a few of both in the waiting room. I explained to the receptionist that I had been diagnosed with cancer, and wanted a second opinion. Her usual curtness morphed into something akin to low-level panic, and she fell into formulaic behaviour by stutteringly saying I needed to have my temperature taken, the usual first step for all visitors. I smiled, saying that as I'd already been diagnosed with cancer, I didn't think my temperature was much of an issue. Minutes after, I had a comfortingly matter-of-fact conversation with the on-duty doctor, and an appointment was booked with the Otorhinolaryngology Head and Neck Department for the Thursday morning.

When we got there on the Thursday, I was greeted by a very chirpy doctor around my age, called Dr Nishi, and a rather sullen-looking younger doctor. Dr Nishi explained that they'd like to do another biopsy, just to make sure, which meant the back of my throat had another little lump removed. They claimed to have sprayed the area first with the anaesthetic, but again it seemed as effective as a splash of aftershave. The biopsy, and the CT scan, confirmed the results from Fujisawa Hospital: stage-4 oropharyngeal cancer, with a 5.5 centimetre main cancer behind the tonsils, smaller cancers in two of the neighbouring lymph glands, and some build-up of cancer cells in more distant lymph glands. I'd have to undergo more scans and procedures to check that the cancer hadn't spread elsewhere. Dr Nishi sat Mayu and me down and explained that, while I was most welcome to have the treatment at Fujisawa Hospital, as a member of Todai I was entitled to have my treatment here instead. The University of Tokyo Hospital (Figure 13.1) is world-renowned for its innovative approaches and eminent oncologists. It would mean more travel, but it was a simple decision.

While this was good news, the prognosis was apparently not. Once all the results were back, Mayu and I had a two-hour meeting going over the situation and the plan with the two doctors. Dr Nishi's usual chirpiness was replaced with an earnest will to make us grasp the reality, and he explained with great clarity that my chances were 50/50 at best. Still, this was more positive that the 20–80 odds I'd been told at Fujisawa Hospital, and I warmed quickly to them. 'You've got the job!' I said to Dr Nishi, telling him with a grin that Fujisawa gave me only a 20 per cent chance, so the treatment must be better here. He smiled, humouring my attempt at humour. He was, however, at pains to stress that these are just odds, and it would all depend on how I reacted to the treatment.

13.1 The University of Tokyo Hospital to the left. My room was in the left tower.

Statistics and the cancer patient have a somewhat paradoxical relationship. At times you feel like 'I'm not just a dot on a graph!', and at
other times you want to ask, 'But where am I on the graph?!' S. Lochlann
Jain, author of *Malignant: How Cancer Becomes Us*, talks about how patients
can learn 'what to say to be seen as a person, not as a statistic'. This can
involve learning the right instrumental language to get the right levels of
medication. Paul Kalanithi, a neuroscientist who was diagnosed with ter-
minal cancer at the age of thirty-five, and who wrote *When Breath Becomes
Air: What Makes Life Worth Living in the Face of Death* during the last year of
his life, talks of one cancer patient making sure she always wore her best
socks. This is so the oncologist sees she is someone worth treating as an
individual. So maybe I should have bought the new shoes. But the other
side of the paradox, the wanting to know where we are on the survival
chart, is according to Kalanithi, beyond our grasp: 'Getting too deeply
into statistics is like trying to quench a thirst with salty water. The angst of
facing mortality has no remedy in probability.' For me, this meant learning to tolerate the profound uncertainty a cancer diagnosis gives birth
to. In intercultural communication, much is made of the importance of
'tolerating ambiguity'. Ambiguity is inherent in new contexts, where our
expectations of usual behaviour may not be accurate, for example when
we visit a new place (or interact with a new Discourse). Cancer creates a
different order of ambiguity, which at times is intolerable.

The treatment, we were told, would involve two week-long periods
of intensive chemotherapy, with three types of drugs being fed intravenously twenty-four hours a day, followed by thirty-five days of radiation
treatment. The treatment could not involve surgery because the cancer
had spread so much into the tissue in my throat. I still wonder how it's
not possible to notice a lump in your throat the size of a very generous
piece of sushi.

I would be an in-patient for the chemotherapy and have to stay for
some time before and after each of those 24/7 chemo runs, but would be
an out-patient for the daily dose of radiation. Dr Nishi emphasised that
the treatment was extremely intense, physically debilitating, with severe
short- and potentially long-term side effects. I would lose weight, I would
lose my sense of taste, my salivary glands would stop working, I would
lose my hair, I would suffer from fatigue for a long time, I might suffer
from depression, my ability to work in the future might be permanently

affected, I would feel illogically cold all the time, and the pain from the radiation would become excruciating. The chances of a secondary cancer further down the line, caused by the radiation, was also a possibility. The chemotherapy drugs were toxins, and some patients suffered anaphylactic shock, which could be fatal.

Dr Nishi also said most of these side effects should eventually pass, or at least lessen in severity. I couldn't help noticing the irony that the treatment causes such pain and misery, but the tumour none. If we could have come to some agreement, the generous piece of sushi could have sat contentedly behind my tonsils forever, and I would happily have left it there. Sadly, you can't negotiate with a lunatic parasite bent on self-destructive colonisation.

Dr Nishi then told us that I could be admitted the following week, and that the hospital would be in touch. He advised me to contact work immediately to let them know I would be away for some time. It looked like the treatment would take around four months, meaning I could go back to work in February if the treatment was successful, and if I was up to it. He said at least I was relatively young and, barring the obvious, in good physical condition.

He then asked if there was anything we wanted to know. I think he'd been talking for about an hour and a half when he finally asked if we did have questions. I was so glad that Mayu was there, because there were parts that were beyond my Japanese listening ability. It felt like information overload, layered with the challenge of its being transmitted in a second language. But it wasn't just that; looking back now, it was clear I was to have no active role in either the decision-making about the treatment, or the process of the treatment. I was being positioned as a passive agent in all this, 'We the medical team will do this to you, so best you lie there and don't move.' Again, Paul Kalanithi captures this beautifully, in terms that warm a linguist's heart: 'I had passed from the subject to the object of every sentence in my life ... as a patient, I was merely something to which things happened.'

In Chapter 11 I introduced the concept of Discourse with a big D as a way of understanding our social identities. I think this concept can also be applied to capture the experience of being a cancer patient. Seeing oncologists and other cancer healthcare professionals as a Discourse, with their own ways of doing things, their values, practices, expertise, tools, and so on is not much of a leap, but perhaps seeing cancer patients (and carers of patients, like Mayu) as a Discourse is less obvious. S. Lochlann Jain talks of the 'grammar of cancer' which I think has a lot of parallels with what I'm suggesting here. They argue that being told you've got cancer means

> ... learning a whole slew of unwritten codes for how to be a sick person. All this work of learning how to negotiate one's personal and social identities that are usually learned over years – such as how to live as a white or brown person, how to live as a gendered and queer person, as a child, or an adult, and so on – all this needs to be learned quickly as one is learning how to cope with the diagnosis of a life-threatening illness.

With Discourse, we have a primary Discourse, the one we grow up learning as a child, and all the secondary Discourses we learn later in life (profession, hobby, etc.). I think Jain's list of stuff you learn while growing up, about our race, gender, sexuality, form part of our primary Discourse. The 'grammar of cancer', which needs to be learnt very fast, and had unwritten or tacit codes and practices, is to my mind a secondary Discourse.

For different cancer patients there will be differences in the Discourse, for instance, relating to their prognosis. One of my friends was diagnosed with stage-0 bladder cancer, had an operation, and was basically able to forget about the whole thing. Another dear friend had an aggressive brain tumour, and was given less than a year to live. Doug, we miss you. But there are also differences in terms of how active people want to be in the decision-making over their treatment, or in terms of the technologies and tools they'll need (or better, *choose*) to engage with. I'll talk more about this idea in later chapters, but suffice it to say at this point I didn't mind feeling that I was being taken care of, and the decisions about my treatment taken out of my hands. The sense of chaos was overwhelming, and Dr Nishi's forthright but jolly approach was a balm to my mind.

After thanking Dr Nishi, Mayu and I headed straight over to my department, about fifteen minutes' walk across campus, to talk to my colleagues about my taking time off. I'd recently moved buildings, and the administrative staff I was managing as part of my new internation-alisation role hardly knew me. While telling the person in charge of schedules that I was going to be taking four months off because I needed medical treatment, I couldn't help sensing some incredulity on his part. Whether this was down to my apparently direct Japanese over such a massive request, or whether he thought it shocking that a new person in a role, however senior, would have the temerity to announce they were taking such a long time off, I was not sure. And I didn't look sick at all. We collected the necessary paperwork and wandered off to get a coffee and talk things through.

As we walked out of the building, I bumped into one of my postgraduate students whom I'd taught the previous semester.

Hi Mike-sensei, how's it going?

Oh, you know. I smiled, and there was a pause as he studied my expression.

I'm really looking forward to your classes this semester. Are they starting next week?

Er, I won't be teaching that module I'm afraid, hopefully there'll be a replacement lecturer.

Really? How come?

I'm sick, and I have to go to hospital.

Oh, is it serious?

I stopped for a second, looking at him, not knowing what to say. Eventually I just said, 'Yes'. He also paused, staring at me, said something about hoping I would be back soon, and then walked into the building. Mayu reminded me of this conversation after the treatment had finished, saying that she realised that this is how people die, how they pass into the memories of the living: the well usually move on. She felt that in this student's mind, who was a very good guy, I was already becoming a ghost. Yes, someone towards whom he might feel a lingering warmth and sadness, but someone who was, for practical purposes, in his past, an 'other' from another time. She said she realised at that moment that our new life was starting, that we were moving into a different existence.

Mayu also noticed that some people began to talk about me in the past tense once they'd heard the news – 'Mike was such a nice guy, that's awful.' She wanted to scream at them 'He's not dead!', but in many people's minds cancer is final, shifting all cancer patients into the waiting room of the deceased, into that other place.

As the past may be a different country, so is this Kingdom of the Sick. The future was beginning to change, in that we could predict with considerable certainty what every day of the next four months would involve, much more so than usual. And with the repetitions of this routine, the present and the future of this period seemed to merge. But then the future stopped in four months' time, we couldn't know what was after that. While I felt lost in that uncertainty, I could sense that Mayu was looking for ways beyond it. I think it was on this day that she decided to contact Maurice.

CHAPTER 14

Maurice

What is the meaning of cancer? One of the main areas of linguistics is concerned with understanding how language becomes meaningful in different contexts. Indeed, one simple definition of 'meaning' is 'language in context' – and if you take language out of context, it no longer has meaning. So when my colleague Richard Gwyn states, 'Illness is constructed, reproduced and perpetuated through language', he's not suggesting that illnesses are reproduced in the biological sense, but in the sense of how we understand them, how we engage with them, what we let ourselves do (and not do) about them.

I mention context here because cancer is one of those events that seems to bring a new collection of expectations and rules with it, but also a set of new possibilities. Cancer is a context, and it is something we do – in the Introduction, I asked if we might usefully see it as a verb. Whether we do or not, cancer is very much a new reality, shaping time, space, physicality, relationships, and opportunities. Some freedoms may be lost, and there is the shadow of life itself being lost. But standing in this shadow, and with Mayu gripping my hand, I glimpsed that all was not lost, not yet.

Cancer patients often talk of how the disease inevitably means you relate to people you know somewhat differently. In the Introduction I talked about interpersonal relationships becoming like intercultural ones because you have become something of an other to friends and loved ones. Your new sense of otherness is, perhaps, Janus-faced: cancer separates you from some people and brings you closer to others. I think the new context of cancer enables some relationships to gain a meaning renewed, and one imbued with renewal; a meaningfulness that would not have been possible before cancer. This group can include nurses and other healthcare professionals, but also people we know personally but perhaps didn't really 'see' before the diagnosis. One such person for me was Maurice Joosten.

The first few times I met Maurice, I just considered him a taciturn, skinny guy who smelled nice and looked the part of an artist. A couple of attempts at conversation hadn't resulted in much, and I'd left it at that. Mayu had talked to him more than I had at the informal get-togethers a few neighbours had set up so their children could practise English (Maurice has a child around Julia's age). He'd turn up regularly at the weekly events, and he seemed to have a knack of engaging the kids in flights of imagination, getting them to act vigorously as spiders and all sorts. Once I'd been diagnosed, Mayu decided to ask him round, as she had a vague but strong feeling he might be able to help in some way.

Maurice is one of those people for whom time does not seem to be a quantifiable commodity, a commodity that many of us see as something to 'spend' or 'waste'. Things take as long as they need for Maurice: time is elastic and some things require a lot of time for a good result to be achieved. This is very much the case when he's giving up his time for others, despite having a family and three professions (sculptor, scent architect and yoga teacher). Though 'professions' sounds rather transactional when applied to Maurice; 'vocations' might capture his commitment more accurately.

'There is no point being frustrated about this, the frustration is caused by a misunderstanding of time', I can imagine him thinking if I said something about wasting his time. I say thinking, because he'd be too sensitive to others' feelings to state it as baldly as that. He'd be much more likely to smile and say, 'It's OK, I'm not so busy today.' I found this quite disconcerting at first and had to remind myself that the guy sitting in my house was here to help me, even though we'd been talking for two hours and there were so many things I hadn't got done, never mind what he hadn't. This was especially so when the time left to me might have been no more than a few months. But over the course of the treatment and beyond, my sense of time also shifted. This was very much Maurice's influence, and I thank him.

On the first afternoon he came round, it was a typically sunny early October day, warm without the humidity of summer. We talked for some time about the diagnosis and proposed treatment and he had a good feel of my throat. The gland on the left side was clearly swollen, and my neck was flabbier than it deserved to be. No doubt it was the toxins that were congregating there. After talking for half an hour or so, he said we could try a bit of yoga, looking around my living room as he spoke. 'Why don't we do it on the roof then?' I suggested, and he thought this a great idea.

The session lasted around an hour, and was the most gentle form of yoga I had done or seen. Not that I was much of a yogi. For most of the session we lay on our backs, looking up at the clear autumn sky, and the movements were minimal and slow. After a few deep breaths, Maurice began by saying, 'Feel the mass of your body ... your head ... your hands ... your legs ... as if your whole body sinks, melts into the ground. Notice the changing sensations from your feet, to your knee, to your upper thigh ... you can abandon all control ... inhale, turn up, straighten the back, raise the head slightly from the floor, move forward ... inhale deep and completely exhale, and give it time to finish. In every exhalation there is a giving up, no holding on, no resistance.' This was then followed by a long silence, and the message resonated with me through the silence. It communicated a relevance to my situation; a brief glimpse that resisting my diagnosis would not help me at all. Throughout our sessions, Maurice would repeat this message of 'there's no resistance, accept the condition as it is', and while it usually followed instructions to move into a physical posture, it related to more than the physical for me.

We then carried on with some very gentle bodily movements, focusing strongly on the breathing. Maurice modelled the breathing, and his exhalations had a guttural sound (also termed 'the ocean breath', or Ujjayi breathing). This surprised me at first, but later through practice, I realised that this happened when breathing very slowly and deeply in a relaxed state. It's similar to the sound actors make when they slowly, peacefully pretend to pass away on stage. So it's not one to practise in front of the kids when you have cancer; but on our secure flat roof, accompanied only by some kite-hawks circling high above and the odd insect buzzing past, there were no such concerns.

Each session involved many opportunities for self-reflection on the feelings, physical and emotional, of the moment. In recent years I've practiced mindfulness daily. Now I can appreciate that Maurice's sessions were a very meditative type of yoga, with a lot of emphasis on awareness of the breath with the body in stillness. And the context of cancer lends itself well to an awareness of the now, the point of mindfulness. With cancer, you are forced into the present, there is only the brutal reality of now. Also, because you fear you have no future, you may regret so many wasted moments that pad the past. Mindfulness offers a way of taming these torrents of perceived time, the torrents that a cancer diagnosis brings. For me, these sessions with Maurice meant I could begin to feel less like I was being overwhelmed by the reality of the now. I could begin floating on these torrents, and at times even gain some satisfaction from the insights I was gleaning. In his poem 'Auguries of Innocence', William Blake talks about time in a sense that I think captures this shift:

> To see a World in a Grain of Sand
> And a Heaven in a Wild Flower
> Hold Infinity in the palm of your hand
> And Eternity in an hour.

In the same poem, he repeats, 'Some are born to sweet delight, some are born to endless night.' While this may be true for some, I think for most of us, we graft and shunt between the two extremes. Thanks to Maurice, I could see that the place I chose to live was partly in my own hands. Through his exhortation to forgo resistance, I could indeed begin to accept my condition on an emotional level. This did not mean I resigned myself to dying. In fact, as I learnt to accept my condition in its entirety, my belief that I would not die of this cancer diagnosis became stronger.

After about thirty minutes of practice, Maurice brought the first of our many sessions together to a close. I felt a calmness I hadn't expected. I opened the door and shouted down to Mayu that we'd finished. I then popped downstairs to make some tea. In the kitchen, she was shocked when she looked at my neck. The swelling had gone down so much. I got a mirror and it was definitely different. The flabbiness seemed to have lessened, and even the swollen lymph node seemed smaller. All three of us liked this sign.

As we drank our tea on the roof chatting, a praying mantis jumped onto Maurice's arm and sat there peacefully for about ten minutes. He didn't seem particularly surprised. One of Maurice's other roles in life is as a creator of scents from essential oils, for instance from the sublimely scented *hinoki*, or Japanese pine. This meant he always smelled beautiful. I don't know if the praying mantis thought Maurice was a *hinoki*. He looks a bit like a tree, a supple tree with thin but strong branches and a shaggy growth at the top. I've since learnt that praying mantises signify meditation and patience in certain religions. Indeed, the term 'mantis' comes from the Latin meaning 'prophet or seer'. It was one of those incidents I had during my recovery that seemed pregnant with meaning, one that signalled my moving into a new context.

When we finished our tea, Maurice came up with a radical suggestion. How about I delay going into hospital for a couple of weeks, to allow me time to prepare myself for the imminent ordeal of the treatment? Maurice has written about this time, recalling his impression of me: 'The first time I visited Michael at his house to start the practice, he looked devastated, like a sentenced man with fear and despair in his eyes. You could clearly see the emotional impact of such a verdict on the level of the mind/body.' That sounds about right.

I contacted the hospital, and they said delaying by a fortnight would make no difference to the overall prognosis. Just making this decision meant I was doing something, and it was a first step out of the chaos, the 'devastation'. Along with Mayu's health regime, my own exercise routine which involved running, swimming, and weight-training (I didn't think I could cope with talking to people at football), Maurice's yoga sessions and the work on metaphor I'll describe in subsequent chapters, we had embarked unknowingly on what is now termed 'prehabilitation'. Prehabilitation involves the patient preparing the mind and body before they endure something like major surgery, or cancer treatment. The cancer charity Macmillan talk of five key areas in prehabilitation: physical activity, eating well, mental well-being, drinking less alcohol, and quitting smoking. Parts of the NHS are now investing in it because it is shown to have significant long-term benefits in terms of recovery, and also overall mental and physical well-being. At the time, Mayu and I weren't sure there was a long term for me, but as we had nothing to lose by postponing the treatment, this is what we decided. I'll let Maurice have the final word on the changes he saw over this period:

> Michael became more open and tried out new and unknown paths, exploring all kind of different treatments and at the same time surrendering himself to the long healing process and the fight for his life. The time he took out and reserved for himself before going into hospital helped him

to recentre and reconnect to reality. If the body and mind are already defeated beforehand, there is little healing possible. Very quickly in the week when we daily practised, there was a clear perceivable change when his life force seemed to return, where he was being present again, open and combative, more centred, grounded, and engaging.

Thank you Maurice, thank you Mayu.

CHAPTER 15

Framing

I am a hypochondriac who got cancer. According to Dr Arthur Barsky, author of *Worried Sick: Our Troubled Quest for Wellness*, most people ignore many bodily sensations whereas hypochondriacs do not. When hypochondriacs have an upset tummy, they attribute it to some serious condition, such as potential stomach cancer, or a headache as a sign of an oncoming stroke. So when a hypochondriac like me is diagnosed with something very serious, part of me says, 'See! I was right!' It's a bit like the old joke of the inscription on the hypochondriac's tombstone: 'I told you I was sick.'

A little time after the initial shock of the diagnosis, I was reminded of a line by George Orwell in *Down and Out in London and Paris*. There is, he notes, a certain amount of consolation to be found in the fact that you have hit rock bottom. 'It is a feeling of relief, almost of pleasure, at knowing yourself genuinely down and out,' he writes. 'You have talked so often of going to the dogs, and you have reached them, and you can stand it.' On some days, the better days, this was how I felt about the cancer diagnosis, and I imagine I'm not the only hypochondriac to react like this. But on reflection, I never did reach rock bottom, not really. I always had hope.

The mind is a many-layered tool. When I reflected on my reactions to cancer during the fortnight of 'prehabilitation', these layers became more apparent. This in turn allowed me to develop my sense of agency concerning the disease. These are some of the layers that navigated my understanding.

Layer 1: I function as a hypochondriac.
Layer 2: I realise I function as a hypochondriac.

Layer 3: I feel darkly amused that being a hypochondriac means having cancer is not so shocking.

Layer 4: I am aware of the irony of 3, and that such a reaction is not set in stone.

Layer 5: Because of Layer 4, I am aware that others could have different reactions.

Layer 6: I develop the insight, based on the awareness realised in Layers 4 and 5, that the *relationship* I have with cancer is, to some extent, in my own hands.

Layer 7: I intentionally develop a relationship with cancer that benefits me.

In other words, if I could feel amused about the hypochondria–cancer dynamic, I can feel pretty much anything about cancer. I saw that I was not just passive in the whole diabolic carnival, but I could have some input in how I wanted to deal with the situation. In particular, I could choose the relationship I wanted to have with my cancer. The very act of seeing it as 'my cancer' was, in itself, a change. I was in the process of othering my cancer less, by seeing it as mine, part of me.

After realising I was at least partly in control of how I felt about cancer, I had a second insight: I could also decide to communicate with my cancer. The yoga sessions with Maurice on my roof in the warm autumn sunlight, and the long chats afterwards, very much helped create the ground for such insights. I'm using the word 'communicate' here in the sense of talking to yourself, but not in the out-loud sense. It is the mindful difference between, on the one hand, shouting angrily, and on the other having a nurturing conversation with yourself about your current feelings of anger. It's more than just internal dialogue: it is also deciding the terms of reference, or what in psychology and linguistics is termed a 'frame'.

'Framing' concerns the way we interpret and then interact with different situations. For instance, if a friend says, 'I hate you', but does it in a way that lets you know they are joking – through a smirk or by intonation – you will interpret this as being said in a playful frame and not be offended. The frame affects the meaning of what is said, but it also affects the way we see the world at that point in time. A frame is really a set of expectations, a context. Each frame will lead us to ignore some things while adding value to others. This is because the expectations you have about something will very much affect the way you perceive it, interpret things related to it, and communicate with it. Even the common initial reaction to cancer of being shocked and scared, well represented in the Macmillan advert where patients are seen falling to the floor following diagnosis, is a frame.

I had to work out how best to frame my relationship with my cancer, and this would involve these two conversations: one with me, and one with the cancer itself. And I knew that heightening my sensitivity to this new absurdity ('talking to cancer'?!) was going to be central to the way I communicated. This felt good, because the absurd is often funny, and funny in dark places is nearly always good. Also, the absurd frees us up from the constraints of the frame of the normal. And living in what Christopher Hitchens called 'Tumourtown' is not normal.

When you find yourself in Tumourtown, you're making adjustments to living in a place you'd rather not be. It involves learning new words and ways of talking to navigate your way through this alien place that is your new home, and trying to communicate with people who see you as different, some of them suddenly so. As I discuss in the Introduction, there are layers of othering going on in many directions, between you, your carers, the cancer, and so on.

Framing helps explain a lot of these changes that have suddenly arisen, not least through the way the intercultural perspective operates at such times. The way I see a situation, what my expectations are, may not be the same as the way my oncologist or my old friend sees it. Through considered communication we may navigate these alternative frames and become aware of our differences, which is a consolation and a hope. As with the best intercultural encounters, once we've understood the extent of our differences, we can more deeply appreciate the extent of our similarities and our shared hopes, and build a shared frame together. Being aware that you may be perceived as an other by some people who didn't see you like that before, or didn't know you before, is a first step to lessening the distance between you. I realise that for some people with cancer, this might seem like an extra burden. Each person deals with their cancer in their own way, and this was mine.

F. Scott Fitzgerald said that the test of a first-rate intelligence is the ability to hold two opposed ideas in mind at the same time and still retain the ability to function. This may be so, but according to some psychologists, we suffer what is termed 'cognitive dissonance' when we hold two or more contradictory ideas, values or beliefs. I think psychologists are talking here about people in 'normal' frames, in the Kingdom of the Well. When you are life-threateningly ill, then you're plunged into a state of cognitive dissonance, or absurdity, or chaos. We might say it's a Frame of Chaos. Partly this is because you are confronted with a society which you walk around in, but are now outside of.

As an other, you are by definition a member of a different culture. Cancer is a culture with different practices from most people, like having chemotherapy treatment, but the culture also affects things like the way you perceive future time. The whole concept of future is fractured, so things like advertising, or career plans, make little sense. You consider future parenting responsibilities from the perspective of an absent parent. I had the idea of recording some videos for each year of my girls' lives until their eighteenth birthdays, where I imagine what they're up to and tell them I love them. But then I wondered whether this might darken their birthday fun. It might even become something they secretly dread, an obligation to a half-forgotten man. Then there are the more existential questions. What strengths, or indeed weaknesses, will they carry into adulthood that are my responsibility, but which I won't be there to nurture, or clumsily atone for?

We live so much of our mental lives in the future, in a future we imagine with certainty. The sudden cancer-induced awareness of this future's precarity is like being abruptly interrupted in a conversation, and realising the other person is absolutely right. Perhaps all you can say after a thoughtful pause is, 'Oh, OK'. In that sense, a cancer diagnosis really is a conversation stopper. The inner conversation over your future-self ceases to be a topic in the bleaker moments, instead morphing into a conversation about the self-absent future. The future will still happen, in the same way your workplace will continue to function after you have retired and your office is someone else's.

I soon realised that these inner conversations were going to be conducted through metaphor, and through stories. Our minds need stories and metaphors to make sense of new things, a theme I'll develop more in the next chapter. It is in this way that language is so much more than a mere vessel through which thoughts are transmitted. Rather, language can work as a frame, like a lens. This lens focuses our attention on certain aspects of the world and enables us to ignore others. The metaphors and stories we use form a key part of the lens and are far more prevalent in the way we construct and interpret the world around us than common sense would suggest. When you wear glasses, you don't tend to notice the lenses.

Once we accept the importance of frames, stories, and metaphors, and the way they affect how we see the world, we can be much more dynamic in the way we negotiate and relate to anything or anybody. It's a question of the right stories, and the right metaphors. Jackie Stacey in *Teratologies: A Cultural Study of Cancer* describes how metaphors can 'rush to the rescue of the subject whose terror is otherwise uncontainable'. And for many people with cancer, what could be more important than that?

CHAPTER 16

Unruly

The oft-quoted opening of Susan Sontag's *Illness as Metaphor*, is a powerful reminder of the inevitability of sickness at some stage of our life:

> Illness is the night-side of life, a more onerous citizenship. Everyone who is born holds dual citizenship, in the kingdom of the well and in the kingdom of the sick. Although we all prefer to use only the good passport, sooner or later each of us is obliged, at least for a spell, to identify ourselves as citizens of that other place.

I think the emotional truth of Sontag's message is that being seriously ill does indeed feel like being a citizen of a different place. As I've discussed already there are different rules, people treat you differently, and you have to interact with different people. You can become slightly invisible to some people, while provoking sudden tears in others. You learn new words to communicate and develop a detailed knowledge of things that were perhaps heard of, but not understood. Some things that were very important are no longer so. And while some freedoms are withdrawn, there can be opportunities. We enter a new Discourse, and part of that Discourse involves having the right metaphors.

During the two weeks following the diagnosis, I realised I had to come to terms with my 'new normal', that of being a citizen in a strange and frightening land. The feeling of being overwhelmed meant I was struggling to cope. I was indeed 'haunted and hunted'. I quickly noticed that the predominant way of seeing cancer (the common-sense perspective) seemed to be as a battle, with the cancer 'attacking' you, or treatment 'attacking the cancer', and then you need to 'fight' the cancer, a gladiatorial battle that ends with either you or the cancer killed. Also, cancer is often seen as something alien and invasive. While I can understand these metaphors, for me they didn't ring true. For some people, these cancer-as-war metaphors do seem helpful. But for me, cancer was a part of me, my body had created it from itself (with a little help from my behaviour and environment). So seeing the cancer as something alien, and something that I needed to fight, didn't ring true. I started thinking about what would make sense to *me*. What kind of metaphor would allow me to communicate with myself, and communicate with my cancer, in a way that seemed natural?

I'm aware that for many people, the way I'm talking about metaphor may seem odd. Surely metaphors are just the flowery bit of language that we find in poems? That's how I used to understand metaphor, but now I see it very differently. Now, I think metaphor underlies the way we see the world. It was reading the highly influential book *Metaphors We Live By* that changed my mind. The authors make two points: we use a lot more metaphorical language than we think we do; and, more contentiously, metaphor isn't just an adornment to our communication, it provides the underlying structure for how we conceptualise the world.

In other words, we see the world through metaphor. One of my colleagues at Cardiff University, Lisa El Rafaie, has researched how metaphors are employed in graphic novels about illness, including cancer (Figure 16.1). She argues that many of our everyday metaphors are inverted or reversed when we enter the 'Kingdom of the Sick', as a way of making sense of our new reality. Our bodies, now dysfunctional, can seem alien, absurd, or grotesque, and metaphors can help us make sense of that alienness. Below is an example of one such metaphor in a graphic cancer narrative that Lisa analyses. The author, Jennifer Hayden, is showing her reaction to a breast-cancer diagnosis.

While the way we think affects our relationship with cancer, we cannot think our cancer away. Indeed, scientific evidence strongly suggests that your attitude to your treatment does not have an effect on the success of the treatment. This is a sobering finding, one that casts a stark light on the efforts of charlatans who profit from cancer patients' suffering in the form of snake-oil remedies, such as healing cancer through positive thinking. But our way of thinking can definitely affect what we *do* during our treatment (smoking or not smoking, for instance), and how we *experience* our treatment. This explains why there is a such an amazing range of responses to the reality of having cancer: many feel dread and loathing, others may feel love towards their cancer. And if I had to choose between

16.1 One of the pages of the graphic cancer narrative 'The Story of My Tits', by Jennifer Hayden.

seeing cancer as a battle or as a journey, then it would definitely be as a journey. But I chose neither metaphor, and instead created one. At the time I thought I was a bit of a genius, hitting on such an idea. Since then, I've found out it's not that uncommon, and linguistics colleagues at Lancaster University have made some excellent resources relating to this approach, for instance an online 'A Metaphor Menu for People with Cancer'.

For me, it was important to decide on a metaphor that was rooted in my experience. I'd never been in a battle, I didn't like the undertones of battling it (nor did Sontag), and the journey metaphor struck me as a bit passive, a bit like being on a conveyor belt. Thinking about what I knew, what I had done in my life, something related to education seemed most natural. And something that helped me feel as if I was an active agent in the situation, not just somebody to whom things are done. I hit upon the idea of having some teacher-student relationship at the core, but one with some difficulties, and decided upon CANCER AS AN UNRULY CLASSROOM. This involved me being the teacher, and the cancer being my students. Rather naughty, rebellious students at that. Like all half-decent teachers, I'd like to think I care about my students. I want what's best for them, especially when they may not know what is best for themselves, or are doing things that are detrimental to their well-being or success. As someone who was a bit of a mixed bag of an undergraduate student myself, I had some experience of that student perspective, too, and I've always been drawn to disengaged students who give the slight hint that they do, deep down, want to study.

What did it mean, to frame my cancer as an unruly classroom? It meant that I could talk to myself about it without seeing it as something wholly negative, or wholly alien. Every classroom unfolds as a dynamic between the teacher and the students. It meant I had hope, because all classes, even the ones that get off on a terrible footing, can improve. I know that from bitter experience. And it allowed for a giggle sometimes, because most classes benefit from a bit of humour now and again. But apart from talking to myself, this also allowed me to talk directly to my cancer: the unruly students needed to understand that there were various things being done to them to help them learn to be a better class. My 'prehabilitation' was a case in point. And being a better class would really be in the students' interest, if they could be persuaded to take a longer-term view.

Some things might seem shocking to the class, as they would involve tough love in the form of pain or restraints. These included poison in the form of chemotherapy drugs, burning in the form of radiation, no foodstuffs beyond those of a macrobiotic diet, and exercise in the form of, well, exercise. I could visualise that the classroom in my neck would be a very settled and engaged class by the end of the process – they wouldn't be unruly any more because of all the things being done for their benefit. There might be one or two unruly bits of behaviour now and again, but provided these didn't develop, everything would be OK.

I have already talked about how the intercultural concept of 'the other' seems to shed light on different aspects of having cancer, such as people suddenly perceiving you as an other, as the outsider. The French poet Arthur Rimbaud wrote the phrase 'Je est un autre', which would roughly translate as 'I is an other', in a letter to his friend Paul Demeny on 15 May 1871. It's a phrase remarkable in its marriage of form and message: normal grammatical and phonological conventions are over-turned, as are the normal social conventions, by his existence. As some-one with cancer, this line seemed to have a special resonance. In some cultures, cancer can lead to being ostracised in society, and many would recognise the silences that accompany the stigma or taboo of a cancer diagnosis. But there's also the way you may perceive your own tumour as an other, an alien outsider who is far from welcome. For some people, continuing to otherise their cancer may be the best way for them to deal with it mentally and emotionally. In the Lancaster metaphor menu, one example is 'I want to fight. I don't want it to beat me, I want to beat it.' But for me, changing my relationship with it, through the class-room metaphor, helped me develop a much stronger sense of agency. Gradually I came to see my cancer not as something that was other, I came to see it as part of me. Again, in the cancer metaphor menu, one that chimes with me is this one: 'Cancer is part of me, the cure for can-cer is accepting it, to heal is to convince the cancer cells to sing in tune with the rest of the body.'

There's the old joke that insanity is hereditary, you catch it off your kids. In my family's case, the same might be true of neck cancer, as my mother developed it some years after I did. She didn't have the HPV ver-sion, though, more the traditional heavy smoker+heavy drinker variety. At the time, I talked to her about my classroom metaphor, and how it had helped me reframe the relationship. She agreed that the 'cancer is war' metaphor was unhelpful, because it would make her see cancer as an enemy. And the problem with enemies is that you are afraid of them. So she decided to frame the cancer as a friend, a friend who is visiting for a short time. Her take on it was that she didn't need to have a really specific identity for the cancer, just not positioning it as an enemy was the main thing.

For people with leukaemia, developing a relationship with cancer provokes specific challenges, because the cancer is not a separate 'thing' like a tumour, it is running inside you. In an academic article titled 'When Cancer is the Self', one patient who uses the nickname

Luke for her leukaemia describes her situation in these impressively combative terms:

> It's in my blood. Yeah, in my blood. Yeah. I also had a tumor. I called him Tommy. Tommy the tumor. And Tommy and Luke came to the party and they weren't invited, so I had to evict them, and they left. And they took their shitty friends with them.

Other people talk about loving your cancer. The point is, you can't decide whether you have cancer, but you can decide how you frame it, in a way that chimes with you, and influences whether (and how) you communicate with it. This then affects how you emotionally respond to the situation, and how you continue to negotiate life. For while the metaphors we live by may not affect the success of the treatment, they most certainly affect how we choose to live in the time we have.

CHAPTER 17

Sanshiro

Many think that Tokyo by daylight is an unbeautiful place. I do wonder if it's to do with the lack of nature, especially compared to other great cities. Around 40 per cent of Hong Kong, for instance, is made up of woods, parks, and gardens, whereas in London it's a third. Tokyo, by comparison, features a dismal 7 per cent of green space. When I conjure Tokyo in my mind, it's an endless expanse of three-dimensional concrete, grey spikes, and flats, and widths. But there are flecks of beauty in the greyness, and one of these is Todai's main campus. It was built on the grounds of an old Samurai family's palace, and at the heart of the campus sits a large pond, built in 1638, and designed in the shape of the Chinese character for heart (kokoro, 心).

The pond (Figure 17.1) is encircled by a path that glides up and down, offering views of the pond and the nature that grows around it. It takes about fifteen minutes to walk the circuitous circuit, a walk I would often take when needing a break from my desk or lecture room. It is a place of considerable beauty in all seasons, but in autumn the changing leaves of the various trees around the pond attract photographers and naturalists from all over the country. The pond is nicknamed *Sanshiro*, after a famous novel in which the pond features. Along with the Big Buddha at Kamakura, and the banks of Sakai River, it is a place that always brings me some peace. By coincidence, the writer whose novel *Sanshiro* provided the nickname for the pond was another source of peace for me.

Regarded as one of Japan's greatest novelists, Natsume Sōseki engaged with themes that resonate today – such as cultural tension, the social cost of industrial 'progress', and the pain of personal isolation. He lived during a period of immense change in Japan, was a professor of literature at Todai,

17.1 Sanshiro Pond in autumn.

and between 1900 and 1903 was sent by the Japanese government to the UK as 'a literary scholar'. At this time, Japan was sending abroad many of those it considered its elite, after the period of self-isolation known as the Tokugawa period (1603–1868). The aim was to 'catch up' with the scientific, medical, and cultural developments that Japan's isolation had not allowed the country to even witness. Sōseki described this rush to modernise, 'The Olympics of the Insane', acutely aware of the social and cultural loss that such changes would, and did, engender.

Sōseki had an unhappy time in London during his three years there. In *Patient X*, David Peace reimagines a conversation between Sōseki and his acolyte, Ryunosuke Akutagawa (author of *Rashomon*). Sōseki is recalling his time in, and his feelings toward, England.

[Sōseki:] 'There is a part of me wishes they would wipe the place off the map.'

'Was it really such a terrible time, Sensei,' asked Ryūnosuke.

Natsume Sōseki closed his eyes, closed his eyes for a long time, and when he opened them, opened them at last, they were red-ringed and damp. 'I often wonder if I did not die back then, out there, and all of this...' – he waved his hand across the desk, towards the shelves, at the glass doors, the garden outside – 'if all of this is not the dream of a dead man ...'

'He paused, eyes closed again, then said, 'I know very well the things people say about me, said about my time in London; that I shut myself in my room, that I cried in the dark, that I suffered a nervous breakdown, how I had lost my mind and gone insane.'

One definition of art might be the creation of beauty and meaning from conflict, contradiction, and pain. While Sōseki clearly suffered personal pain, not least through the racism and othering he suffered during his time in England, the fruit was an enduring collection of literature.

I came across these novels at a critical time. I had started teaching English in Tokyo at a language school for adult learners in early 1994, not long after graduating, and by the following winter, my honeymoon with Japan had ended. I was frustrated by the way I was constantly seen as a *gaijin* by people, and an English one at that. Growing up, I'd always seen myself as half-Irish, but I never seemed to be able to get my Japanese students to grasp this layer of complexity. And it was really hard to make real friends who were Japanese. It didn't help that my Japanese was pretty rubbish, but I was too self-righteous to appreciate that factor. Nor was I aware that it is a challenge for all newbies everywhere to make friends with the locals.

There were offers of intimacy, this being a conversation I had several times, sometimes while waiting for a train, or reading a book in a café:

Hello, my name's (Takashi), can I be your friend?

Hi. Er, can I ask – why do you want to be my friend?

Because I want to practise my English/because foreign people are cool/because I really like America/because I want to leave Japan.

Such conversations further reinforced my sense of alienation, and by early 1995, after a year in Japan, I began to think about leaving. In hindsight, the ability to just up sticks was a reflection of my privileged position, but again it was years before I appreciated that. When I talk about alienation, I'm not talking about 'culture shock', which is often used to describe the various stages of living in a new place. In the well-known culture-shock model, you pass through four stages: honeymoon, frustration, adjustment, and finally acceptance. So at first everything is rosy, all new and shiny and exciting. Then, once the novelty has worn off, you notice the little (and big) irritations, your inability to communicate effectively, and so on. I remember hitting this stage about six weeks after moving to Tokyo, when I was twenty-four – it seemed that strangers (i.e. the population of Tokyo) suddenly stopped being friendly. Of course, it was me who had changed in some slight but perceptible way, probably the expression in my eyes had lost some of its guilelessness.

The third stage of the culture-shock model is where you gradually adjust yourself to your new environment, which lays the groundwork for the final stage, of 'adaptation': you fully accept the customs and practices of the different culture, and become integrated. In Japan this adaptation should involve going through ever-increasing degrees of *amae*, a state of harmony and interdependence with others – accepted by and accepting of all things Japanese, while gliding around in a state of near nirvana. Sadly, this just isn't the case for any sane long-term resident of Japan I've known, or anybody anywhere actually. It's true that to have any hope of a reasonably happy long-term existence in a different culture you need to adjust and accept (or learn to ignore) different practices and customs, and there is a special joy in the knowledge of such flexibility. But I never found this a smooth or straight road.

In the space of one hour in public in Tokyo, I may go through a greater range of emotions that I would in a day or a week in London. Rather than stages of culture shock, going from honeymoon through pain to eventual calm acceptance, I think the final, long-term stage is an ongoing veering between jollity and 'cultural fatigue'. This fatigue is not like shock at all, and may manifest itself in suddenly struggling with everyday things. Carol Ann Duffy in her poem 'Foreign' captures the sense of sudden, numbing alienation you can feel despite having lived in a place for twenty years:

> And in the delicatessen, from time to time, the coins
> in your palm will not translate. Inarticulate,
> because this is not your home, you point at fruit.

In early 1995, some months before I met Mayu, I started flat-sitting a friend's place in Shimokita. Andy and I worked together in the same branch of a language School, also in Shimokita. He was thin, tall, pale, with delicate features and an askew stance. He remains one of the most intriguing people I've met. Like a poem on legs, knowingly dishevelled in his Issey Miyake suits, he was a fascinating mix of the urbane and the local. I'd say he was born to live in Tokyo, an individual artifice reflecting the metropolitan one, although his place of birth was Midwest America.

Andy would punctuate his natural inertness with moments of flickering energy. He would sit in silence between lessons in the tiny staffroom, and then suddenly pick up his guitar and play with a furious brilliance for two minutes. He could never be coaxed to play, it only happened spontaneously on his terms. On our many nights out in Shimokita he would dance, but each move was never quite completed. It was existential angst in motion, a left arm fighting gravity to rise upwards, but then falling to his side, as if suddenly bereft of all will. Such a move might then be followed by him windmilling his small glass of beer with his right arm three times without spilling a drop, then the windmill morphing into a bent elbow and wrist, enabling an elegant sip. The way he communicated was a study in euphemism. As the night pushed past midnight, and I'd be keen on exploring a different bar, Andy would gently smile and say, 'Yeah, I think I've had enough fun already.' On some nights we'd return to his flat to play chess. These were great struggles lasting an hour or two, played out to Thelonious Monk or John Coltrane in the background, which I never won.

I remember at the time one of our students in the language school saying she wanted to live abroad, because foreigners were all so interesting. She'd clearly made the inductive error of thinking the likes of Andy and my other colleagues were typical citizens of their home countries. I told her, 'No, no, the people in this language school are not normal at all. In fact, I think people who move abroad are far from typical. If you go to the States or wherever, you'll meet lots of people like there are in Japan, you know, all very normal.' Another student agreed, saying he'd spent a year in Australia. While there he'd met several Japanese people who'd moved to Melbourne or Sydney, and they were all quite 'odd'. Rather like Jackie-san, whom I was to meet later in 1995 for the first time, Andy was an other who seemed to revel in his otherness, dancing outside the constraints of normality.

Andy had decided to return to the US for a few months to finish his degree in Film Studies. He needed to complete just two modules, and for some reason hadn't done so ten years ago. Perhaps it was another instance of him suddenly becoming inert just before completion. I took the train with him to the airport, and remember asking if he ever wrote letters. 'Sure. I even send them occasionally.' I returned to the two-room flat, and filled seventeen large rubbish bags in the first two days of living there. Clearly, along with the letter-writing, cleaning was an occasional practice.

Along with the jazz CDs, Andy had a fine collection of books, including many translations of Japanese novels. Before leaving he advised me to read some Mori Ogai and Natsume Sōseki, and over the next months I duly obliged. The simplistic, stereotyping scales fell partly from my eyes, as their characters struggled with the tensions of the traditional and the new, the known and the untested, the conservative and the progressive. I began to understand why the things that frustrated me were not about me at all, but were the same forces that operate in all societies, just in different guises. I understood from Sōseki that if I ended up like the character Sanshiro, who moves to Tokyo but doesn't really develop during his time there, that was my responsibility. While I didn't start agreeing to be 'friends' with random strangers, I hope I became more sympathetic. And back in 1995, I had no way of knowing that ten years later I'd start teaching in the same university where Sōseki had taught English Literature, walking around Sanshiro Pond (Figure 17.2). Or that sixteen years later I'd be escaping to the pond between chemotherapy treatments.

Despite having spent more than seven years working on the Todai campus come autumn 2011, and walking around Sanshiro Pond at least once a week, it had never really registered that the university hospital was a ten-minute walk away. It's true that this isn't unusual in cities, with spatial proximity being no guarantee of frequency of footfall (or as a normal person might say, just because you are close to somewhere in a city, that doesn't mean you'll go there). Plus, I'm particularly unobservant. For instance, Medical School Building 2 had an excellent Italian restaurant on the Thirteenth Floor, with views of the hospital and beyond. I'd often eat at the restaurant, looking out at the hospital without realising what

17.2 Watching the girls at Sanshiro Pond just before admittance to the hospital. The girls are watching carp.

it was. At the edge of the hospital is the university sports ground with an Astroturf football pitch, where my colleague Petr and I used to play on a Thursday afternoon with students. Again, it hardly registered that there was a huge hospital next door.

Once I was admitted to the hospital as a cancer patient that was the end of the afternoon walks round the pond, the Italian lunches, and the football. While I could look out, I could no longer touch. But when I wasn't plugged into the chemotherapy machine, I'd secretly escape in the early morning to jog around the pond and the football pitch. This was despite strict instructions to stay in the hospital at all times. Once one nurse on the neck ward, who ended up obtaining an intricate knowledge of my rear end, saw me returning just before she started her shift, but kindly looked away. I guess it must have made a difference from patients sneaking out to have a crafty cigarette.

CHAPTER 18

Admittance

Delaying entering the hospital meant that, two weeks after the second confirmation of my cancer, I was now in much better physical and mental health. This was mainly down to Mayu and Maurice's support. I had swiftly lost the excess weight I always put on over summer, I felt energised, and I was accompanied by a nascent mindful perspective. Maurice's yoga along with my developing cancer-metaphor were providing a degree of calm confidence I could not even have imagined a fortnight before. I was learning to navigate the vagaries of my inner and outer absurdity. Without knowing it at the time, I was developing my new Discourse. I was also about to start developing a new side of my Discourse, interacting with the powerful Discourse of oncologists with their own strange tools and practices. It didn't start well.

The day before I was to be admitted to the ward, I had to have a couple of tests. Mayu drove me in, the first of many such drives from the Orange House to Todai Hospital. We parked on the roof of the hospital, and eventually found the ward. Floor 10, South Wing. It was the newest part of the hospital, with pristine walls, floors, and lifts. We had to sign in to enter the in-patient wing, and took the swift lift to the tenth floor. The nurse directed me to the examination room, where the chirpy Dr Nishi welcomed me, and a rather surly junior doctor grunted something. I was invited to sit back in the chair, rather like a dentist's, and then a trainee doctor produced a cable with a camera at the end of it. That description would also work for a Pentax SLR attached to a garden hose, and it might as well have been. She attempted to insert the endoscope, which in reality was a little over half a centimetre in diameter and slightly more bulbous at the end, up my left nostril. It felt like she was trying to push a sharp stick through the top of my nose. I grimaced and groaned as she struggled to make any headway, and the longer the ordeal lasted, the more flustered she became. I felt sorry for her, but the pain was becoming unbearable.

Jesus, that really hurts! I shouted, sweating away.
Sorry, sorry, she muttered, sweating away.
It's impossible, there's no way that's going to work. Ow. Ow.

As I began to writhe noisily in the seat, I could see Mayu smirking in the doorway. It was worse than her foot massages. At this point, the surly junior doctor told me to calm down and 'take it like a man', or words to that effect. I fixed him with my less watery eye and told him where he could shove the camera if he liked, in my best Shimokita-street dialect. Mayu let out a loud laugh. My initiation to Floor 10 was not going so well. I was clearly not conforming to their expectations of how a new patient should behave.

'Unbelievable', the surly one said, and at this point Dr Nishi, grinning, said that he'd take over. With a bit more gel, a gentle twist and a steady force, the cable gradually crept around the top of my nostril and down the back of the throat. It was deeply uncomfortable, but far preferable to what I'd just been going through. Uncomfortable is much better than stabbing pain. Dr Nishi and his colleagues had a good look on the screen, and took some shots of my throat. I then had some more blood tests, and we were told to come back at midday the next day. A nurse led me out of the examination room, and showed us the room that would be my temporary home from tomorrow.

Because of an insurance policy I'd forgotten about but Mayu remembered, we received 1 million yen. This meant we could afford a single room, rather than a bed in a shared ward. The room cost 10,000 yen, or around £70, per day. If the treatment went to plan, I was going to spend around four weeks here, then a break of a couple of weeks to recover at home, then another three to four weeks as an inpatient. Such long stays in Japanese hospitals, while expensive, allow for different kinds of healing relationships to develop. I saw this in how the staff engaged with patients – not just monitoring our health but building connections that made the ward feel more like a community than an institution.

The next day we moved into my new home. The tenth floor was L-shaped, with the entrance, examination rooms, canteen, reception,

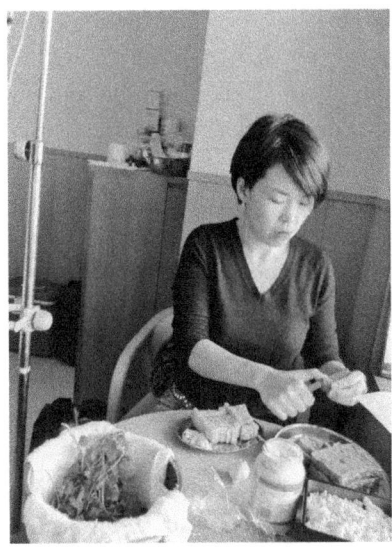

18.1 Mayu preparing my lunch.

and offices on the vertical part of the L, and the rooms on the horizontal. My room was about half-way along the horizontal. I took in about thirty books, and lined them up along the windowsill, imagining long periods of solitude where I would read. I ended up reading only one. We also brought in a fantastic contraption from Maurice's work – an elegant battery-operated essential oil burner, about the size of a cigarette packet, that released gentle bursts of Maurice's *hinoki*-pine scent. Along with all the usual stuff (new pyjamas, jogging clothes, regular clothes, olive-oil soap, an iPad, and slippers), we had an impressive amount of gear. Once we'd unpacked, a couple of the nurses came in to admire our efforts, commenting on the lovely smell and presciently smirking at the ridiculous number of books. I remember feeling slightly indignant at their ridicule, as any preening academic might.

Mayu was keen that I should eat the hospital food as little as possible, and to keep me on a macrobiotic diet. In came the rice cooker and a bag of organic genmai rice, plus a cooler box of fresh produce (Figure 18.1). Officially you weren't allowed to cook in your room, but the nurses and doctors all turned a blind eye and a tempted nostril to Mayu's dishes. One of the stereotypes about Japan is that rules are always strictly enforced, but it wasn't the case with the cooking. After several days of Mayu arriving with her cooler box slung over her shoulder, the nurses and receptionists starting enquiring about what delights Mayu was to concoct that day. Keen not to waste food, Mayu would dig into my hospital lunches as I enjoyed the colourful macrobiotic fare, saying they reminded her of school dinners.

Despite the rocky start, I still smile when I think of the staff from Floor 10. While not all their patients had cancer, many did, and that meant some passed away there. On the day we moved in, a group of family members dressed in white PPE were leaving the next room, some crying, others staring at the floor. The next day, a different patient moved in. It must be an environment where only resilient staff can thrive. But thrive is what they seemed to do. They were constantly jolly, highly organised in their work, and usually had time for a chat.

Like most longer-term patients, it was the nurses I got to know best. One nurse, 'Nurse Souda', seemed to be very taken with me from the moment I entered. She started with the compliments about my face, and within a couple of days the compliments had moved to my physique. Interestingly it didn't seem to matter if Mayu was there or not – when Mayu was there, she said it to her, and when she wasn't, she told me. Another nurse, 'Nurse Kitamura', who I think was the head nurse, kept the conversations more on-topic, but ended up with a far more intimate knowledge of my body than either of us would have wished. Then there was 'Nurse Shimizu', with whom Mayu and I developed something of a friendship. She had had short careers as a model, then a singer, before recently going into nursing. She was also quite a foodie, so the three of us ended up discussing our favourite places to eat and listen to music in Tokyo. Mayu's encyclopaedic knowledge of rock music, cynicism towards music companies, and recent experiences as a local radio DJ could usually be counted on to earn the trust of a musician. These nurses and their colleagues made us and the girls feel at home, and I will always appreciate the many kindnesses and moments of laughter we shared.

My mother and sister both worked as nurses, and the time I spent on the tenth floor brought home to me the practices of healing that nurses embody. The gentle, stroking hand on my back and comforting word *daijobu* ('it's OK') as a camera was inserted down my throat and into my stomach, without which I'm not sure I could have coped. The indignation of another nurse on finding my name had been misspelt on the door to my room, saying how our names are reflections of our individual selves. The quiet encouragement towards my quirky exercise regime, and the warmth they gave to my family. We felt valued as a family, and I felt valued at this most threatening of times. The oncologists saw my cancer, the nurses saw me.

Mayu had an hour before she needed to drive back home to pick up Maya from Kiddie and start cooking dinner. We took the lift down to the ground floor so she might grab a coffee (herbal tea for me) and noticed that there were security guards near the lift entrance. We asked the receptionist why they were there, and she told us that the granddaughter of the emperor was sick with 'flu, and was staying in the adjacent wing. The two wings shared the same entrance and lift area, so the guards would be there as long as the child was. After Mayu enjoyed a coffee and a sandwich, while I sipped my chamomile tea, we wandered through some darkened corridors to the exit nearest the car park. Just before the exit was the ward for children with cancer, which we hadn't noticed when we arrived. Inside the glass door were various parents hugging their little ones goodbye, many of them with bald heads and attached to ominously large orange drips, the bags of toxic chemicals bigger than their heads. We said our subdued goodbyes just beyond the view of the children's cancer ward, and Mayu walked quickly through the rain to the car. I walked slowly up to my single room, with a complicated, guilt-tinged sense of relief that it was me and not my children here.

CHAPTER 19

Hair

Who are you, and are you always the same person? At twenty, I was happy to be seen reading Sartre or Nietzsche with my thick crop of chestnut curls and furrowed brow, searching for the authentic me. But as I've aged, and read more widely, the world has persuaded me to ask, is the search for this authentic-self misguided? Aren't we, in fact, a mix of various intersecting identities – white, middle-aged, middle-class professional Mike, short *gaijin* Mike, aggressive footballer Mike?

As a person with cancer, one of the struggles is trying to navigate the constraining views others may have of you, and to make a space for yourself, to find a little agency in the chaos. This may be a space to momentarily forget about the diagnosis, or it can be much bigger than that. It may also be deeply inflected by other aspects of our identity. Sexual minority women of colour, for instance, often face barriers relating to cancer diagnosis, treatment, and even survivorship that are not faced by other groups. But stories of profound agency exist, too, such as the *The Cancer Journals* by Black lesbian poet 'warrior' Audre Lorde (1980). Following her mastectomy, she refused, despite considerable pressure from doctors and from society, to have reconstructive surgery or wear a prosthesis. This refusal she frames positively, healing and empowering her: 'I also began to feel that in the process of losing a breast I had become a more whole person.'

I read a research article the other day about Black doctors in US hospitals. When they do something patients approve of, this is typically attributed to them being a doctor, but when disapproval occurs, this is usually put down to their Blackness. Doesn't this mean that different aspects of our complex identities are, at particular moments, more 'seen' than others, and for reasons that may be beyond our control? We might also

ask (or sometimes hope), are some of these different intersecting identities, such as white male Mike, relatively more fixed than others, such as
cancer-patient *gaijin* Mike?

These are big questions, and perhaps something as mundane as hair
can shed some light on them. For me, hair is something of a mystery. As
I get older, I am not intrigued by hair-loss so much as hair-movement.
It's true that hair-loss is a fact for many, with healthy adults losing seventy
to one hundred hairs a day, and not all heads replacing them. My head
being a case in point. But what I mean is, while hair does disappear from
the typical parts of my head, it also appears in alternative places, like
the base of my back, or randomly around the shoulders, or even in the
darker crevices. So while there is definitely a general thinning going on,
there is also a movement, a redeployment from desirable to undesirable
locations. Along with gravity weighing heavier on features, muscles atro-
phying at the slightest excuse, and your parents' mannerisms usurping
your own, the fickleness of follicles form part of the increasingly discord-
ant orchestra of ageing.

With cancer treatments, there are the well-known violent attacks
on hair. Surgery to the head requires a bald surface, chemotherapy
often causes hair-loss, as can radiation around the head or neck. While
I wouldn't be having surgery, the other two treatments would mean my
hair would be changing. Dr Nishi warned us of this, and said that there
was a hair-salon on the ground floor of the hospital if I did decide to
have a trim. That seemed odd to me – why have a trim if your hair is coming out? I hadn't realised that chemotherapy makes it fall out from only
some parts of the head, in clumps. Like clumps you might grab in your
fist from a busy hairdresser's floor. I was also told I could try wearing a
wig, but didn't consider this too seriously (Figure 19.1).

I'd just finished the first week of chemo, and I was taking my morning
shower in my hospital bathroom, following a secret run around Sanshiro
Pond. The shower was what's known as a 'unit bath', a standard en-suite
feature in many Japanese hotels and apartments. The ubiquitously beige
unit is about three feet by two feet by three feet, doubling up as a com-
pact bath and a shower. I started to lather my hair with the olive oil soap
Mayu had bought for me (I was to stay away from the industrial-strength
stuff provided in the bathroom), and when I looked down at the yel-
low bath floor, there were two sizeable lumps of dark-brown curly hair.

19.1 Trying on wigs in Fujisawa.

I put my hand to the side of my head and pulled gently, easily removing another clump. A laugh escaped in surprise, and I was about to call out to Mayu to let her know. Then I remembered she wasn't there. I was alone in my temporary home, with my ludicrous hairstyle, and she was back in our real home in Fujisawa. A spike of poignancy went through me, not so much from the sudden loss of hair as the realisation that there was to be no sharing through the showing of it. I stood watching in silence as the wide sinkhole gulped down the clumps.

I came out of the shower and studied the new gaps on my head. I was a bit disappointed where they were, as I'd been hoping for other places to be bald. My hairline had been slowly receding for some years, and a general thinning was starting on top. Dr Nishi had told me that the places where you lose the hair eventually enjoy quite vigorous re-growth – so I was hoping that it would fall out around my crowns and at the front. Instead, it fell thick from around the sides, the very places where growth was still virile. Looking in the mirror, I gently pulled at it the top, hoping; it stayed stubbornly intact, unchanged.

I've been left with an ever-thinning front and top, and chemically induced extra-curly growth on the sides. This means that if I let my hair grow, it now self-styles into something resembling greyish broccoli on the sides with a wispy top. I keep it short. When Mayu arrived later that morning to find me with a completely shaved head, she complemented me on my well-shaped skull, and gave it a gentle oil massage.

The radiation also led to hair-loss, but the changes have been, on the whole, more welcome. From a young age I had a hairy neck, especially at the back. I always hated it, but the radiation has ensured it never grew back. And now the skin is very silky to the touch. The hair has never grown back at the front of my neck either, thus providing the bonus of not needing to shave that part of my face. It's not completely perfect though. If you look at the hairline at the back of my head, you will notice it is uneven, like a barber has slipped with the razor. For the first year or so following the treatment, the line across the whole of my head was so high it resembled the base of a monk's tonsure. There's a lot to be said for scarves.

While I was far too wrapped up in my own circumstances to consider this, looking back at my hair-related experiences and reactions, I can see that things might be different for a different person with different lived experiences. For me, losing my hair was not a very threatening thing, not because I am brave or unselfconscious, but because there were few serious implications. It didn't threaten my relationships, my career, or my place in society. But it's a well-known fact that for some people, hair-loss caused by cancer-treatments is a very scary thing. Some surveys among women put it up there with fear of mastectomy. In 2011 I couldn't understand that view. In fact, in my ignorance I may have dismissed it as a sign of misguided vanity.

While I could joke about my hair-loss and even find silvery-grey linings, I've come to realize that this casual attitude is itself a privilege. For many cancer patients, hair-loss carries far more serious implications than mere appearance. This made me think about how different aspects of our identities – gender, race, class, age – shape not just our experience of cancer, but our ability to cope with its effects.

Returning to the questions at the beginning of this chapter, it's clear that cancer-related hair-loss affects different people in society very differently, and therefore different groups will feel and have very different ideas about it. It goes without saying that, in general, women are held to stricter and more prejudicial beauty standards than men but looking solely at gender tells only part of the story. For instance, one study shows that the fear of loss of hair is greatest among young Black women.

If the study stopped there (as many quantitative studies do), some might assume that young Black women are more vain or more concerned with physical appearance than other genders and ethnicities. While this and other studies argue that young Black women in predominantly white societies might indeed be conscious of their physical appearance, and beauty norms can vary according to ethnicity and culture, attributing this fear purely to vanity would be an instance of the type of discrimination borne of ignorance. Dr. April-Louise Pennant, an expert on Black British women's experiences in education, explains that hair carries particularly profound cultural and social significance for Black women.

A key reason cited in the study is security, including job security and relationships, specifically 'problematic work and relationship issues, fertility decisions, and poor support when transitioning into survivorship'. One of the main work-related issues is that losing your hair is a sign you are having cancer-treatment, and in many insecure work environments, cancer patients are not protected. Members of the Precariat, on zero-hour or temporary contracts, are the easiest to fire. Many young Black women find themselves at the intersections of race, age, gender, and class that multiply disadvantage them, so for some losing their hair may mean losing their job. I'm not implying this is the case for all Black women, or that race or gender completely determine our experiences. But if you're a young Black woman working on a zero-hours' contract for an unempathetic employer, making light of losing your hair probably isn't an option.

What I experienced as a minor inconvenience can, for others, represent a threat to their professional standing or cultural identity. Whereas for me? Well, male professors evidently don't get laid off because they go bald. Men like me can make light of hair-loss because it really doesn't matter.

CHAPTER 20

Routines

Hospital life is fairly routine, and I developed further routines in the spaces between the institution's routines. My day started at around 6.30am with a blood pressure and pulse test, the former always fine, and the latter constantly causing surprise at less than forty-five bpm. Then off to the scales in the corridor for my daily weigh-in. Next the bathroom to pee into a measuring cup, and record on a sheet the amount I'd urinated. I had to do this every time I peed, and that was often. As I was desperate to wash the chemotherapy out of me as quickly as possible, I drank copiously. Apparently, I broke the Ward record for most pee on a day, several days in a row.

For breakfast, I'd join the other patients in the Ward cafeteria, at the end of the corridor. The shutters opened up at 8.20am, releasing the heady smells of the traditional Japanese breakfast: fermented soybeans, miso soup, pickles, grilled salmon, and boiled rice. There was little conversation in the cafeteria, although the patients who were on the ward for less serious treatments were inevitably more talkative, and gravitated automatically to each other. The cancer patients seemed to move within a solitary silent space.

Cancer patients undergo a daunting number of blood-tests. My blood tests were fine at the beginning of the stay, with ease of access provided by the obvious veins in my hands and wrists. But by the end of the week of chemo, the nurses and doctors were struggling to find any. It was like they'd siphoned me dry. One junior doctor spent around fifteen minutes scraping inside my wrist with a syringe, searching in vain for a vein. The pain drained the little energy I had left, while my wrist darkly glistened with many shades of the rainbow for days afterwards.

In the days before the chemotherapy started, I'd sneak out for a jog before breakfast around Sanshiro. Once that was not an option because of being attached to the orange bag and monitor, I'd walk around the inside of the hospital. One problem was that if I ventured further than about forty metres from the lift, the alarm on the monitor would go off. It was just too disconcerting for the passers-by to see this skin-headed little foreigner with a furrowed brow walking round with an ominous orange bag and a ringing alarm. Having breached the limits of my incarceration, perhaps they thought I was doing a runner with the bag.

Some people clearly did know what the bag meant. When walking past a mother and young son one morning, the son asked his mother what the bag was. She whispered, a little too loudly, 'He's got cancer. He may die soon so don't stare.' I walked past without showing I'd understood. The words of this stranger shuddered through me, and I felt my inner classroom become very unruly. But sometimes you just have to carry on walking.

As well as Mayu, David was a regular visitor, coming most days in the week. On a couple of weekends he'd take our girls home to stay with him and his family, meaning Mayu could stay the night in my room. For our usual weekday schedule, Mayu would arrive around 11am, make me lunch, and we'd talk until around 2pm. David would arrive just before she left, and stay with me till around 4 or 5pm. Having a private room meant that this most private of people was comfortable, and we could talk about all manner of topics: football, Foucault, UK politics, Japanese politics, writing, films, comedies, and back to football.

But most of all I remember David recounting the times he'd got into trouble, much to my amusement, usually through no fault of his own. He just has that kind of demeanour, it seems, one that doesn't fit in, even in Yorkshire. Perhaps especially in Yorkshire. Another one for whom home is not a place. On the first visit he told me about the time he was walking down the road in Huddersfield, near where he was born and grew up, when a car suddenly stopped just in front of him. The driver walks up to David, looks squarely at him for a second, and punches him in the face. At this point it's worth knowing that David is the most tender of people, so very gentle. A crime novelist whose novels keep him awake at night. The guy's girlfriend then jumps out of the car and screams at him, 'What the fuck are you doing?', to which the boyfriend replies, 'I couldn't help it. I just saw his face and really wanted to fuckin punch it.' A complete stranger, and that happens. In German, there is the word

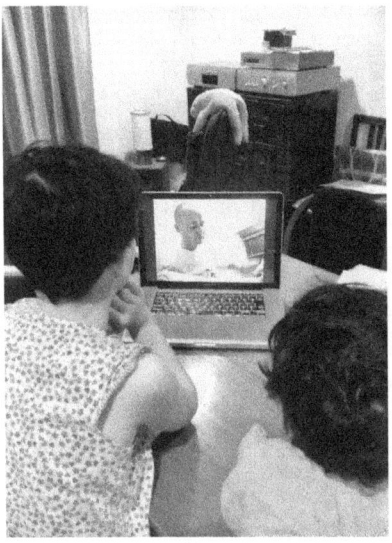

20.1 The girls and me Skyping before their bedtime.

Backpfeifengesicht, meaning 'A face badly in need of a fist'. Poor David, to have such a face, in such a place. But at least the event, in its retelling, lifted the spirits of a cancer patient.

I had other visitors, too. Maurice came in several times, and we'd make a space just wide enough for the two of us to lie down on the floor by pushing the bed towards the door for a yoga session. A nurse would invariably come in at such times. As well as Maurice, my colleague and friend Petr would also pop in, usually later in the day after his day's work. Petr took on the role of jester, telling me ridiculous stories or bringing me little gifts such as farty cushions. All this from a man whose research on social network analysis is internationally respected.

From before lunch to dinnertime I was busy fitting my social life in between tests, and then I'd also have some chats via Skype with friends and family in the UK once they'd woken up there. In the evening, after the usual tests, I'd Skype the girls (Figure 20.1), and then sometimes settle down to watch a TV series on DVD that David had lent me. The dark humour of *Curb Your Enthusiasm* hit the spot, and for when the girls were around, *The Simpsons*. I tried *Tinker, Tailor, Soldier, Spy*, but my chemo-fuddled brain couldn't keep up with the plot. On the iPad I'd

20.2 The girls enjoying the university campus just before I was admitted.

start to read academic articles on throat cancer but couldn't usually manage more than the abstract. The row of books on my windowsill would sit there mocking me. I only read one book in all that time, *The God Delusion*, by Richard Dawkins.

On weekends, Mayu would bring the girls in, and sometimes we might have a wander around the University campus (Figure 20.2). The first time they came, we all seemed nervous, not our usual selves, and I felt a guilty relief when they'd gone. But from the next day, we relaxed, and the girls basked in the warm attention of the staff on the ward. Little Maya in particular was very happy, as she'd always had a liking for hospitals. Once we'd eaten, the girls would wrap themselves in the blankets on my bed, adjust the positioning of the mattress to a suitable angle, and watch a couple of episodes of *The Simpsons*. After dinner, they'd have a bath in my little bathroom, brush their teeth, and then get changed into their pyjamas. Maya would often then nod off on my bed, and I'd carry her down to the carpark on my shoulder while pushing the drip with the other hand. Mayu told me that Julia would always promise to stay awake for the drive, but inevitably lose the battle. Once home she carried them

20.3 My face, swollen from the chemotherapy.

into their beds, and would then sit in silence looking out of the living room window across Sakai River.

Apart from a night of high temperatures (a slight reaction to the chemotherapy), the hair-loss, the mouth that looked like it'd had a Botox lip-fill (Figure 20.3), and increasing levels of nausea over the three weeks, I was perversely enjoying aspects of my stay. I didn't have to work, I was spending a lot of time with a few people I cared a lot about, and I was sensing a level of gradual control in my upside-down world.

After I'd been in hospital for a couple of weeks, I remember the jolly Dr Nishi and the younger doctor coming into my room. After checking all my data, Dr Nishi announced:

Mike, you really are amazing!

Huh, why do you say that?

Well you get dressed every single morning, you exercise as much as you can, all that kind of thing. Your fluid consumption is fantastic, what an effort. And I hear you've even been doing yoga in your room! I've never seen someone deal with their cancer treatment like this.

At this point the younger doctor, who at the beginning of my treatment had tried to scold me for being a wimp, chimed in.

Yes, amazing. It's really impressive. You're a tough guy.
Oh. Thanks very much.

Dr Nishi then continued with the praise.

Yes, it's not just your physical reaction. Our Japanese patients just sit around watching TV all day in their pyjamas. They're so passive. You are so vigorous, so positive. So British patients are like this, eh.
Er, I'm not so sure about that. I'm just keen to feel in control. You know, 'embrace the challenge'.
Yeah, yeah, that's right. British people must be great patients. It must be good to be a doctor in Britain.

In Chapter 13, I quoted S. Lochlann Jain's definition of 'the grammar of cancer', and of the cancer patient having to quickly learn the unwritten codes of how to be a sick person, while dealing with a life-threatening illness. As I mentioned, this to my mind is part of entering the Discourse of being a cancer patient. I think my Britishness had virtually nothing to do with my navigation of this new reality. But that's the way cultural (mis)attribution often works: we see some different or unexpected behaviour, and the person doing it is different according to some category (race, gender, nationality etc.), so we think the second (in this case my Britishness) explains the first (my active engagement). As the saying goes, correlation does not equal causality – just because I'm British, that doesn't explain why I do things that are different from most Japanese patients. I probably do things differently from most British patients, too.

Along with a fairly optimistic, curious disposition and the resilience-inducing support from my loved ones and carers, I'd put my 'dealing with it' at this point more down to the ability to navigate ambiguity, an ability I'd developed over many years learning to live in another country. But the earlier events of the year also seemed to have played some role in preparing me. Priming is a concept from psychology that explains how our subconscious reaction to a new thing can be influenced by a previous reaction to something else. It's as if the earthquake and its aftermath had primed me, or rather Mayu and me, for this new disaster. Both threw us into chaos, the earthquake relatively more external, but nonetheless still chaos that needed a response. And we responded in similar ways to both: get as much information as possible before making informed, joint decisions; question authority; laugh, especially when panic appears; accept that platitudes like 'live each day' take on a special resonance; don't be passive, act.

Along with dealing with the present reality in the hospital, during my evenings alone I resolved for things to be in place for my family's future, in the event of my not being part of it. This played a huge part in enabling me to achieve some degree of control over my internal chaos, the chaos in my mind. The irony being that accepting the possibility of not being part of the future helped subdue the chaos that the prospect of my absence had thrown up.

Most important, I thought, was Mayu getting an MA. If she had a postgraduate degree then finding appropriate work to engage her fine brain would be easier, and she could support the girls in many ways. Apart from being the sole carer and breadwinner, she'd also need to be the sole role model. When we first discussed her studies in the event of my death, Mayu thought she should give up on the idea. I strongly disagreed, telling her I thought it was probably more important for her to do the MA if I wasn't with her any more. And if I was dead, my life insurance would at least mean she'd be able to pay for it.

I was entitled to take a sabbatical the following year, after seven years of work at the University. But if I was alive, I'd need funding for the year abroad. Some of my research has involved working with engineers, particularly examining communication and culture in engineering contexts. One of the advantages of doing interdisciplinary research with engineers is potential access to research funds. Compared to the humanities and social sciences, engineering is a different world, the rich and the poor relations of academia.

One engineering colleague who saw the value in interdisciplinary collaboration, and in communication research more specifically, was Professor Yozo Fujino. He is one of the world's leading structural engineers, who amongst other things, accurately predicted the vibration issues with the London Millennium Bridge before any feet crossed it. Apparently enough people walking across a suspension bridge will get it swaying dangerously, a phenomenon termed 'pedestrian-induced lateral vibration'. He was on the panel who originally interviewed me back in

2005 for my post at Todai, and we'd become increasingly friendly after that. One of those multitasking, force-of-nature individuals, who still plays tennis in his seventies and looks like he's in his mid-fifties, he has time for everybody and is another person who seems to value *honne* above *tate-mae*, disarming honesty above bland courtesy. The emperor has awarded him prizes for his research, and he's adored by the hundreds of Japanese and international students he's guided through their degrees and early careers. He'd been one of the first colleagues I'd told about my diagnosis. I emailed him just before entering hospital about my desire to take a sabbatical in the coming year, and to ideally attract some funding to support my research trip.

He replied, saying he knew of several potential sources of funding, and that because I was a permanent employee of Todai, I was eligible to apply. Over the week I was having my chemotherapy, he would run over from his office at lunch, his beautifully prepared lunchbox and chopsticks in-hand, wolf the food down in less than ten minutes and explain to me and Mayu what should be emphasised in any bid. Mayu and I would take notes as he offered his advice. He'd then get up, remember to ask me if I was OK, listening carefully to my brief answer. I could sense he liked the idea of my applying for funding from my hospital bed when in such a predicament. It was the kind of thing he might do. But neither of us knew that in less than a fortnight, my chances of going anywhere in the future would shift from 'possible' to 'very bleak'.

CHAPTER 21

Emperor

When it came to the Japanese royal family, I was happy to just listen to the comments of others. A bit like being able to have no opinion about a sport I take little interest in. But as a permanent resident, I inevitably had to engage with the abstract entity on some occasions, as all residents do. Thankfully Japan doesn't expect permanent residents to swear an oath of allegiance to the monarchy, but sometimes there's no escaping the weight of certain institutions.

Politically, I think it's fair to say that Mayu and her parents are somewhat of the Left, which can manifest itself through some gentle ridiculing of the Japanese royal family. Jackie does an impression of the late Emperor Hirohito, an impression involving high-pitched, ponderous delivery, and vacuous phrases, along the lines of:

> *It is with certain feelings that I acknowledge these things have come to pass. That they have come to pass is evidence that certain things have happened. All happenings have causes. Such things having happened evokes inevitable emotions, which I am sure we can all share.*

On more than one occasion, upon starting his act I've seen his friends laugh uproariously while others leave in disgust. The act is his remembered version of the radio broadcast Emperor Hirohito gave to signal Japan's unconditional surrender in 1945, the first time in history an emperor's voice was heard by the general populace. While I didn't come to hear the Japanese emperor's voice while I was having treatment, I did hear his wife's voice.

In the many narratives about Japan in the overseas media, the domestic tension around its institutions is not one that has received much attention. I doubt it's unique to Japan: the media does not tend to deal in complexity when portraying 'the other', often favouring broad, super-ficial strokes that do not perturb stereotypes. Indeed, the media often actively employs stereotypes to communicate its message. When people outside Japan consider the Japanese relationship with its royal family, I'd imagine that the Second World War, emperor-worship, and perhaps the problematic national anthem (*Kimigayo*) are what typically spring to mind. *Kimigayo*, meaning 'His Imperial Majesty's Reign', divides opinion in Japan, because of the connotations with the Second World War, and also because the lyrics are so arcane as to be very hard to understand (a bit like the emperor's speech declaring the surrender).

The national anthem once caused me a very stressful morning, culmi-nating in one of the most unexpected experiences of my time in Japan. In hindsight, the stress was caused by my own stereotypes about how Japanese people behave in formal events. It was the morning of Julia's entrance ceremony at Katase Primary School. I'd taken the day off work, got dressed in a suit and tie, and put Julia in a pretty little grey suit – even Mayu wore a dress. Once we'd taken Maya to the nursery the three of us wandered over to the school. The expected mix of happy grandparents, slightly stressed parents, and nervous-looking children milled around out-side the rickety school hall, that tripled up as a gymnasium and a theatre.

Once we walked inside, Julia was gently taken off to sit at the front of the hall with her new classmates. She already had a few friends from her short time at Kiddie Nursery. Mayu and I found some inconspicuous seats near the back of the room. I smirked at Mayu, watching her inevi-table struggle with such formal events. At times like this she brought to mind Leonard Cohen's line, 'Like a bird on a wire, like a drunk in a mid-night choir, I have tried in my way to be free.' I could sense her bristling desire for it all to be over soon, and to replace the dress with jeans.

On each small seat was a programme for the morning's ceremony. I glanced through the long litany of speeches and performances and songs. Then at the end, the national anthem. Ah, I hadn't expected that. To make it easier for everyone, they'd printed the lyrics on the pro-gramme. I nudged Mayu, pointing to the programme. We looked at each other, and she raised her eyebrows, showing she hadn't expected this either. I knew she'd be in a quandary, too.

Around this time, the national anthem in schools had been receiving a lot of attention in the Japanese media, as the ruling LDP Party had decreed that all teachers had to sing it at special events. The decree had caused consternation in society, as many felt it smacked of more emboldened nationalism on the part of the government, led by then Prime Minister Shinzo Abe. Parents were not forced to sing it, but as I expected everyone else to, what should I do? I already stood out, being one of only two white people in the hall of hundreds. If I was in the UK, I would gladly refuse to sing it. But I wasn't in the UK. Should I sing *Kimigayo*, a song with lingering militaristic connotations from an often glossed-over period of Japan's recent history? Could I get away with just standing and not singing it? If I stayed seated, that would probably be seen as hugely disrespectful. And I couldn't embarrass Julia on her first day. I imagined her getting bullied at school because her *gaijin* dad had insulted Japan. Could I get out before the end of the event, feigning sickness? I was beginning to feel a bit sick. The ceremony dragged relentlessly on and on to the final point of the programme. Still I had no idea what I should do when the teacher announced it was time to sing the national anthem.

All the teachers stood up, many clearly reluctantly. They were on the stage, facing the audience. It was at that point that it didn't happen. I didn't get up, not because I'd resolved to make a moral non-stance on the issue, but because nobody else stood up. Nobody except one elderly woman, who I assume was a grandmother of one of the kids. The other hundreds of parents and grandparents stayed seated. Apart from the clear, steady voice of this elderly woman, and the barely audible mumblings and shiftings of the teachers on stage, there was seated silence in the hall. Hundreds of parents refusing to sing the national anthem, or even to stand for it. I saw at least one teacher on stage with tears in his eyes, and Mayu and I exchanged incredulous glances. I have no explanation of why this communal refusal happened. But for me, it illuminated how culture is indeed a practice, something that people do. And if people stop doing something, then that can eventually change a culture. It also illuminated how shaky my own stereotypes were.

While my experiences of this event might be termed monarchy-at-a-distance, when I was an in-patient I had much closer dealings with the royal family. Firstly the granddaughter of the emperor, and then the emperor himself, were treated one floor up from my ward. The eleventh floor of my wing was reserved for the family. The entire floor.

I wondered at the time if I'd banged loudly on my ceiling whether they would have heard.

I'd like to say quickly that they have the right to excellent medical treatment, as does any Japanese citizen. After all, I wouldn't want the infamous Japanese ultra-right wing blockading my house with their black vans blasting out wartime music and threatening my daughters. Nor did I begrudge the fact that the royal family have an entire floor of the hospital wing to themselves, reserved for themselves at all times, at tax-payers' expense (I include myself here).

But I also have to say, in a spirit of honesty and openness, that there were inconveniences caused by their presence. For instance, foreign or unusual-looking visitors were given a hard time entering the building. And several of my visitors were both foreign and unusual-looking. It's probably not much fun going to see your friend having industrial levels of chemotherapy forced through his little body at the best of times, so I can imagine being harassed by very large scary men in dark suits and sunglasses wouldn't exactly incentivize the visit. So hats off to those of you who made the journey! My friend Petr, a Czech national, seemed to get a particularly hard time, perhaps because he's not a small guy himself, having once been the first non-Japanese captain of Todai's sumo-wrestling team. In other words, the security guards harassed the guy who was so well integrated into Japanese society that he'd become the first foreign captain of Japan's national sport at its most venerable university.

Petr now lives in Sydney.

During the Emperor's stay, there was at least one and often two of these very large, statuesque, sunglassed men in the small lift, as well as several stationed around the ground floor. The orange chemo-bag was like a chemical passport, providing a certain freedom to move around without being hassled, and on the one occasion someone did try I rather spat the dummy. I was sitting just outside the side entrance, not far from the lift, having just said a glum goodbye to Mayu and the sleepy girls. At that point, one of the guards came over to me and said I had to go inside. I refused. He stood up straighter, towering over me, and said very directly and very quietly that I must go inside. Looking directly up, I rattled my chemo bag at him, shouting that I didn't have to do anything he said as I'd probably be dead in a few months. I then asked him why he was wearing sunglasses at night.

At this point he took a step back, clearly processing some unexpected input and reconsidering his options. His tone changed, and explained that the emperor's wife was about to leave the hospital, so could I just move further away from the entrance for a few minutes. I did as he asked, saying he could have explained that in the first place. As I watched this graceful elderly woman seemingly glide past the row of bowing hospital staff, my own small confrontation with institutional authority ended in respectful compromise. My next confrontation, this time with the medical establishment, was to prove far more bruising.

CHAPTER 22

Shock

The emperor left the hospital about the same time my first week of chemo was coming to completion, and the hospital seemed collectively to sigh in relief at the return to normality. The congestion around the lifts and corridors reduced, meaning the doctors could again swiftly rush down to the convenience store to buy the poor-quality sandwiches or bento boxes on offer, visitors were not harangued, and odd-bods were once again free to wander around.

There was a strong sense of liberation once the orange bag of chemicals was no longer my constant partner. I was able to wander around freely, and after a few days I felt good enough to escape for a light jog around Sanshiro Pond. I even began to explore the area on foot, including a beautiful neighbourhood called Yanaka, which has since become very popular with foreign tourists. It is one of the few areas of Tokyo that was not destroyed by the firebombing of the Second World War, or by subsequent property developers. I still had to stay in the hospital for another ten days to ensure there were no adverse reactions, but after this I could return home for a fortnight to recuperate, before the next round of chemo.

The next round of chemo. When explaining the treatment plan to me, Dr Nishi had stressed that the chemotherapy would not rid me of the cancer, but the two intense rounds should reduce it a bit. But now, after the first round, I was having the intriguing thought that the second round might not be necessary. My glands seemed normal in size again, and 'robust' is probably the best word for how I felt.

I also had a growing feeling of foreboding. As someone who has trained himself to live in his head, too much probably, I am not given to overly trusting my emotions as a guide to action. Fear may be a reaction

I have to many things, but learning to ignore it, even to fight with it sometimes, had worked out quite well for me over the years. And yet I couldn't
shake off this strong feeling that the second chemo was not going to do
me any good at all. I spoke to Mayu, Maurice, and David about it, and
they all encouraged me to see if I could persuade the doctors, at least to
see if they might do a scan to check the situation.

I hadn't appreciated at this point the degree to which you are in a
system when you have cancer treatment. There is a template, a flow chart
as it were, and you flow along in the pipes of the chart. You might bang
along the sides a bit with an adverse reaction to treatment, and in some
cases you might have to be removed from the chart altogether, but the
one thing you can't do as a patient is change the chart.

To me, it seemed quite simple: I had reacted very well to the treatment, so rather than undergoing another course of intense chemotherapy, with all the short-term and longer-term dangers that the treatment
presented, surely it was worth bringing the scan forward to now?

I'm sorry Mike, but that's the treatment plan for all our patents. Patients have the
CT scan after the second course of chemotherapy.
But Dr Nishi, I am sure that the cancer has got a lot smaller – I can't even feel any-
thing in my neck any more, inside or out.
Look, your type of cancer receives this treatment plan, it's as simple as that. And there
are risks with CT scans as well you know. You shouldn't have too many of them.
OK, but then why did you repeat the CT I had at Fujisawa hospital just a week later?
Well, we needed to verify the results.
Hmm. I'm happy to pay for the scan, Oh I do anyway. But I really feel it's not neces-
sary to have the second round.

The doctor looked at me, and I could read in his eyes the question,
'Are you an oncologist now?' It was a fair question, but I was where I
most hated to be: trapped in a system I did not agree with. I was also
aware that I was trying to persuade him in my second, less persuasive
language. In Chapter 13 I quoted S. Lochlann Jain talking about the
need to learn 'what to say to be seen as a person, not as a statistic'. In
English, I can train people how to do this, but in Japanese I was failing.
And I had no evidence to support my argument – that could only be
provided by the scan I couldn't get. I felt disempowered, like a case and
not a person.

'The research shows a double dose is most effective in the majority of cases', Dr Nishi said.

'But I'm not a case!' I screamed inside.

My relative powerlessness was being made painfully clear in the one-sided struggle between his oncologist Discourse and my Discourse as a cancer patient, one operating in a second language. Doing a bit of yoga in my room was one thing, but questioning the path laid by clinical trials was not to be countenanced. He held all the cards. And we both knew I wasn't going to throw my hand in, the evidence was too flimsy. I could find no clinical trials that supported my suggestion, which would be persuasive in his Discourse.

There was nothing for it but to get back home, get myself as fit as possible, and come back for Round Two. The night before I was to leave the hospital, David took the girls to his house to stay the night, and Mayu stayed in my hospital room, officially on the camp-bed the staff had provided. The next day we packed up my books and the rice cooker, my clothes, and took them to the car. David brought the girls back to the hospital, and Mayu drove us back to sunny Fujisawa. In the back sat the girls, happily telling me about their night and the points of interest along the route they now knew better than me.

After a few days of eating well between runs and workouts at the local gym, we decided to spend a weekend up in Hakone with the in-laws. Jackie and Hisako were waiting for us in the driveway when we arrived, and on looking at me Jackie said, 'Wow, cancer seems to become you Mike. You look great.' Hisako slapped him on the arm, while suppressing a smile, saying, 'There you go again!' Over each dinner Jackie enjoyed a good few drinks, while expressing his condolences for my abstinence. 'Poor Mike, poor Mike', he kept repeating, as he took another smiling sip. The girls, wallowing in the bounteous love of their grandparents (Figure 22.1), seemed to lose that half-second of silent sadness that had become part of their reaction to everything, while Mayu and I did very little indeed.

All too soon, I had to return to the hospital. I brought far fewer books this time, just *The God Delusion* and a couple of novels. The staff had organised the ward so that I could move back into the same room, and they gave us a very jolly welcome. The welcome was appreciated, and yet I was unable to shake off that feeling that I shouldn't be here. I don't

22.1 The girls relaxing with the grandparents at Hakone Shrine, some time before our troubles started.

mean that chronic state of cognitive dissonance that comes of having cancer, but this was a much more specific, here-and-now feeling of discomfort. But I was on the treatment conveyor-belt, and that was that.

David resumed his weekday visits the day after I arrived, and was pleased to see me looking so well. I had even managed to get a slight tan during my fortnight out. I took off my shirt off and flexed my biceps. I informed him I was weighing in at sixty-four kilograms, with body fat at around 9 per cent, in other words athletic levels. My intelligent scales announced my body-age was now thirty, over a decade under my physical age. We both grinned at the irony, and I think he managed an additional grin at the resilience of my vanity.

Once again, I had to spend some days as an in-patient before the treatment started. Mayu came in those days until David arrived, and then on the day the chemo was to restart, Julia had an important swimming competition, and wouldn't be in. Chemo Round 2 was going to be the same as Round 1: three types of drugs, intravenously, for twenty-four hours a day for a week – 168 hours of uninterrupted chemotherapy. I'd begun to rationalise my sense of foreboding as natural fear, my mind's awareness that it was under threat from the toxic mix in the orange bag.

David had arrived at around 10am, and was sat in the armchair as usual next to my bed. As the nurses put the connector in my vein on my wrist, he looked up at the corner of my room. I was still tickled by his squeamishness, this famed narrator of humanity's brutalities unable to watch an intravenous drip being put in. But the event seemed to remind him of his own discomfort, as he launched into a story about the time he was stopped going through Customs with a vicious hang-over, and the steady fall that led to a full cavity search. The doctor came in and administered the first two types of chemotherapy while David continued his yarn. I was in hysterics, and hardly noticed at first the strange heat building in my chest. It was about the point where poor David was being bent over on a table and being told by a very large, smiling Customs official that this shouldn't hurt too much. David looked at me, stopped mid-sentence, and asked with concern if I was OK. All the blood in my chest felt like it had rushed up into my skull. I had the strongest urge to sneeze, but sensed that if I did, I might pop. I shook my head in response to David's question. He asked if he should call the doctor, and I nodded.

He pressed the emergency button, and a nurse I hadn't seen before came in, asking formulaically as she entered if everything was OK. She'd stopped mid-sentence. Looking at my face, she started to hyperventilate. My head had turned beetroot in colour, apparently. David shouted at her to get a doctor. 'Now!'. She snapped herself out of her petrification. The desire to sneeze was becoming so strong I had to pinch my nostrils together and try not to breathe, a good trick all hay-fever sufferers learn. David held my other hand, telling me to hold on and that the doctors would be here soon.

Within the next few minutes, my small room came to resemble a packed hospital staffroom. I remember counting three doctors and seven nurses bustling around me, putting me on oxygen, removing the chemotherapy drip, injecting me with some things, wheeling in a big machine that went 'ping', and talking too fast and too technically for me to be able to understand much. I tried to sit as still as I possibly could, afraid that any false move would lead to something very undesirable. David sat there throughout the whole afternoon, and called Mayu once it looked like I was not going to explode like a cartoon tomato. Poor Mayu, the one day she didn't plan to come was the one day I came all too very close to dying. I sent some pictures later in the day of me smiling through the oxygen mask. They were meant to reassure her, but in hindsight I can imagine the mask may have got in the way of that. She arrived at the hospital late in the afternoon, having got Jackie-san to look after the girls.

David left at around 8pm, when things were looking a lot better than earlier in the day. He gave me the gentlest of hugs, not wanting to break me, and gave Mayu a more robust one. Over the course of the evening, my heart began to slow down, but I could get no sleep that night, despite being tired beyond words. Every time I was about to nod off, my heart started racing again. I reacted like someone had suddenly appeared and screamed 'Fire!' in my ear. Mayu, lying in the camp bed next to me, watched as I drifted between these uncomfortable states. But by the second night, I could sleep some. And over the coming days my pulse began to return to normal.

I'd had a severe allergic reaction to the chemotherapy, an anaphylactic shock. It can be fatal, and I was saved by the quick reactions of my friend and the fine staff of Floor 10. Chemotherapy Round Two was stopped, meaning in the end I only had 30 of the planned 10,000 minutes of intravenous toxins. A few days after the reaction, I was wheeled down for a scan to see how much of the cancer now remained. The doctors were amazed when the results came back: the tumours in my glands had all but disappeared, and the main one in my neck had dramatically reduced in size. Dr Nishi said he couldn't remember seeing such a good reaction for this type of cancer from chemotherapy. I felt like saying, 'I tried to tell you this!', but smiled instead. It was still fantastic news. He then laughingly reminded me that while my original prognosis was 50/50, he was pretty confident that I was now in the good 50 per cent.

I stayed a few more days in the hospital following the reaction, for observation and tests, and Mayu came to spend the last couple of nights in my room. On the final night, I was allowed to go out for dinner, provided we were back by 10pm. We found a small Italian restaurant in the pretty Yanaka neighbourhood. It was the type of place that justifies claims about Italian food in Japan rivalling that in Italy. I had spaghetti in garlic, saffron and tomato sauce, followed by tiramisu, freshly made that evening. It was the richest, tastiest meal I'd had in months, and I could hardly talk when devouring it. We wandered slowly back to our private little room hand in hand, replete and beyond relieved. In hindsight, I was also totally unaware that the chemotherapy had only been the warm-up act, rather like the children of the awful relative from years before.

CHAPTER 23

Stuck

Mayu and I woke up at around 6.30am. The sun was rising with its usual autumn brightness in the cloudless blue. I was sunny inside, too, being giddy about all aspects of the oncoming day: saying farewell to the little room, the staff, the tenth floor; Mayu driving us up to Hakone, where we'd have a reunion with the girls and Mayu's parents. All in the context of my improved prognosis. The cancer was still present, I was still in considerable danger, but glimmers of hope were breaking through the chaos.

The nurse knocked on the door, and entered quietly, to take my blood, measure my blood pressure and pulse. It was Nurse Shimizu, and she chatted happily to Mayu and me about our plans for the day, involving a hot spring in Hakone and a lazy dinner with the in-laws and children. She said how jealous she was. Like a gleeful boy I even told her we'd had pasta and tiramisu the night before, and she noted the details of the restaurant saying she'd visit there some time. As she was leaving the room, she said all I needed to do was have a poo, and then I was free to leave. 'No problems there!', I quipped, saying I was a timely defecator. She smiled, with a hint of 'too much information' in her eyes.

After a cup of tea and some rice and pickles, I felt ready for some bowel movements, but when I sat down there was nothing doing. It felt like a plank of wood had been attached to my bum-cheeks, most firmly. I'd never had constipation in my life, so I didn't feel a great deal of panic yet. That was in the post. I pushed, and then pushed, and then really pushed, but still nothing doing. I tried the wash-let toilet, putting the bidet jet on level 10 and pointing it directly at the puckered eye, to see if that got things moving. Nothing. Confused, I left the loo and sat down with Mayu. Having lived together for around sixteen years by this time,

Mayu had a most intimate knowledge of my bowel movements, and was as surprised as me. 'Not to worry', she said, reminding me that she regularly had it with the onset of her period. We sat on the bed, drinking coffee to see if that would get things moving.

At around 7.45am Nurse Shimizu came in, and upon hearing that I hadn't done the deed, suggested an enema might be an option. I laughed out loud at the absurdity of someone with my alacritous arse needing an enema. She then said she'd be knocking off in fifteen minutes, so she could do it now if we wanted. Mayu and I looked at each other, and I said I was sure I'd be OK with the natural method, it was just a matter of time. I smiled and thanked her for all her help over the past two months, feeling silent relief that her lasting memory of me wouldn't be that level of institutional intimacy with my hairy pink behind. After she left, I went back to the toilet and pushed and pushed and pushed, but again, that plank was not for moving. 'Fuck', I said, as I inserted the tip of my finger up my bum, and had an unpleasant wiggle. Once more with the bidet, but still no change. I went back to the bed and said to Mayu we should wait a bit more.

I was meant to be out of the room by 10am at the latest, as another patient would be coming in later that day. By now it was 8.45am, and all that I had achieved were some red cheeks (in my face) from pushing, and the cleanest bottom in those parts from prodigious use of the bidet. I was now beginning to get very concerned, as I'd never had such a sensation before, this feeling of trying to push a brick through a letterbox. Nurse Kitamura had replaced Nurse Shimizu, and she persuaded me that an enema was the wisest option. In my ignorance, I had no idea what an enema really involved, or how it worked. Mayu agreed that this was the way to go, so I timidly lay on my side, knees curled up into a foetal position, and grimaced. 'Hold it hold it!' They shouted, as I ran to the toilet and expelled the enema almost immediately. Only the enema. 'You need to hold it in there!' But I couldn't I said, it had to come out. I knew I sounded like a petulant child, and it wasn't surprising because I felt like one at that moment.

Nurse Kitamura then suggested she try her finger. My stomach went cold at the thought, but she and Mayu and persuaded me into accepting the option. It was another demonstration of the power of institutional Discourses to vaporise the agency of the institutionalised, the finger almost a metaphor in itself. The equivalent of my whole unruly classroom being mercilessly caned, its protestations of innocence gleefully ignored.

Not that I was having such high-brow thoughts at the time. I returned to the foetal position, and whimpered as she entered my innards. My warm inner glow at the breaking of the day was now replaced by utter naked feebleness, and an exploratory finger which seemed like a frozen bratwurst. During her intimate explorations she kept a running commentary. 'Yes, definitely there! Oh yes it's very hard, you're definitely constipated (*No shit, Sherlock*). Let me see if I can hook my finger round that bit there (*what!?*)... No, no, can't get a hold of that. Let's try again (*Please don't*)... Yes, ah, missed it, let's try again...' After about ten minutes of this quite remarkable discomfort, she gave up. Nothing was coming, except my tears. She suggested we try another enema, but by this stage, after what was such physical intrusion, all I could do was hide my head in the sheets. 'Can you give us some time?' I pleaded, and she agreed. The word 'enervating' shot across my mind. It's one of those words I often get confused about. It somehow sounds wrong, being too close to energy, rather like 'restive' sounds to me like restful and festive. But at that moment its meaning was as clear as my tears.

By now, I was so drained and injured that walking to the toilet took a long, tender time: a journey made on tiptoes. With every step I felt like an out-of-tune tuning fork being clobbered by a brick. It was all far too much reality. Once I had my upper lip stitched without an anaesthetic by an angry doctor following a rugby game, and at this point I would have preferred that. Another forty-five minutes passed, the same routine of pushing and bideting and swearing, and now sweating a lot with fear of another enema, or worse, The Finger. I knew I had to get this damn brick out, and it was going to be through inserting another body up my bum. The Finger option was excruciating and demeaning, whereas the enema was not excruciating. Mayu explained that with enemas, you had to pucker up and keep them in for as long as you can. I resolved that this was what I had to do. Pucker up. Pucker up.

We called Nurse Kitamura back, and asked for another enema. She told us we could keep the room till 11am, but we'd really need to move to another room if things hadn't changed by then. So, we had a little less than an hour. The only room with a spare bed was a room for four people. And a shared bathroom. This was another incentive to steel up the puckering, and make sure the brick was delivered down where it belonged, in the toilet I'd been paying Y10,000 a night for. I really didn't fancy introducing myself to a ward of sick guys by whimpering on the bed in front of them as Nurse Kitamura enemised me. A nightmare scenario ran through my mind. I'd be in the shared room, the other three men watching me not managing to hold in the enema till I got onto the toilet. The toilet itself might be busy. Or the doorhandle might come off in my frenzy to sit down, and I'd be stuck on the middle of the room, all the guys looking at me, as this crying small foreign bloke crapped the biggest turd they'd ever seen before their very eyes. No. it was coming before 11, and that was that.

I resumed the foetal position. I needed to think of some time when I'd steeled myself for something difficult, and achieved the desired outcome. Completing a PhD in four years while working full time, emigrating, and raising two small kids didn't seem that relevant to the current predicament, I needed something more visceral. My mind flashed back to the time I won my cross-country 'colours' at school. The school was in a village built on a plateau, and the school course was a vicious six miles of journeys up and down the sharp valleys that dropped from the plateau. The first time I represented the school on this course, like most of the runners I vomited and couldn't finish. Our coach, Mike Tolkien, who also happened to be my English teacher, was disappointed. When I explained I'd been sick, he said 'Just carry on', as if it was the natural thing to do. Six weeks later, we had another match competing against the best runners from ten other schools. Once again, after about four miles of the valleys, I puked the same black, acidic, tar-like bile. But this time, after it had all gone, I started running again, puked again, and finished in the top five. Tolkien, smiling widely, awarded me my 'colours'.

This time around, I was going to win my enema 'colours', I knew it. Nurse Kitamura did her digital business, and I embraced the enema. My innards were machinating, like a heavy boot in a tumble-dryer, but still I held on. Sensing the anal apex, I stumbled up off the bed. Mayu and the nurse jumped up to support me. 'Take care, don't stop!' I pushed the door to and collapsed on the loo. It all arrived. Oh, the joy! A crescendo of vast waves sprung from the bowl as the thing thudded down. 'Yes!' I croaked, rising above my ego-ravaged state in pitiful triumph.

Twenty minutes later I had showered, dressed, and we were saying our goodbyes to the remarkable staff of Floor 10. At the lift, I shook the hand of Nurse Kitamura (hoping she'd washed them). I had to support myself on Mayu's shoulder as the aftershocks kept punching me in the gut, and elsewhere. It was not the departure I'd imagined, but we were leaving. If things went according to the plan, I wouldn't need to spend another night in hospital. Instead, I could start the next stage of the treatment, the radiation. But like the second chemotherapy, I was beginning to wonder about this.

CHAPTER 24

Resisting

But Doctor Nishi, you've said yourself that the cancer had largely disappeared from my glands, and the one in my tonsils has remarkably reduced in size. Are you 100 per cent sure that I have to have the thirty-five doses of radiation?

Well it's true the chemotherapy was very successful. But there are a few traces of cancer still in the glands, and in the tonsil area. And anyway radiation is part of the course of treatment for this type of cancer.

So I have to have thirty-five doses of radiation.

Yes. That's right.

And if the chemo hadn't reduced the cancer in size, I'd still have thirty-five doses of radiation.

He moved slightly in his chair, and paused before confirming. I smiled.

Sorry, but that's a bit ludicrous, isn't it?

The prescribed number of radiation doses for this course of treatment is thirty-five.

The conversation was reminding me of British middle-class rules of behaviour you're expected to follow even though they are at times arbitrary, the rules I did not miss at all … 'You have to hold your glass like that because that's the way it should be held.' I remember learning as a Philosophy undergraduate that these are tautological arguments, being circular. A very poor kind of argument, but in the hands of the powerful, quite sufficient for their needs.

I'm sorry doctor, but that doesn't make sense. It's as if the patient's personal details don't matter, you get the same dose whatever.

Mike, you're a clever guy, sure you know that that's the way medicine works. We look at the most effective treatment for people with this type of cancer, and give them that. We can't be tweaking things for individuals.

OK. So I might lose my sense of taste forever, have permanent side effects of various kinds including greater chances of secondary cancer, because the system is inflexible.

We sat there in silence, and then I told him.

To be honest doctor, we're thinking of not having the radiation at all. As you said, the cancer has pretty much gone already.

He raised his voice.

Listen. Your type of cancer cannot be cured by chemotherapy alone. And if we don't get all the cancer cells, when they come back, which they will, they will come back very aggressively. Now is our chance, our one and only chance, to get rid of all the cancer cells. This is it. Can't you understand? I can see you British don't like following rules!

I ignored the final comment.

We're thinking of having a second opinion.

The voice become even louder, the exasperated anger shining brightly through his eyes. I could sense I'd threatened his professional self-worth. And as is usually the case in such intercultural encounters between professionals and their 'clients', I wasn't so much threatening his personal sense of professional worth, but the institution he represented. And who was I to question the value of this great institution? Who asks for a second opinion when they are lucky enough to be cared for at the University of Tokyo Hospital? The emperor chooses to be treated here, for crying out loud! And perhaps he thought I was disrespecting the institution of medicine itself.

What? You've already had a second opinion! This is your second opinion.

I stayed silent, looking at him. He'd never raised his voice like this before, and I sensed he was a bit shocked at himself as well. As he calmed down, he agreed it was my right to have a second opinion, but that he was sure they'd say the same thing.

Around the time I was having the treatment, this was published in a research article:

When patients resist a physician's treatment recommendation, they create an opportunity to actively participate in how a treatment recommendation ultimately emerges as acceptable. This implies that through their responses, patients demonstrate a limited form of agency to actively participate in treatment decisions.

I'm not convinced Dr Nishi had read this. And far from feeling like I was demonstrating some agency, I felt the opposite at the time. If my cancer was an unruly classroom that was showing signs of genuine improvement, it was like the headmaster had just barged past me and was preparing to punish the whole class because their shirts were not tucked in properly.

It was mid-November, so Mayu and I still had a week to decide about having the radiation. We spent much of the week reading up on radiotherapy and neck cancers, discussing the options, and asking friends' opinions. But most of the conversations were in my head. The decision would have to be mine; I couldn't ask someone to make this one for me. I had to examine my motivations and make the decision for the right reason. The right reason being one that I could live with. And ideally one that would mean I could live. But would living mean I couldn't live well? And what is the formula for weighing the quantity of years against the quality of years?

I was scared, confused. The fear was not like the dreadful calm I'd felt following the 11 March earthquake when confronted with the choice of crossing the river together or alone to get Maya from the nursery. This was a fear banging around in my guts, forming a different gravitational system that pulled me this way and that. The list of potential side effects was a long and hard road. I flinched when I considered them, the impact they could have on my life. I liked kissing Mayu, and more importantly I think she liked kissing me. But could I assume she'd take pleasure in kissing someone with no saliva? And the breath issues. Xerostomia, the condition of chronic dry mouth, is often accompanied by bad breath. In the US, they typically remove all teeth before radiation to the neck area, and then replace the lot with dentures. It's because of the much-increased threat of necrosis, where the jaw tissue gets infected from a bad tooth, and begins to die. Then there was public dining: I might never feel comfortable eating in restaurants. Who wants to eat with someone who can't swallow properly, and who can't taste the meal you are sharing?

Oh, you're having soup again. You must really love soup! How is it today?
Hmm. I have no idea – muddy maybe?

There is also the potential permanent cancer-related cognitive damage, termed 'chemobrain', which is more of a risk for those having radiation around the head or neck areas. Many professionals who've undergone chemotherapy and radiation to this area of their body cannot return to mentally demanding jobs. They just don't have the brain power any more. It sounds very similar to the cognitive aspects of long COVID. Then there is the increased threat of a secondary cancer. And these were some possibilities if the radiation actually worked. Rather a lot of reality for a hypochondriac.

But I was also frustrated by the system itself. The dosage did seem extreme for what were now far fewer cancer cells, so few that they hardly showed up on a scan. The treatment was developed for non-HPV oro-pharyngeal patients, the old smokers and drinkers who had developed the far more tenacious type of tumour. Recently, there is increasing clinical research about de-escalating the treatment for the likes of me (HPV+, young-ish, and healthy), to reduce the toxicity of the long-term side effects. But in Tokyo in 2011, there were no such discussions that I was privy to, and my inexpert attempts to start them provoked the disdain of the experts. And few do disdain like an expert. In my frustration I was reminded of the nurse's joke, told to me by my mother the midwife: 'What's the difference between God and a doctor? God doesn't think he's a doctor.'

I was also still smarting from the unwilling road I'd taken to the second dose of chemotherapy, the one that caused severe anaphylactic shock. I'd been dealt with by the 'system', that system that can make you feel like a number, or a cog in a big machine, or something on a conveyor belt. All these metaphors show the depersonalising experience of cancer treatment when you are your most vulnerably personal, an isolated, fragile, fragmented self. I was right (admittedly with scant evidence) when I said I felt the cancer had got a lot smaller, and the doctors wrong when they'd dismissed this. I'd said I'd wanted another scan, and they'd said that wasn't part of the treatment programme: I would receive my scan after the two cycles, and that was that. I ended up having only thirty minutes of the second cycle of chemo, having a very-near death experience and also for a while, getting a dodgy ticker (chronic atrial fibrillation). And then having the scan show my intuitions were correct. Now they were saying I had to have thirty-five doses of radiation because that's what it says in the book. It was immaterial who I was, what my situation was, how big my tumours were. I was just a point of data on a graph.

These were the thoughts going round my head when deciding what to do about the treatment. But how much of this was really just a natural desire to run from potential pain and suffering, and how much was rational concern over the likely benefits? If my main reason for not having the radiation was that I was scared of the side effects, but I was confident that having the radiation would prolong my life, that didn't seem like a good enough reason not to have it. I would still be able to love and raise my daughters, Mayu and I would be able to build a different life together but still a life together, and I would work in some way. I'd met plenty of academics who seemed to be working on the same research article for years, I could always become one of those. And the internationalisation work didn't require a great deal of brain power, rather smiles, positivity, charm, and some strategic vagueness to respond to any tricky requests.

I also knew this one-size-fits-all process is how modern medicine works, and generally modern medicine works very well. It is the culture of cancer treatment, or certainly was at the time. Patient-centred care, where patients are involved in treatment decisions, was not really evident in this institutional culture from what I could see. But I knew how cultures work, they constrain choices, and they censure those who try to do things differently from 'the way we do things round here'. Like me, the oncologists operated within and were controlled by this culture. So my frustration with the staff at this point wasn't fair. They didn't make the system, they were in many ways as constrained by it as I was. Their Discourse was a very powerful one, one that had helped halve the number of deaths from cancer in the past fifty years. And they had saved me, so far.

I now resolved that my best chance of a longer life involved allowing them to continue trying. I felt that I'd explored all the options but hadn't put myself in danger in exploring them. A week later I started radiation treatment. After thirty-five daily doses, provided I made it through the treatment, I would be able to have a scan and tests to see whether it had worked. At that moment, I couldn't have imagined just how much of myself I would have to sacrifice because of that resolution, or whether with foresight, I would have made the same decision.

CHAPTER 25

Shrinking

The radiation department in Todai Hospital is in the basement, three floors down, and has an entire floor to itself. There is only one lift you can take, hidden away behind a side-corridor, far from the prying eyes of the healthy. On entering the floor, you will be greeted by the invariably welcoming receptionists. After taking your card and processing the information they give you a file and invite you to sit in the waiting area down the corridor, until your name is called. There are around thirty seats in this area, some plants, and a couple of TVs. They are always on, always showing NHK Channel 1, always with no volume. In the seated area there are radiation patients and their families. Because you have treatment at the same time each day (my treatment was at 1.45pm), you see the same people, although they may have started their series of doses before or after you. As far as I could tell, I was the only non-Japanese person having treatment. During the regular visits, you see the effects of treatment on other patients and their families as they endure the process, as they must with you. We end up being darkened mirrors of each other's states, and perhaps fates.

Of the many families there, two stay in my mind. The first was an elderly couple, probably in their seventies. Neither of them was having treatment, but we never saw who they were accompanying. They would look kindly at Mayu each time they saw us, and acknowledge her through a slight bow of the head. As with all other people in the waiting area, no words were exchanged. What is there to talk about in such a place?

The other family was a husband and wife, probably in their late fifties. They were a strikingly handsome couple, both very tall and slim, and very well dressed. Mayu wondered whether they might both have been models or actors when younger. The woman's treatment started about a week or so after mine, so we disintegrated at a similar pace, though in different ways. By around week five she was struggling to walk, and was now emaciated. By week eight, my final one, she was in a wheelchair, looking decades older than when she had arrived. The husband had also aged, his elegant posture replaced with something more brittle and bent as he pushed the wheelchair silently back and forth.

IMRT (intensity modulated radiation therapy) is the advanced type of radiotherapy I received. Unlike standard radiation, the radiation beams conform to the 3-D shape of each individual tumour, meaning a stronger dose of photon and proton beams can be applied to the affected area. It also means that less damage is caused to the surrounding healthy areas. Receiving this type of radiation was the main reason we wanted to have the treatment at this hospital. Fujisawa Hospital also offered radiation treatment but it was the standard type, which was more likely to cause severe permanent damage to the whole area being treated. As I mentioned in Chapter 24, the short- and long-term side effects of radiation to the head and neck area can be significant, and that is still the case with IMRT, effects including a higher risk of secondary cancers. Not long after starting the radiation, I made a Faustian pact with my body. I could endure the treatment and the long recovery, provided I could reach an age where my daughters would be relatively independent. If I could survive to sixty, I reasoned, I would be very content indeed.

When having radiation treatment, the importance of not moving was impressed upon me, verbally and physically. The first stage of the treatment involves having an individualised thermoplastic mask made, a wonder of modern science. It's initially a very hot sheet of plastic mesh that is moulded firmly to your face, shoulders, and chest by the radiologists as you lie on the treatment table. Once cooled, which takes a few minutes, it clips into the table, and then surgical tape is attached to the mask, showing which areas are to be irradiated (Figure 25.1). The radiologists draw a circle on the tape with lines through it, like a target, showing the places on which the laser should focus. My mask had one target just below my lower lip, another under my chin, and a third over my main lymph gland on the right side. I can still trace where the laser escaped out the other side, because there at the back of my head it looks like a barber has prodigiously slipped with the clippers.

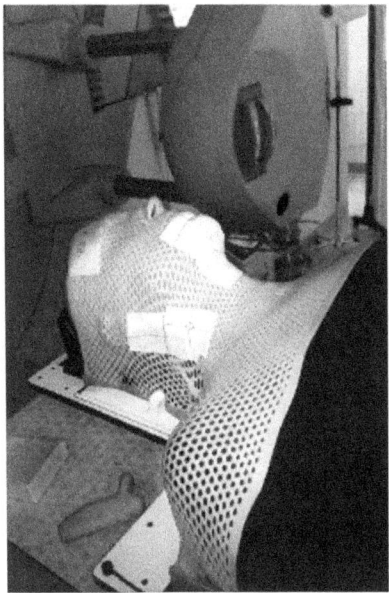

25.1 Me in the mask, early days.

There's another strip of surgical tape across the forehead part, with each patient's name on. When not in use, my mask took its place with the other masks on the shelves in the radiation room. Once in the mask, it's impossible to move, and the large laser goes about its business, noisily circling above you as you lie there. As I lay there in the first weeks, I'd practice the mindful breathing Maurice had taught me, stilling my body and mind. But as my body shrank, the mask seemed to grow. My breathing became shallower and shallower as the weeks progressed, for fear of moving too much, and with the shallower the breath, the deeper my sense of unquiet.

If the original cancer diagnosis was like an earthquake, the treatment was like a series of powerful aftershocks. I've mentioned the inevitable physical disintegration that this treatment causes. My disintegration was not gradual, it felt jagged. Rather like a well-crafted horror film, where the opening scenes are really rather comforting, before you are suddenly thrust into a very different mood, a different frame of existence.

I was reminded of the events of 11 March: we were all happily looking forward to the holidays when the earthquake hit. But the type and degree of suffering was so different: Fukushima caused so many deaths,

25.2 After the run, a few days before I started radiation.

and so much trauma across society, but in reality did not traumatise me or my family; it scared and threatened us, but we were among the lucky ones, unlike so many. This cancer and its treatment was causing no difference to society, but the trauma was intensely personal, threatening to change the lives of the few people I dearly loved.

And yet, apart from the odd bout of heart tremors, a hangover from the anaphylactic shock, I was in great shape when the radiation began. I was at my ideal weight of sixty-four kilograms, and felt supremely fit. Mayu's macrobiotic cooking, the range of supplements, the foot massages, the daily gym workout, swim or run, abstaining from any alcohol or caffeine for months, and the absence of work all combined. There's a photo taken outside of the Orange House just after I'd been running (Figure 25.2). It's a few days before I started radiation, and I don't think I've ever looked as healthy.

The first treatment, which like all sessions on the table lasted around ten minutes, went off painlessly. As indeed did all the opening blasts. Then, after three weeks of treatment, I suddenly lost about five kilograms. Eating had become very difficult because of the pain in my throat, but the weight loss seemed more fundamental than just reduced food consumption. My body was now in a battle, and it did not seem metaphorical. It was fighting against the poison of radiation, and using my body mass as fuel. I kept up my regular gym visits, and when I went to the gym to do some weights the following week, I could see the staff looking quizzically at me. I quipped that they probably saw me as a bad advert for their gym – here's a guy who pumps iron and it makes him much skinnier!

A week later I lost another five kilograms, but I wasn't making jokes any more. I was struggling to eat any solids, even with the blue packs of morphine I'd been prescribed, and the foul-tasting packets of Terumi, a kind of food supplement, became my primary source of calories. One advantage of gradually losing my sense of taste was that I didn't have to taste that stuff. Strawberry-flavour, indeed. But as my sense of taste receded, the pain in my mouth increased. It was like having an electric wire inserted into my tongue, with my throat burning. Which of course it was; radiation is heat. I couldn't stop myself whimpering as I tried to eat at the table with Mayu and the girls, so one evening I took my dinner into the TV room and closed the door. I stayed eating there for the next few weeks, hoping that they couldn't hear my noises.

Many cultures draw a distinction between the body on one hand, and the mind (or soul) on the other. The biomedical model that informs clinical cancer care is predicated on such a dualism, and may ignore the mental side of things when it comes to problems of the body. I was being given a harsh lesson in an alternative philosophical position, one that rejects the dualism of mind and body, one that argues for our embodied nature of mind. Rather than having a body, I am a body, and part of that body is my mind. And this mind can only exist, can only understand, can only perceive the world, through the body. Changes in our world therefore change our embodied mind, such as the metaphors we use to make sense of the world, the Discourses we see ourselves belonging to, the stories we tell. Cancer was a radical change to my world, radically changing my embodied mind.

Alongside my physical disintegration, my mental fortifications were starting to falter. By fortifications I mean especially the stories I told myself, about myself. These weren't just comforting fictions – they were how I understood who I was: teacher, father, athlete, academic. Now, as my body changed, these familiar narratives started slipping away. It was as if my communication with myself had changed, as if I had become something of an other to myself. My thoughts and feelings, my intrapersonal communication, was becoming intercultural.

My initial reaction to the diagnosis was one of emotional chaos, but love, support, and hope meant I could begin to move away from this chaos, to start making a new Discourse. This new Discourse had made use of old, positive stories I told about myself, such as being a teacher, being physically active, being reasonably physically attractive, being a caring and active parent, having an agile mind, and being combative when threatened. Now, my body and mind were entering a new kind of chaos, a chaos in my mind resulting from the alien chaos of my body.

It was a new sense of that otherness within, what Freud called *unheimlichkeit*, a not-being-at-home-in-your-own-body. It was like moving from solid ground to ice – not just the physical uncertainty of each step, but the psychological shift that comes with it. On solid ground, you walk without thinking, confident in your body's abilities. On ice, every movement becomes conscious, tentative. Your awareness of your body is coupled with a sense that it could betray you at any moment. Even standing still requires constant adjustment. This was how I felt – a constant state of flux, of darkness, never quite finding stable footing in my own body or mind.

With this new chaos, brought on by my reaction to the radiation, my earlier stories were starting to make less sense. Exercise was becoming impossible, I was doing less with the girls, I was physically withering by the day, my brain was feeling befuddled, and rather than being combative, I was beginning to realise that enduring is sometimes all you can manage. It was like someone had turned the lights off in my unruly classroom and I had no idea what the students were doing. All I could do was be present.

CHAPTER 26

Supports

Cancer is like culture, it's tempting to blame it for every problem we encounter. But as cultural differences are often not the cause of many failed international business relationships, so cancer does not always cause every physical issue. Some issues may have been lingering around for years before any cancer appeared. Lingering in the background of our daily lives, erupting gently and then gently dissipating across time and space. Like farts.

But perhaps farts are unfairly maligned. There is indeed literature on the subject, such as Jonathan Swift's 'The Benefit of Farting'. At 120 pages it's tempting to call Swift's piece short, until you remember the subject. One joke I heard recently compares farts to children: we can enjoy our own while we quietly recoil from other people's. Might this reflect some deep psychological truth, an inverse Oedipal complex of the arse? Freud himself was certifiably entertained by the man known as Le Pétomane, who could play 'Marseillaise' through his backside.

The professional flatulist has a long history, which like so many things, is shared across seemingly different cultures: St Augustine, for instance, wrote in the fifth century of performers with 'such command of their bowels, that they can break wind continuously at will, so as to produce the effect of singing'. In the Tokugawa period in Japan (1603–1868), during which the national borders were uniformly closed, its nationals' sphincters were certainly not: *heppiri otoko* ('farting men') earned good money, and competitions between them (Figure 26.1) have been captured for austerity in woodblock prints.

My own, admittedly amateur, fart story concerns one of the many supports we used to alleviate the after-effects of my cancer treatment. For neck-cancer patients undergoing radiotherapy, damage to your salivary

26.1 Woodblock print of the professionals and the unfortunate cat.

glands is one of the toughest symptoms to deal with. Saliva, how precious you are! Even with IMRT, the very focused type of radiotherapy I was lucky to receive, you're still looking at a year or two with drastically reduced saliva, and for many survivors there is permanent damage. As winter 2011 approached, I had no way of knowing, provided I survived the treatment, what degree of parched mouth I'd be left with. And anyway, I had a more pressing concern. Once asleep, I'd violently wake up every hour to my racking cough. It was like someone shoved a powerful hairdryer in my mouth while I was dreaming away. I wasn't particularly aware of this at the time, but the noise would also wake my girls up in their bedrooms.

Mayu, lying next to me, was suffering silently in the noise. And suffering between the noises, with any period of silence making her wonder if I was still breathing. We both usually need a lot of sleep, and the days were giving her enough challenges without this. Dr Nishi recommended a humidifier, so once back home we got on our bikes and cycled off to BicCamera, the ubiquitous electrical supermarket. The Fujisawa branch contains nine large floors of technological goodies, including a sound-proofed room with around seventy sets of hi-spec speakers, a whole floor of TVs, and another floor for naturalists and stargazers, full of cutting-edge, digitally enhanced equipment.

We went straight to the floor full of air conditioners and related items, and found a fine selection of humidifiers – from the hand-held to the fully installed type. We plumped for a brown portable option, about as big as a medium-sized suitcase. One of the attractive features was a traffic-light system to tell you about the humidity in the room – red meant very low humidity, orange meant low humidity, whereas green meant the room was sufficiently juicy. On red, it would automatically shift into top gear and thrust out moisture-filled air until the room, and I, were unparched. A full tank of water would get our bedroom through the night in the dry Japanese winter and spring. In summer the natural humidity in the Tokyo area turns unchecked rooms green with mould, and summer seemed a very, very long way away.

After a few nights of using this humidifier I found I was definitely sleeping a bit better. One night, around 3am, I woke myself up when I let out a loud, fruity fart. Almost immediately the humidifier revved up, the light switching from red to green, completely missing out orange. Clearly, I'd messed up the mechanism with my natural gas. The poor machine must have interpreted the stinky air as dry air, which it certainly wasn't. The smell woke Mayu up, in a state of exhausted anger. There she was having not just her ears invaded but her nostrils, too. But when I told her about the colour change, she fell into a fit of giggles. The next evening, as I was reading to the girls before putting to bed, I felt a certain rumble in my tummy.

Girls, do you want to see some magic?

Ooh, yes, Daddy, yes!

Quick, come into my bedroom and turn the light off. I'm going to change the light on the humidifier without touching it. Do you think I can?

No way!

Okay. How about you bet me a bedtime story, if I can do it you two have to tell me a bedtime story instead.

Okay!

Okay.

Watch that light. And Maya, you hold the remote control so you know I'm not tricking you. OK?

We sat there on the bed in the dark, and I let rip. 'No, Daddy, no!' they cried, but I told them to hold firm and watch the traffic lights. Once again, straight to red.

They fell off the bed laughing, and then for weeks after, when anyone felt a certain feeling, off we went to 'check' the sensor. I seemed to have

26.2 Learning to drink miso soup through a straw.

the most 'power', as the girls or Mayu could usually manage merely a change from green to orange.

Apart from this wonderful piece of technology, we also found a range of other supports. It's a tricky business navigating all the advice you receive when in cancer-world. I mean, you'll try anything but at the same time you don't want to do anything that will put the treatment and so your life at risk. The risks of potentially fatal anaphylactic shock are much higher for those on chemotherapy, and mixing the prescribed toxic chemicals with unprescribed medicines can kick off that unwanted process. But it's not only drugs. With a debilitated immune system and weaker constitution, the advice is to stay away from many foods, too, such as raw shellfish, certain processed meats, and blue cheese. One food I didn't stay away from was soup, although I ended up taking it through a straw because of the pain in my mouth from the radiation (Figure 26.2).

The challenges are compounded because everyone seems to know someone who claims they were cured by drinking aloe vera, or praying, or meditation, or indeed foot massages. Apart from the praying, I tried all those. One of our neighbours said that loquat leaves, either brewed into tea or attached to the sick part of the body, have healing properties.

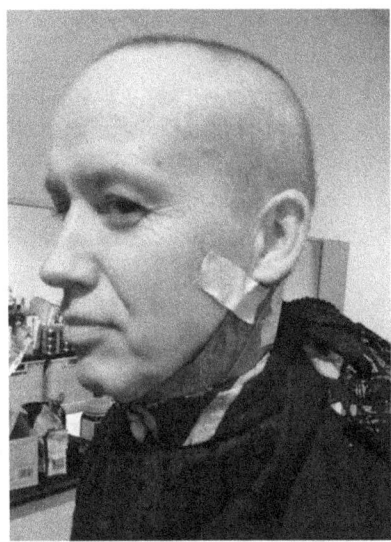

26.3 With the loquat leaves strapped on.

Loquat is a fruit tree native to China, and widespread in Japan. It is indeed rich in antioxidants and helps the body fight against free radical damage. I drank so much loquat tea (it tastes like a stale rooibos) that I will never touch it again. One evening, Mayu tenderly strapped the brittle, sharp leaves to my neck with surgical tape, then wrapped them up with her mother's floral silk scarf (Figure 26.3). The confusion of the silkiness and the sharpness was too much for my tender skin, so it was just the once. And it looked ludicrous.

Aloe vera is another plant that grows well in Japan, and in our area it seems to be everywhere – from our garden, to the shopping streets in the city centre, to the grassy plots behind the beach. Big plants, with thick dangling leaves two or three feet long. It is miraculous: it has both anti-oxidant and antibacterial properties, accelerates wound-healing, including sores in the mouth, and can even reduce constipation. It's not the prettiest of plants admittedly, but when my mouth sores were at their worst, I found it gave more solace than the morphine. I'd wander down to our little garden, tear off a strip of a spiky, rubbery leaf, and suck out the jelly inside. When shopping in Fujisawa, I'd even break off leaves on the plants lining the streets when I'd find myself in too much pain, like some furtive bitter-jelly addict. The clear inner-solids have virtually no flavour, but the green lining of the leaf can be bitterly acidic. We'd put it in smoothies, and I'd rub a leaf all over my neck area after the daily radiation dose. Aloe vera, nothing comes near her!

Well, acupuncture maybe. My mother had first put me onto acupuncture after it had cured her pathological fear of flying. Following a visit to her local acupuncturist in her hometown in rural Ireland, she no longer had to find that sweet spot between very drunk and unable to walk without assistance when boarding a plane. It was a blessing for all concerned.

Once other therapies such as foot massages became impossible because my naturally unimpressive pain threshold had been trounced by the radiation, Mayu suggested I try acupuncture. Replacing a stick of pain with sharp needles seemed to fit with the absurdities of the time. She found a local practitioner in Fujisawa I could cycle to, an elderly quiet man whose 'clinic' was the type of age-warped wooden building you wouldn't want to be in when a big earthquake comes. You enter by sliding an old wooden door, push through the curtain, and could be confronted by one of the other customers in the process of undressing. Two or three customers would be sitting further along, in their underwear, with the treatment area close enough to be touched while sitting on the bench. All in silence, with smoky clouds of the medicinal dried herb moxa threading its way through our carefully piled clothes. I always felt an increase in energy after the visit to this peaceful, dilapidated space.

Although I didn't really think about it at the time, these alternative treatments were all suggested to me by Mayu and her father, and originate mainly in China. It's an understatement to say there's a complicated relationship between the two neighbours, but the long and fruitful influence of Chinese culture on Japan is evident in many spheres of life, for instance food, writing, or medicine. *Kanpō* (漢方), which translates as Chinese medicine but is the Japanese modified version of Chinese medicine (think ramen), is integrated into and can be paid for using Japan's national insurance system. During this time, I made use of all the four main branches: acupuncture, moxibustion, food therapy, and herbology. Jackie-san, a fellow-hypochondriac, has always kept a prodigious, generously shared supply of various Chinese herbological medicines in his home (mainly pills and teas), so much so that I nicknamed him 'The Chemist' – a nickname that seemed to annoy him. Like Mayu, he's good at giving it, not so good at taking it.

I'm also aware that I wouldn't have been introduced to, or perhaps been so open to, certain alternative medicines if I hadn't been so long in Japan, and if someone other than Mayu had introduced me to them. In our thirty years together, it's only the rare occasion where I've felt that Mayu and I are culturally different. This is because in my mind culture is not something we have, but instead something you do, and we tend to react to things in similar ways and act similarly, often in unison. But Mayu's knowledge and acceptance of *Kanpō* was something she'd acquired during her upbringing in Japan, something I hadn't experienced. I have no way of telling what the effect of *Kanpō* was on my cancer, but I do know that it often made me feel better, and it felt good to be doing something, and perhaps it felt good for Mayu to be doing something. For these reasons alone, I'd say this instance of cultural difference was welcome.

CHAPTER 27

Christmas

When we had our first Christmas in the Orange House, we took Julia to BicCamera, where there was a wonderful range of children's toys. She wanted to buy some Sylvanian family pieces, the cute little animal toys, which would represent the four of us. The staff member encouraged her to buy four of the same kind, the rabbit family I seem to remember. Instead, she bought the father from the husky family, the mother from the cat family, one kid from the squirrel family, and the other from the rabbit family. 'But they're not the same', the staff member quietly protested. Julia looked quizzically at her, saying these were the ones she wanted as they looked like each of us.

The notion of 'third spaces', where people with different cultural practices interact and make a new, hybrid culture, is popular in intercultural communication. It strikes me that being bicultural and mixed-race is a regular negotiation, a conversation with the world around, to make third spaces, new identities, new ways of doing things. Christmas, celebrated in the Orange House in a country where less than 2 per cent of the population is Christian, and where Christmas Day is just a regular workday, might be seen as another third space. We transported customs from the UK, such as Christmas carols on CD and crackers brought over in suitcases, but most of all I like to think we nurtured that spirit of kindness and love that pervades this time of year. Japanese New Year has a similar feel, of kindnesses shared, so for us Christmas and New Year merge into a long happy holiday.

Although Christmas is not a public holiday in Japan, schools and nurseries are closed at this time of year, as families wind down for the New Year holiday. On Christmas Day, the girls would wake us up early, too early for comfort but the pain of a 5am start was usually eased by the jollity of their bustling, bursting expectancy. The presents for the girls had been put under the tree, which we'd set up together a few weeks before, the pile slowly decreasing in size as they got older. But at the ages of eight and five, the pile was still considerable, a shiny avalanche below the tree's fake branches.

Maya had asked for a T-shirt and poster of Motörhead, having become obsessed with the song 'Ace of Spades'. This was my fault. Mayu's parents, who like her are great singers, had a state-of-the-art karaoke system, which we were all expected to use. Being a bad singer, I had taken (before cancer) to finding karaoke tunes I could move energetically to, compensating for the sounds. Along with Elvis's 'Suspicious Minds', to which I did a high-octane impression of his early Las Vegas performances, the headbanging 'Ace of Spades' had become a firm favourite. Particularly with Maya, particularly the headbanging.

The poster had arrived the night before, a massive glossy image of Lemmy, the lead singer. But what we hadn't noticed when ordering it was the writing at the bottom of the poster: '99% Motherfucker, 100% Son of a Bitch.' We carefully folded it back so she couldn't read that till later in life. Unfolding that was the first thing she did (Figure 27.1). She looked at the long words, thankfully with incomprehension. 'When you're older you'll be able to read them,' I said, hoping that I'd be there to see it.

Every year Mayu would film the unwrapping of the presents by the buzzing, busy girls, while I helped with unwrapping, assembling stuff, and tidying up the wrapping paper. This year, it was a struggle to even crumple up the wrapping paper. I helped, but could rarely manage a smile before falling back to the reclining chair. I was becoming a shell, an emptied exoskeleton. At night I now had to sleep on my back because my legs were all bone, and lying on my side meant resting cold, hard bone on bone. I had eaten nothing solid for a week, and the treatment carried on regardless. Because Christmas Day was on a Sunday, I had a break that day, but I'd be back in the mask for Boxing Day. The mask that now was loose around my diminished shoulders and chest. I was now down to fifty-four kilograms, around a 20 per cent loss of body mass in the space of a few weeks.

After the girls had finished unwrapping, I sat in the reclining chair staring out of our living-room window. It was another crisp, clear day,

27.1 Two angels.

Mt Fuji glistening white, and the ocean steel blue. I could pretend I was thinking wistfully of Li Po's poem:

> *The birds have vanished down the sky.*
> *Now the last cloud drains away.*
>
> *We sit together, the mountain and me,*
> *until only the mountain remains.*

But I wasn't. I felt no closeness to the beauty of the mountain, it was just an enormous block of stark, cold, whiteness. I felt ripped out, tired beyond tears, and all the thoughts of comic absurdity that had kept me going earlier on in my treatment had departed. I stood up from the chair so that I could get a blanket, but forgot to hold onto my pyjama bottoms, the new pyjamas we'd bought for my hospital stay. Instead of laughing as they fell to my knees, I could only sigh. I pulled them up and fell back into the chair.

Mayu stared at me for a long time, and I looked back at her. Along with the grey bags under her eyes, grey streaks on the left side of her hair had appeared. She brushed off my question about the hair, asking me instead about the thing I'd been trying not to consider.

Mike, do you think you should stop treatment?
I thought for a time, and said, *No.*
Well, how about having a stent in your stomach? That way you can get some solids inside you.
But I'd have to be hospitalised in that case. No. I just need to keep going.
But you can't eat. Whenever you try you scream.
That's why I eat my meals in the small sitting room.
But we can hear you through the door. When the girls hear that they start crying. I don't know what we should do. There's nothing I can do to help.

I didn't know what to say. I sat there in silence, staring at our beautiful wooden floor.

I need to call my parents to wish them a Happy Christmas.

Mayu looked at me, seemed to decide against saying something, and walked downstairs.

I called my mother first, and kept it brief. I said I was doing OK, and told her not to worry. The treatment was going fine, and we were having a nice Christmas. I was thankful that she didn't ask much, or talk too much. I then called my father.

How are you doing sonny Jim?

I told him I didn't know what to do, that I felt so weak, so emptied. I began to weep. He listened, and unusually didn't turn the conversation to himself or utter something castigating. The anguish poured out of me in bursts, and he sat at the other end of the phone catching and cradling my pain. Like a kind parent, quietly consoling a small child who has been robbed of something they cherish.

For Christmas Dinner, I had booked a table at the Piny restaurant next to the river, part of the well-known Piny Bakery. Going out to dinner was the last thing I wanted to do, but I'd booked it so that Mayu would get a break from the kitchen. I'd usually cook dinner at Christmas, but that wasn't an option this year. It had been a long time since I'd cooked anything. The questions were swirling in my head. Would I be able to eat anything? Would I end up whimpering in pain? What kind of company would I be? Mayu sensed my apprehension and asked if I wanted to cancel. I knew the girls were excited about going, the food was always excellent, and their remarkable appetites could be satisfied with the four courses plus the range of breads, cakes, and patisseries that were on offer.

We wandered down to the restaurant at around 5pm, just as the sun was setting across Sakai River. The restaurant had been decorated with the usual red Christmas stuff, as is usual across Japan, and a large fake Christmas tree sat next to the two-piece band. The quality of the music was in direct contrast to the usual quality of the food. The pianist kept hitting the wrong keys for the song, as indeed did the singer. Mayu looked at me in earnest, and said, 'I think she's even worse than you.'

We knew the staff here well, being regular patrons of the bakery. They encouraged us to eat as much as possible, using the hospitable phrase often reserved for guests at your home, *enryo naku*, or 'don't hold back'. I smiled at the irony, my levels of cancer-fuelled solipsism rising. The rich smells of freshly baked bread, creamy soups, roasted meats, and good coffee initially enticed me, before I remembered. I looked around the restaurant, and there was only one other family there, with it being an early Sunday evening. I was relieved, thinking that if I did make a sound at least there weren't too many people present. The server came over, and she was the daughter of one of Mayu's neighbourhood friends. She smiled as she approached us, and I was thankful she didn't look at me too long. Mayu's friend later told us that she'd gone home after the shift shocked, saying I looked 'like a skeleton'.

The first course arrived, pumpkin soup. I steeled myself to eat it, and was shocked to find that I could. The soup was going down, and without any noise from me. It was at this point that I realised what a deeply vain person I am. And then it dawned on me that vanity can be a strength in certain circumstances. In the same way that being of a belligerent disposition may be an advantage in the context of war, I realised that being vain can be an advantage when in public. I screamed at home because, in reality, I could; but there was no way I was going to scream in a restaurant, embarrassing my daughters in turn. I was reminded of a Monty Python film where the ghost of the unfortunate host says, 'to serve salmon with botulism at a dinner party is social death for me', seeming to care more about the damage to her reputation than actually being dead. This was different, but only by a degree.

One (British) reviewer of this book commented, 'How very British of you' upon reading this. Yes, it does tie in with the 'stiff upper lip' stereotype, but I've always had a decidedly wobbly upper lip. I recently read Angela Carter's biography of her dear father, a man prone to tears, and from whom she learnt to equate lachrymosity with emotional depth. She'd find me deep, very deep. I imagine some (not all) Japanese reviewers might have a parallel reaction to my ability to eat. They might say my many years acculturating in Japan meant an increased ability to endure (*gaman*), that most valued of Japanese values. Again, I'd disagree. I'm just very vain. Like a stopped clock, stereotypes may look accurate now and again. But like a stopped clock, I'd say even when they look right, they're not. As a stopped hand on a clock cannot represent the movement of time, so a fixed image of a group cannot capture the dynamism and diversity within.

I found I could finish the soup, and even eat some bread soaked in it. Yes, the pain was still very much there, and I could hardly taste anything except for that soil-like flavour. But ever so slowly I could finish the bowl. Mayu and the girls were shocked. The next course arrived, a white fish in sauce, and again, I got through it. Each small mouthful gave me a little more strength, a little more warmth. I felt happy, the cliché of turning a corner rang true, and I knew what I had to do to get food inside me: eat in public. I wallowed in my happy vanity, feeling that I saw a way out of the dark.

As I managed to eat in the restaurant, I realized my unruly classroom was learning new behaviours. In private, the students (my cancer) were still chaotic, but in public, they showed remarkable restraint. Like a lucky researcher, I had accidentally discovered how a different environment could produce different behaviours. My vanity was becoming an unexpected teaching tool – the students might misbehave at home, but they would maintain decorum in public. Julia asked me why I could eat, and I told her enigmatically that I was learning how to teach my cancer to behave. She paused, looked quizzically at me, shrugged, and returned to devouring her pudding. Eating out was to be a new practice in my cancer Discourse, I resolved.

Walking home along Sakai River, I noticed again how normal everything looked now, nine months after the earthquake. The river was calm and lapping low. Boats were bobbing gently against the bank, the myriad reflections of well-lit homes cascaded across the water, children were laughing unselfconsciously, and some people were happily already the worse for wear. Just as society had found ways to cope with disaster through small, accumulated acts of normalcy, I wondered if I, too, was discovering my own path back – not to the old normal, but to a new way of being. A nascent third space perhaps.

As we walked home, the girls chatted happily about the good food, the awful music, and what film to watch together. Once there, with Maya on my lap, and Julia and Mayu sandwiching me in warmth, we watched, again, Ghibli's glorious *Spirited Away*.

CHAPTER 28

Ending

One of the positives in having cancer in Japan was the improvement in my bilingual vocabulary, specifically medical jargon. All the words that the Fujisawa oncologist had kindly translated for me, the ones I didn't even know in English, I could now use fluently in either language. 'Oh yes, the severity of the side effects of radiation is higher because the cancer has metastasised', I could nonchalantly utter in Japanese while sipping herbal tea with a colleague who didn't speak much English.

As I found myself using more medical terminology, perhaps more than was appropriate sometimes (like when a colleague was trying to eat their lunch), I wondered about what this meant. Was I, like many cancer patients, trying to distance myself from my failing body? Researchers have observed that patients often adopt medical language as 'a mechanism of resistance' against seeing themselves as one with their deteriorating bodies. I'm not sure this was the case for me. I think I really liked to sound more fluent in Japanese. And while I hated the treatment, I still saw my self, my cancer, and my tattered body as parts of me, central tenets of my interpretation of the Discourse of being a cancer patient. My cancer metaphor, that central part of my Discourse, hoped to coax these three into supporting my longevity. My unruly classroom was gradually approaching that limbo period before the exam results were known. But there were still taxing classes to be completed first, radiation classes, which required resolve to get through.

As for the side effects of the treatment, they were marching on. Although I was becoming less and less active, we kept to the same evening routine: while Mayu sorted the kitchen, I'd bathe the girls, get them in their pyjamas and into bed, and then read to them. We practised typical Japanese bathroom etiquette in our typical Japanese bathroom: proper shower first, then get in the bath, making sure to carry in no suds. While showering, the girls would take great pleasure in slapping my now negligible bum. Maya, giggling, said that it was like a slice of thin ham. Julia thought it more like a sandy puddle on the beach, having the same tension and sound when slapped. While I did manage to read to them, short stories were now spread over a couple of nights, or I'd ask Julia to read part of the story.

I had a week's break from the radiation during the Japanese new year holidays. We spent most of it up in Hakone, giving the girls a chance to be pampered by their grandparents and Mayu a chance to recuperate. But how could she recuperate, as I aged by the day, withdrew by the day? The effects of the radiation were continuing despite the break, meaning I was in pain, weak, and becoming less communicative (Figure 28.1). As I sat in a chair looking out on her parents' garden with her behind me, I'd see in the window's reflection the concern etched on her face: her thinning, beautiful face.

Radiation restarted on Monday 8 January, and there were seventeen more sessions scheduled before completion. On the Tuesday we had a

28.1 In Hakone over the holidays, showing signs of wear and tear.

check-up with Dr Nishi. 'Oh, you're not looking too bad at all!' he said as I entered the room. One of the key insights of linguistics is that the possibilities of what you can say in a conversation are largely dictated by what is uttered immediately preceding your turn. Him opening with this positive evaluation framed the conversation in these terms, meaning it was hard to get him to understand that I might (to him) look acceptable, but was far from feeling it.

I can understand that part of his job was to get me through the treatment, and words of apparent encouragement might seem the obvious way. Also, he'd seen a lot of people at this stage of the treatment, so he was in a position to judge. But I felt, Mayu and I both felt, trapped in the tyranny of positivity that surrounds cancer patients. Why is it not OK to say you're not OK? Mayu was becoming more and more worried about me, as my energy, my body, my personality, continued to wane. A few days after the treatment had restarted, she again, more gently but more persistently, broached the subject of my stopping the treatment.

At what point does your love for someone mean that the kinder thing is to let them die, rather than see them suffer? What kind, what temper, of love is that? I knew what Mayu was weighing up when she suggested this, the potential loss of so much in her life and the life of our daughters. Stopping the treatment after slightly more than half of the doses didn't mean the cancer would definitely come back, but it would have raised the chances. 'Mayu, I can't stop the treatment', was all I could say. I could find no words to say why.

Increasingly, apart from the time in the car seat when Mayu drove me to and from the hospital and the time spent there, I sat in the reclining chair in the living room of the Orange House, staring out of the window in silence. I was cold in my bones, whatever I wore, and the fatigue was overwhelming. The strawberry drinks now tasted of nothing, everything tasted of nothing, even water, but they all had the effect of acid on my tongue and throat. We still had the odd meal out, but the resolve required to leave the house was in itself exhausting. And I was aware of how I looked, and made further aware by the looks I received.

Cancer has, in the words of Christopher Hitchens, a harsh way of showing 'the truth of the materialist proposition that I don't *have* a body, I *am* a body'. An academic friend of mine was recently operated on for prostate cancer, had this to say about the short period before and after the operation: 'I entered the hospital as a well-respected university professor, and I felt I left as an old man, carrying a catheter bag, who people looked at and felt sorry for. The change in the sense of self over days is astounding.' For me, the change was a little more gradual, being weeks rather than days, but astounding is a good word for the shift in the cancer-self, that embodied, fractured self, as it perceives itself and is itself perceived.

A couple of weeks before the treatment ended, my friend Jim came to see me. Jim had known Mayu and me since before we had kids. He had interpreted my cancer as a natural travesty, and as an act of defiance, he'd taken to going to Shonan Beach at night and screaming at the sea. In our living room, he stayed for half an hour, before looking earnestly at me and saying his goodbyes. Years later, he told me that after leaving our house, he'd wept as he walked home along Sakai River, thinking he'd never see me again.

As the past may be a foreign country, I noted earlier, so too is sickness. In previous chapters I've talked about the interactions between the cancer patient and the oncologists as being a kind of intercultural communication, with each party belonging to different Discourses. I'd also noticed how communication with the self is akin to intercultural communication, as the chaos within begins to push the normal self out. Now, a third level of interactions shifting into an intercultural frame seemed to be happening, this time at the interpersonal level. In relationships with friends, or even loved ones, the distance was growing, as my reality moved further from anything they had experienced and I collapsed into myself. Becoming an other to each other, there were moments when no bridge could be found to cross that divide.

Looking back, I can see there was also a degree of what Christopher Hitchens termed the solipsism of a cancer diagnosis. It is perhaps inevitable, given that I was so focused on my own health, my own survival. And while I don't mean I succumbed to the 'why me?' type of solipsism, I did become communicatively, emotionally, very introverted. Any thoughts I could muster tended to be about myself, about making things easier for myself, about just keeping going. As I became an other to those close to me, my silence distanced them.

And communicating with people about cancer is inherently hard. I understand this, as I've struggled to communicate well with people about cancer, not only at this time but before I had it, and afterwards. My dear stepmother Grace, who like Mayu's parents showed me unconditional love, had cancer for several years. She died just before Julia was born, and in memory of her, Julia's middle name is Grace. When I'd see her, I'd try to cheer her up by telling jokes, but I could tell the laughing was tiring her out and even causing her physical pain. I stopped, feeling confused, a little shameful, and utterly helpless. In her last months, I gave her a copy of Dylan Thomas's poem 'Do Not Go Gentle into That Good Night', hoping it might give her some strength. She accepted it with her typical warmth, but in hindsight we both knew she was soon to die. Who was I to make such demands on another? Why did I assume she might want to be cheered up, or encouraged to fight against her now-inevitable death? I can see now that all this was more for myself than for her, as is so often the case when it comes to talking to people with cancer.

Some years after my treatment I met someone from school I hadn't seen for many years. Her partner had died the year before, leaving her with two young children. I told her how sorry I was, and mentioned that I'd had cancer myself, but was now OK. Aggressively she replied, 'I hate hearing other people's bloody cancer survival stories.' I don't know why I told her, apart from some clumsy attempt to achieve what linguists term 'interpersonal alignment'. But we were worlds apart: I was alive, her darling was dead; my children had a father, hers didn't.

As I sat in the brown reclining chair in the Orange House, staring out of the window, I just hoped that time would allow for Mayu and I to talk again, like before. I was suffering, she was suffering, and there was nothing to be done except endure. I hardly had the energy to complete a sentence, or to ask to hold her hand. As I looked blankly out of the window, day after day, the world would carry on below. The children would walk past our house on the way home from school, delivery drivers would park and then leave, neighbours would cycle to work or stop for a quick chat with each other.

But I was still just about upright when the last day of the treatment came. We thanked the staff, said silent goodbyes to the other members of the Basement Radiation Club, and we took away the radiation mask as a souvenir (Figure 28.2). 'Not everyone wants to see them again', the radiologist said when offering it to us. It was now far too large, and as I held it in my hands, I noticed the muscularity of the mask's shoulders. 'Then

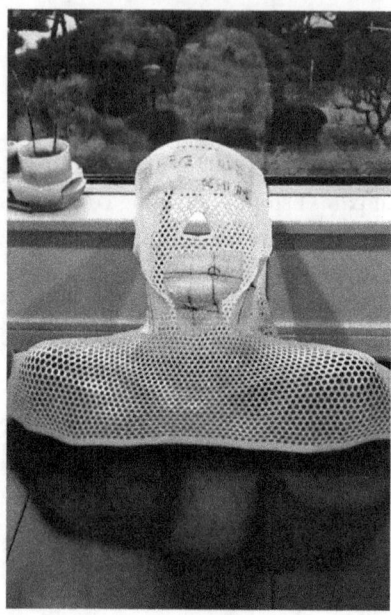

28.2 My mask on the living-room floor, after it had done its work.

you can make the body you want' my friend Jason, a boxer, had said when I'd told him months ago the treatment would make me emaciated. Looking at the mask, I thought I'd be satisfied to have these shoulders back. Mayu carried the mask for me, as we made our way back to the car, a walk that used to take a brisk five minutes. Now it took twenty, with my frail steps and several stops to regain breath.

A week later, I had scans and various tests. Dr Nishi, elated, soon gave us the news that all evidence of the cancer had been obliterated. You're never told you're cured of cancer, but he told me he was confident about my future. 'I told you that you were in the good 50 per cent! Like all our patients, you'll have checks for the next five years, but I think you're going to be fine. Congratulations!' I'd expected to feel euphoric, but in truth I didn't have the energy for intense emotions. The overriding feeling was one of relief. Relief that the treatment had indeed worked, but also relief that I would never again have my neck irradiated. Even if the cancer came back, radiation would no longer be an option. I don't know, at that point, which of the two senses of relief was stronger.

The thing that had been chasing me for months had finally run out of energy before me, but only just. Exhausted beyond measure, I could barely manage to turn round to see its shadow. Mayu and I left Dr Nishi's office and held each other for a long time. 'Thank you' was all I could say in my hollowed-out voice. I was a linguist, proud of my verbal dexterity and knowledge of language, left barely able to speak. But I was alive, and with time I knew I could regrow, we could regrow. We had made it.

Before returning to work I had a gentle month of being fed by Mayu and cuddled by my two precious girls, on my reclining brown chair. I sat there, reacquainting myself with the joy of music, Mt Fuji, and the steel-blue Pacific, learning to speak again. Although much movement was still beyond me, the dual senses of relief increased each day. The coming months would present many challenges, personal, relational, and physical, but I had reached the place which, just a month ago, had seemed so very far away.

CHAPTER 29

Redwoods

Mike-san, good to have you back. We'd like you to go to San Francisco to have some meetings with UC Berkeley and Stanford next month. We're developing links there and want to set up some student exchange agreements.

Oh, I'm not sure I'm up to that yet. Maybe in April or May?

But you've finished the treatment and it was successful, right?

Really, I don't feel very robust at the moment.

You've had a long time off work you know.

It's just I'm so tired even when I get the train to work.

The trip may do you good, San Francisco is nice this time of year. You'll be fine.

Hi, Dad here, how are you doing?

I'm OK, you know.

Good. I think I'm going to come out to Japan to see you all in May. I'll stay for a couple of weeks.

Er Dad, I'm not sure that's a good idea.

No, it'll be fun, we can go out for dinner, you can take some time off work and we can travel a bit.

I've just had five months off work. And Dad, I'm exhausted. And you'll see us in the summer, it's only a couple of months after May.

I'll bring an empty suitcase and you can fill it with some of your stuff. And think, if I don't come now, I won't be able to come back to Japan for almost two years. I love Japan, you know that. Anyway, I've booked the ticket. You'll be fine.

Hi Mike-sensei. It's great to have you back. And the treatment's finished, so you can really throw yourself back into work. You must be raring to go.

Erm I'm not feeling up to speed yet, to be honest, the treatment was quite tough.

But you can forget about that all now, and start working really hard. You've missed a lot of time, haven't you. There's a lot that needs doing.

Yes, but the occupational therapist has said I need to take things very easy for the coming months, while I recuperate. He said I should probably be part-time for a while.

Nonsense! You look fine!

These were some of the conversations I had with family and colleagues within weeks of the treatment having finished. Starting back at work in late February 2012, I was able to manage about an hour or so before I felt my body and brain begin to fade. For the first couple of months back, I'd lie to one group of colleagues, saying I had meetings in a different department. I'd then go to my office, keep the lights off, and rest my head on the desk for an hour or two. Around 1pm I'd get the train home, feeling guilty but too weak to do any different.

And in these conversations with family and colleagues I felt feeble. The environment around my Discourse was in the process of changing, but I hadn't yet learnt to navigate the changes. Whereas interactions with close colleagues and my UK family had always seemed interpersonal in nature, they now took on an intercultural tone, but in the negative, distancing sense. It seemed like I'd moved, or been moved, from being in *uchi*-type relationships, to being *soto*, outside. These people did not understand my condition, and I felt at a constant disadvantage. When I used words like 'exhausted', I meant that at I times could hardly think or move. Five minutes on foot might be all I could manage before having to sit down, a two-minute chat might leave me floundering. They clearly thought I meant I was a bit tired, that's all. A few good nights' sleep and I'd be fine again. We were speaking a different language even though the words were the same, and the identity they perceived was not the one I embodied. At times I felt powerless to make them see. I don't know if they wanted or were able to see – they had their goals, their wants, their pressures, and I was unable to negotiate. The business trips happened, the family-visitors came.

But at least I had someone I could complain to, apart from exhausted Mayu. With my return to campus, David and I restarted having our weekly lunches. The challenge was to find something I could eat, and eat in relative peace and quiet. Quiet for me meant peace for everyone else. Our usual curry was out of the question, as any amount of chilli would make me scream. The blander the better. It wasn't the flavour, as I couldn't taste anything, but I'd realised that fewer ingredients provoked less noise. After a couple of failures with me trying to not make a scene and David looking on concerned, we found that Japanese soba noodles were the best option.

'The fuckin' bastards', was David's response when I told him about the requested San Francisco trip. But as it was my first (and possibly last) trip to California, I resolved to see something of the place. I mean apart from seeing the universities, both of which turned out to be spectacular. I also persuaded the office I needed to fly business class, and ended up on ANA, having my own cubicle with a little door and enormous TV. It eased the pain.

I'd been in San Francisco for two nights when I decided to take the bus up to Muir Woods. It was 11 March 2012, exactly one year after the Fukushima earthquake. And what a year it had been. Standing among the trees, I thought about how both disasters had changed my understanding of permanence and fragility. The earthquake had shown how quickly established routines could crumble; cancer had taught me how swiftly the body could betray itself. But both experiences had also revealed unexpected truths about enduring, compassion, and the openness to others that suffering can enable. Like the Japanese towns slowly recovering from the disaster, I too was learning to navigate a changed landscape, finding new ways to exist in old spaces.

And now here I was in a very old space. The late afternoon sun was cutting diagonals through the deep shards of the trees' bark, bark whose depth is measured in feet, not inches. Standing there I reflected that varieties of cypress, with their fleeting, subtle scents, had accompanied my time with cancer. Foremost was Japanese *hinoki*, thanks to, and indeed on, scent architect Maurice. Now, in this wood on the opposite side of the Pacific, the air was similarly sweet. I was wandering between the California Redwoods, their magnificence deserving of capitalisation. These trees, along with their relatives the giant sequoia, were once the main inhabitants of much of California.

Muir Woods, named after the couple who in the nineteenth century saved some of the last ancient trees from the logging companies, is a place to make the first-time observer giddy. The trees soar into the sky so very high, and are so very wide. Many of them have reached 100 metres or more in height, more than 30 storeys of a building. Reaching eight metres in diameter, some are slightly narrower than a London bus. If not felled by men or nature, they can live for over 2,000 years. They are the tallest, biggest trees in the world, indeed the largest living things on the planet. They speak of another time; to some, they communicate a different experience of time.

As I tried to explore the distant canopy, I craned my neck till it cramped up. I rubbed it vigorously, then craned it again. Over the previous months, other symbols of permanence had begun to resonate deeply within me. For instance, I'd become something of a stargazer since the beginning of autumn – wrapped up in sleeping bags and blankets as I lay on our roof, looking up through powerful binoculars. I spent hours up there on my back, mapping out the Giant Bear as it gradually took over much of the night sky, or learning about Castor and Pollux, Vega and Altair.

My PhD supervisor, another happy atheist, had once told me he loved to look at the stars as it reminded him that there was a time before he existed, and he wasn't upset about that, so why be upset about a time in the future when he wouldn't exist either?

As I stared at these trees, my PhD supervisor's words came back to me. While not so permanent as the stars, these trees are some of the oldest living things on the planet. Each life we live is so little in comparison, and there is solace to be found in their silent witnessing of our mortalities and our struggles.

I'd gone to San Francisco out of a sense of obligation to the job, but the job would still be there even if it killed me. The job didn't care. The university had continued quite effectively in my five-month absence. There were lessons here I needed to learn, not least that saying no can be an act of self-compassion. Here, my weakness in having agreed to the trip confronted me. But that morning I'd had the strength to tell colleagues I needed to take some time off, and then took the bus up to the Redwoods. Having crossed the Golden Gate Bridge and seeing, smelling, and of course hugging these trees, I felt a small liberation.

In my post-treatment Discourse, I was realising that small wins were often as good as it got. Much of the time consisted of struggle, not only with other people, but also internally, intrapersonally. S. Lochlann Jain talks about being 'deflated by tension', the tension between their own awareness of the despair and fear they constantly felt, and the perception of others: 'You're so brave! And lucky!' To me, being brave implies some action, whereas cancer treatment typically inhibits action. On the radiation table you mustn't move, and each session on that table makes all subsequent movement harder. Even the action of voicing words, or conceiving them, can be a struggle.

In an earlier chapter I quote Paul Kalanithi's line about, following diagnosis, moving from being the subject to the object of every sentence in his life. He felt he was no longer someone who did things, he was something to whom things were done. After the treatment, I was now again someone who was expected to do things. But again, this is really just another way of being the object of the sentence: it was others who expected me to do things, I was expecting the minimal from myself. Our frames of expectation were badly mismatched. My unruly classroom was now exhausted and needed rest, whereas some colleagues were thinking it was ready to move on to new challenges. Just as I'd learnt to teach according to my students' needs rather than external expectations, I needed to learn to pace my recovery according to my body's timeline, not others' schedules. My unruly classroom wasn't ready for a new term yet; it needed time to reset, to heal. But I was lucky in my work. I still had a job, a good job, and all things considered a supportive job. Working for an employer that had stood by me, and working with colleagues who I knew wanted the best for me. And even if some colleagues couldn't really grasp my situation, there were many other people around me who could.

At the end of the afternoon with the Redwoods, crossing the Golden Gate Bridge I realised I was seeing the Pacific from the other side. Almost at the same latitude as San Francisco, in Fujisawa Mayu would have got the girls off to school, perhaps glancing in my direction as she drank her coffee in front of the living-room window. Perhaps this was the first time she saw the tulips emerging in our small garden below.

Oh! Where did they come from?!

I said when I got back from San Francisco and stood by the window. She paused, then said,

The girls and I planted 100 bulbs in October for you, while you were in hospital having the chemo. We didn't know if you'd get to see them bloom.

Any distance that had developed between us in the previous couple of months disappeared as I gazed down at the bouncing riot of colours for the first time, holding her hand.

In another month Mayu would receive confirmation of her place at the University of Birmingham. Our friends found us a house to rent in Bournville, cycling distance from the university, and we then arranged places for the girls at Bournville Junior School. Along with the Honorary Research Fellowship at the University of Birmingham, I received the grant for the engineering communication research. Then, after the family visits and variable performance at work, in the summer of 2012 we flew to the UK.

CHAPTER 30

Bournville

Settling into our UK life, Mayu and I had a memorable conversation outside a pub in Birmingham one chilly November evening. I'd recently begun to reclaim my love of dancing, that joy of the bass inside my guts and the high notes sailing through my head finding expression though my body. I'm what you might call a flamboyant dancer. I've had random strangers in clubs stand and clap. Or sometimes laugh. In daily life, I try to exercise restraint, but on a dance floor I anticipate the nuances in a dance track with carnal abandon. Mayu isn't bad, either, tending to stomp and thump to the bass.

Inside this pub there looked to be a disco going on. Wanting to join in and show off our moves, we just had to get past the bouncer on the door.

Sorry mate, you can't come in. She's alright, but not you.

Huh? Why not?

It doesn't matter why. Go on love, you can go in.

Thanks.

Mayu! Wait!

Joking! I'm not going in without you. But how come you won't let him in? He's quite harmless, you know. I'll keep an eye on him.

Haha. Yeah, he looks harmless. Ha, that's what I'm worried about. Look, I can't let just anyone in. It's my job to decide who comes in, see? What's your job then?

I work at a university. Why?

There you go. I bet when you're dressed in your lab coat doing your little experiments you don't let strangers in your lab.

Lab coat? I don't wear a lab-coat. And this is a pub, everyone's a stranger. What's –

Nah, you see that's your problem mate, right there.

In the Introduction I contrast two approaches to intercultural communication, the one employed here that focuses on stereotypes, power, being an other, and the mainstream approach that argues our most important identity is our nationality. This national identity is fixed, and explains why cultural clashes happen. If the mainstream approach to intercultural communication is correct, it's hard to make sense of this situation. From my accent and so on, I was clearly a British man, as was the bouncer (though our accents were very different – his local, mine not). Mayu's English is excellent, but she'd be the first to say she does have a Japanese accent, and is of Japanese ethnicity. Some problem was happening here, which was cultural, but national differences cannot explain it.

While I was a bit shocked to be refused entry, I remember thinking it very funny, satisfying even, that Mayu was welcomed and I wasn't. The situation highlighted the nonsense of assuming national identity trumps all. The world is an increasingly complicated place, and as the linguist John Gumperz argued back in 1996, 'Cultures are no longer homogeneous and language divisions become more and more permeable … speakers of the same language may find themselves separated by deep culture gaps, while others who speak distinct languages share the same culture.' I'm not sure that Mayu and the bouncer shared the same culture, but for the bouncer it was clear where the bigger 'culture gap' was.

During the first few months in Birmingham, things like this happened to remind me that being from a place does not necessarily equate with being part of it, and that not being born in a place does not mean you can't feel at home there. Little Maya's reaction was a case in point. While Julia had, from the offset, been excited about moving to the UK, Maya certainly hadn't. I remember when we told her we would be moving, a month after she'd started Katase primary school along with many of her Kiddie friends, and she lay on the living-room floor in the Orange House gnashing her teeth and wailing. She was settled, popular, and happy in Fujisawa. Why on earth leave for a whole year, to live in a country she'd only visited on holiday? By the time we left Birmingham a little over a year later, her front milk teeth having disappeared, she wept again as she said goodbye to her friends and impressively long line of suitors.

Adjusting to Birmingham life took Mayu virtually no time, her transition being somewhat smoother than mine. Again, the dominant intercultural approach has to tie itself in knots to explain such things. It did, however, take some time for Mayu to adjust to being a full-time MA student, and within the two first weeks of her course starting, the kitchen walls and cabinets in our rented house had been redecorated with colourful Post-it stickers. On each Post-it was a definition of a key term she'd noted from a reading. You'd go to get a cereal bowl in the morning, and inadvertently knock 'transitivity' on to the floor, then have to carefully put it back next to 'triangulation'. I was briefly tempted to jumble up the alphabetical system, for instance by putting 'intertextuality' next to 'cohesion', but thought better of it.

For me, professionally, it was good to be in the UK, not least because I could manage my own work schedule as I liked. I had a personal goal of completing four academic journal articles during the year. In what was becoming a pattern, I worked too hard on them for the initial months, got fatigued, and then had to take a break. But my responsibilities at the University of Birmingham for the Fellowship were undemanding, involving giving a few talks and attending the odd meeting. I could attend any modules or research seminars I liked, and was warmly welcomed by the academics in the English department.

The bigger goal was to heal. And yet I hadn't really considered the challenge of moving to a place where people didn't know I'd recently had cancer. Back home in Katase, and among friends, everyone knew the extent of my cancer, the treatment, and the effect it had had on my life and the life of my family. I was often supported by the palpable sense of injustice my neighbours and friends felt, this awful threat to such a lovely family. My embodied cancer-self had been understood within a community that witnessed its transformation. As with the earthquake, I felt closer to society as a result. Yes, I was born and raised in the UK, but I almost died in Japan and the everyday people of my everyday life there had been horrified by that prospect.

But in Birmingham, I was largely a stranger, a stranger in an unstrange land. Apart my close friend Almut and her wonderful husband Terry, who had found a house for us to rent on their street, hardly anybody knew I'd had cancer. I was just a very skinny little fellow who'd moved back to the UK for a year with his family. The very community that had helped heal me was now on the other side of the world. Each small step – being able to eat solid food again, walking further each day – happened in a place where few understood its significance.

This created a new, different sense of the *unheimlich*, that uncanny feeling of 'not being at home'. But this time, it wasn't in my body, but more a sense of 'not being at home in my country'. I was particularly struck by the double bind of communicating your cancer beyond those you are intimate with. If you don't explain to people the reason why you're skinny, or tired, or moody, or oddly bald, or refusing a lunch invitation, they make their own, probably negative, assumptions. But if you say it's because you're just recovering from cancer treatment, the reactions are rarely what you'd wish for. It's just too big a conversational bomb. Sometimes I felt I'd imposed on the person, as if they didn't want the responsibility of knowing something so personal, something so taboo. Once again, my cancer had meant interactions that might be seen as interpersonal at 'normal' times were now intercultural, with me something of an other. Indeed, the medical anthropologist Deborah Gordon, writing about cancer diagnoses in Italy in the 1980s, argues that a public pronouncement forces the cancer patient 'to enter the world of the "other", thus excluded and no more equal to us'. Unlike Gordon, I refuse to attribute this to national character, such as British reserve or whatever. Had I been diagnosed and treated in Bournville, I'm sure the reactions of neighbours would have been similar to those in Katase.

But appreciating that didn't solve the problem of this double bind. Sometimes I told myself I didn't have to explain myself to anyone at work, or even in my personal life. I thought that silence was my choice, but now I better understand that silence is a social phenomenon, one that is imposed upon us, one we are coerced to submit to. Because at other times, having just survived the ravages of cancer treatment, I felt there was a story that I needed to tell. Because 'just' here holds both meanings so often central to a good story, and the need for the teller to tell it: the relevance of time, and the seriousness of the threat. Telling the story helps heals the mind. And over time, with some old friends and some new ones, I could learn, I have learnt, that story I needed to tell.

It was clear that my Discourse of being a cancer patient was changing, as I was no longer felt like a patient. Was I now 'a cancer victim'? A 'cancer survivor'? 'Someone living with cancer'? These different framings would mean more than just a label, as labels always do. Like many, I tentatively chose 'cancer survivor', hoping I was not tempting fate. But I realised that even a Discourse of cancer survivorship is constrained in

30.1 Just having completed the Birmingham Half Marathon.

many ways, not least in how much you can talk about it, and what you cannot say.

With my developing Discourse of cancer survivorship, and as my body became more robust, I began to return to some of my favourite pastimes. Mayu and I registered for the Birmingham Half Marathon (Figure 30.1). I was pleased with my time of one hour fifty minutes, less than a year after the radiation had finished. Sponsored by generous friends, it was also pleasing to raise a couple of thousand pounds for Macmillan cancer charity, as I'd been making much use of their services over the past year. I've already mentioned music helped me feel more at home in my body. The most astounding live event was Antony (now Anonhi) of Antony and the Johnsons singing at The Royal Opera House in London, with the Britten Sinfonia as her backing band. Mayu, a veteran gig-goer, said it was the most moving, powerful concert she'd ever seen. One of the many five-star reviews in national papers called the concert an original artform.

Meanwhile, something strange was happening with art. Mayu's quip about her liking certain paintings because they were good, whereas I liked them because I thought I should, was funny because I knew there was some truth in it. I liked art, but unlike music or literature, I knew I lacked discernment. But in this time following the treatment, I 'got' one school of art. The distorted figures and savage lines of expressionist art spoke to my experience – how cancer had warped my familiar self into something seemingly other, yet on reflection familiar.

The exaggerated, contorted images, reflecting extreme and often traumatic emotional states, resonated with the way I felt. I found an uncanny affinity between the harsh, jagged lines, the sometimes night-marish features, the unexpected colours, and the emotions that had accompanied me since diagnosis. It was like my emotions were now seek-ing to calmly embed themselves, and these artworks could help. The emotions were sometimes new, and difficult to categorise. Rather than feeling simply sad or lazy or hopeful, these artworks seemed to mirror my new feelings of pleasant sadness, my empowered laziness, my hope tinged with greyish clouds. 'Yes, I've got to admit it's getting better', Paul McCartney brightly coined; 'It couldn't get much worse', mumbled John Lennon behind him.

As has often been the case, I was lucky in my place and time as well, with examples of expressionist art appearing randomly and regularly. Almut and Terry in their house up the road had several posters of paintings by Kirchner and other German expressionists. In June 2013, there was a performance at Birmingham's Electric Cinema of the silent expressionist film *The Cabinet of Dr Caligari* (Figure 30.2), with live musical accompa-niment by Steven Severin of Siouxsie and the Banshees. The Banshees, something of an expressionist band themselves. I discovered the works of Webern and Schoenberg, masters of atonal expressionist music. The dissonance and distorted melodies similarly made sense to and soothed my mind. As much as the running and dancing (when I was allowed in), this art helped heal me.

During these months there was a growing realisation that I was not defined by my cancer. Yes, my body was still brittle, my brain might sud-denly fade in mid-conversation, and energy was a fickle friend. Yes, I am a body, and yes, my body had had cancer, but I was not my can-cer. I did not have to essentialise myself, or let others essentialise me. Rather than being trapped, othered, reduced by cancer, I began to see how, in the fissures created by my recent history, new meanings could emerge. My new-found understanding of expressionist art and music had only appeared because of my cancer. Alienation, anguish, anger;

30.2 A scene from *The Cabinet of Dr Caligari*.

emotions endured by cancer patients, and I felt solace in their visceral representation.

My Discourse was shifting, transforming into something new. I was gradually moving away from being a person with cancer, to being someone who was learning to adjust to life after treatment, while accepting cancer would always be with me. I was learning to live with the realisation that cancer could come back at any time, coupled with the knowledge that cancer can happen to any of us at any time.

CHAPTER 31

Institutions

I recently gave a talk, co-hosted by The Academy of Medical Sciences and Life Sciences Hub Wales, about my experiences as a cancer patient. It was a brilliant event, looking at how cancer-patient care can be improved, with participants from the healthcare system, academia, pharmaceutical companies, and government. The organisers, in discussions prior to the event, said they were keen for me to contrast the UK and Japanese systems and my experiences therein. I said I wouldn't focus on this because, in fact, there were probably far more similarities than differences in the systems, but also that I only knew two hospitals in depth.

In the talk I explained that I'd been asked to talk about the differences, but instead would emphasise the similarities. These include roughly similar survival rates in both countries, roughly analogous treatments for my type of cancer, inspiring levels of professionalism in both systems, and the largely identical Discourses of oncologists, oncology nurses, and radiologists. I noted some differences, such as the differences in post-care in the two hospitals I'll discuss further below, but I framed the whole talk in terms of the overwhelming correspondences: research-driven, biomedical healthcare systems in two outstanding teaching hospitals. Both hospitals clearly performed at a very high level. And in the context of much improved survival rates over the past fifty years, the patient could end up feeling, in both systems, more like a case than a person.

In the newsletter that came out after the event, it said that during my talk I 'reflected on receiving treatment in both Japan and the UK, highlighting the contrasts in patient care approaches between countries'. Hmm. This is, as I've noted before, how culture works: we want to find differences, and then we explain these differences typically at the national level. But it wasn't what I'd said! I'd made it very explicit that I wasn't going to put the emphasis on the differences, because there were so many things that were the same, and I wasn't convinced by (or equipped to talk about) the significance of national-level healthcare differences.

The things that were different were often specific to the hospitals themselves, or to me with my own unique history. For instance, I could use my first language in Birmingham, and this meant I felt more confident in consultations than I was in Tokyo. I could also be more persuasive, such as when confronted by the painful prospect of the endoscope. Yes, I felt a little more agency in Birmingham, but by the end of January 2013 I was now a year post-treatment, and my chances of long-term survival improved as the treatment date receded. By the time I returned to Tokyo in the summer of 2013, I felt more agency again. I was a more expert, confident member of the cancer-survivor Discourse.

Naturally though, there were some differences between the two systems operating at the hospitals. I quickly realised after arriving in Birmingham and having my first consultation there that I had been very lucky in the order of things: the treatment at the University of Tokyo Hospital was fantastic, whereas the after-treatment was paltry; the after-treatment at Queen Elizabeth Hospital Birmingham, was wonderful, but they didn't have IMRT. The oncologists at Birmingham were amazed to see how well the back of my throat was recovering even though the radiation had finished eight months earlier. There was by then little blistering, and they were quick to point out it wouldn't have been like this if I'd been treated there.

In that first meeting with the Birmingham oncologists, I also met the head oncology nurse and a couple of her nursing team, along with a psychologist, and a masseur-cum-acupuncturist. They formed the post-treatment team, and asked me a variety of questions to see what types of support I'd need. Initially I felt a bit unsure of what I should say, but they put me at ease, framing the conversation as wholly supportive. I hadn't been asked such questions at the University of Tokyo Hospital, and Mayu and I had had to make our own way in terms of accessing support beyond the treatment table. Now, I was learning new practices, and about the practices, that became part of my Discourse of cancer survivorship.

They seemed surprised when I said I was feeling emotionally pretty stable – except for the psychologist, who seemed relieved. In fact,

I remember him implying that seeing him might be a waste of both our times, which caused an uncomfortable non-verbal ripple among his colleagues. Thinking about it now, he had patients who had lost their noses, cheeks, jaws, synapses, voices, cognitive abilities, livelihoods, partners, even futures – I retained all of these, so in the world of neck and head cancer patients perhaps he was thinking I didn't have too much to be concerned about.

I told them my main concern, apart from fatigue and skinniness, was dry mouth. My sense of taste, while improving a little, was also still poor. This was especially so with spicy food, which tasted simply metallic. Birmingham, home of the Balti curry, but none for me. For the dry mouth, the oncologist told me, the acupuncturist Paul might be able to help. My question, 'How much is each session?' led to some laughter. Having been deeply embedded in the Japanese healthcare system for so long, I couldn't grasp at first that this treatment was all free.

It was not lost on me that here I was being offered therapies – acupuncture, reiki, shiatsu – that had originated in Asia but were not offered at the University of Tokyo Hospital. But it would also be possible to make too much of this – it was the Queen Elizabeth Hospital's head and neck oncology section that had such a service, supported by the Get-A-Head charity; it was not available throughout the UK's NHS. I had to resist that temptation to generalise, that desire to see something national in what was really a single case. Yes, it was a cultural difference, but not a national-cultural difference. It was a difference in the cultures of two oncology departments in two otherwise very similar hospitals.

Yet here I was, learning new ways to discuss my cancer-healthcare needs in English, things I'd originally learnt to do in Japanese. I booked a session with Paul, but despite my previous experiences with such needles was sceptical about the chances of acupuncture helping my constantly dry mouth. It just felt incongruous that some needles could fix such a big issue. My Japanese acupuncturist has used needles so thin that you barely noticed them. Paul's felt like knives in comparison. But after the first session involving the enormous needles hanging in my ears, there was a tangible difference in my saliva production. After four sessions I could eat mashed potatoes again without the assistance of sips of water. My sense of taste improved as well, and I began to put weight back on, the first time since before San Francisco. After three months I was eating sandwiches. Admittedly with lots of lettuce and a drink and not in public, but it would have been unimaginable just a few months earlier.

As in Tokyo, I still had to have the monthly check. Apart from visually checking the inside of my mouth and throat, the oncologist would stand behind me, feeling around my neck like a frenetic saxophonist, checking for any untoward lumps. And as in Tokyo, sitting outside the oncologist's office waiting to be seen, the fear from my treatment would flood back. Every month, this was the moment when I was most likely to be told my future wasn't what I hoped. But following every check, I would emerge feeling elated, with a renewed sense of my good fortune.

Apart from the Queen Elizabeth Hospital, the other main institution we engaged with during our year in Birmingham was Bournville Junior School. In Katase, the girls would make the very short walk to school by themselves, even from Maya's second day at school. The walk from our house to Bournville Junior School was about fifteen minutes, and involved crossing a busy road. Because Mayu was busy with the MA, I usually walked the girls to school and picked them up at the end of the day. An hour's walk for me each day, which was good exercise. The walk involved going through part of the extensive grounds of Cadbury's chocolate factory. The Cadbury family had built Bournville as a 'model village', to house its employees, and had paid for the school as well. Along with sports fields, quality housing, holidays, and a focus on employee satisfaction, the family-owned Cadbury business was a model in itself, revolutionary for its time.

It's impossible to escape Cadbury's presence when you're in Bournville, not least because the smell of chocolate wafts enticingly around. It's also rather difficult not to notice religion, too. The Cadbury family were Quakers, which informed their ethos of care for their employees, and the Christian practices of the school. Adjusting to this was a bit of a challenge for the girls, after the secular norms of Japanese state education and their godless home. Each day would begin with a religious assembly, which was inclusive enough to say people of all faiths were welcome. Julia suggested this be changed to something like 'all faiths and none', but the request was politely rejected. Otherwise, the girls fitted in smoothly and swiftly, making friends, playing sports, making music, getting invited to birthday parties, and doing well academically. The head teacher had very kind words to say about the two of them when we left at the end of the year.

Before this year, my stereotype was that in the UK you were less likely to come across discriminatory language than in Japan. Being of the white majority in the UK, it's true I wasn't best placed to make a judgement. And this year in the UK made me aware that my stereotype was, like all stereotypes, flaky at best. There were several occasions when things were said to Mayu and the girls, sometimes glossed as banter, sometimes not, that made me have a rethink. With cancer, I'd found that pushing against the institutional practices could feel empowering, even if the feeling might be fleeting. We were about to find parallels as parents of schoolkids.

Get lost, you little Chinese bitch!

Julia was walking down a corridor in the school between lessons, when she saw a boy from her class picking on Maya's best friend, four years' younger than Julia and the boy. She duly pinned him up against the wall, and received in return this response. A teacher walked past, and wanted to know what was going on. Both students were called in to see a senior teacher, where Julia was told off for grabbing the boy, and he was told off for using the word 'bitch'. The only thing the teacher said about the use of nationality as a racial slur was, 'She's not even Chinese you idiot! She's Japanese', which completely missed the point.

In Katase, the girls had experienced similar comments, although instead of 'Chinese', it might be the oft-used phrase 'stupid foreigner' (*baka gaijin*), or 'stupid American'. In response to such comments, Mayu had created a report sheet titled 'Discrimination Incident Report', with the subtitles 'Incident, Time, Place', 'What was said/done, by whom?', and 'What is the school's response?' Any time the girls suffered this kind of abuse, Mayu would type up the information, pass it on to the school and say she'd wait for them (but not wait long) to satisfactorily complete the final section. And to their credit, they did. After this conversation with the teacher, Mayu duly translated this form, I filled it out, and we passed it on to Bournville.

After a week we'd heard nothing, so requested a meeting with the teacher concerned. She said that 'because the girls were half-caste' such things would happen. She also said that middle-class parents at the school would be more likely to get upset about things, whereas it was often the kids from working-class families that said such stuff. 'They don't know any better', she concluded. I wondered if she knew any better than to use terms like 'half-caste', and to justify racism on grounds of class. We didn't get very far, with her terse responses invoking a defensive institutional identity.

Back home, we all talked about the issue, and I suggested that she do something like raise some money for an anti-racism charity. We could invite the school to support it. We hit on the acronym KROOB ('Kick Racism out of Bournville') and decided to raise money for the Show Racism the Red Card charity. Julia's two best friends agreed to do a sponsored run together, I had some T-shirts made with the acronym in big purple letters, and the three of them pretended to do some weekly training for the five-kilometre run. We contacted the school to ask if they'd like to support the event, but they politely rejected the offer. We were welcome to do what we wanted in our free time, but the school did not wish to attach its name to anything 'political'.

It seemed there was more concern about reputational damage to the institution than there was heartful desire to address the issue. Indeed, there was no real issue, according to the (white, British) teachers we spoke to. We'd bumped up against these ingrained institutional practices and were forced (in our minds) to address the issue outside of the institute. Just as the University of Tokyo Hospital couldn't countenance the idea of varying the treatment I'd receive, Bournville Junior School couldn't countenance addressing discrimination directed by, or at, students. Once again, I was left wondering who the institutional practices were there to benefit.

One sunny Sunday afternoon in May, the three children painfully ran most of the five kilometres, having raised a few hundred pounds, and we celebrated by taking them out for a big lunch (Figure 31.1). At home, Mayu filled in a form and sent it to the school, crossing out the final subtitle and replace it with a description of the kids' response and that of the racism charity.

We all loved our year in Birmingham, but I think this was my favourite day. Many years ago, a young Mike and Mayu had promised to teach their unborn children how to push back hard in the face of bullying and discrimination. I was proud of Julia, at heart a timid child, for pinning the bully up against the wall, and I was proud of her and her supportive friends for creating something meaningful when faced with institutional

31.1 Julia with her Bournville besties Rachel and Phoebe having done the five-kilometre run.

intransigence. It struck me how cancer and discrimination have many parallels, not least that they can seem overwhelmingly threatening. But as I had learnt that you can gain agency in the face of a cancer diagnosis and its aftermath, so my daughters were learning that when you are racially othered, you still have choices.

CHAPTER 32

Return

The point of this book has not been to tread that well-trodden path of cancer memoirs, showing how cancer made me realise how special life was. I was pretty keen on life in the first place. But at the same time it would be disingenuous for me to claim that having cancer and coming close to death at a really unwelcome time did not alter me. I was weaker and stronger, and remain weaker and stronger. Physically weaker, but I hope stronger in the sense of having a greater appreciation of those around me, and of being strong enough to be kind to myself.

Some might say I wasn't so strong to begin with. Years before my cancer, Mayu informed that I had helped her engagement with feminism in our first years together. This was achieved through being such a multifacetedly hopeless male. Apparently, I inadvertently went about breaking the stereotypes of what a man should be able to do. I couldn't drive, do DIY, was too small to be much of a physical protection, sneezed incessantly and irritably in pollen seasons or when a cat appeared, had a ludicrous lack of directional sense and would then panic when lost. 'Ah, men like this exist as well', she noted. But with the cancer, at least I had excuses for any weakness now.

I hope the strengths I have gained through the experiences of the earthquake and cancer are more powerful empathy and compassion. I think they have made me more understanding of others, especially those I now recognise as suffering. Before cancer, like many people who have not visited Sontag's Kingdom of the Sick, I just didn't notice as much, and dismissed much that I did. I didn't notice people missing eyebrows and eyelashes, or might not grasp the significance of an elderly mother dancing with her adult daughter in a pub, with tears in their eyes for no apparent reason. Following the earthquake, seeing so many families suddenly, permanently, displaced from their beautiful homes, homes like the Orange House, brought home how close we all are to unexpected disaster. Suffering reminds us that we share far more than separates us.

Cancer, in particular, has also made me realise the need to be more compassionate to myself. But the need for self-compassion was borne not so much from kindness as from necessity. I don't know why I got cancer, but I knew that doing too much and exhausting myself might risk bringing it back. Learning self-compassion I have found difficult, perhaps because I was socialised into that masculine way of pushing myself hard, and eventually learnt to do it effectively. But although it's been a rocky path and one I often forget to take, it is the right one.

The most overwhelming feeling on returning to Katase in the summer of 2013 was one of homecoming (Figure 32.1). Back in Katase and Todai, I was walking in my previous footsteps, albeit in new shoes. Even before reaching the house, the glittering cleanliness of Haneda Airport was comforting in its familiarity, as was the pristine, punctual train back to Fujisawa. On entering the Orange House, shining brightly in the summer sun, I was greeted again by the nostalgic smell of warm wood – the wood of the floors, of the stairs, of the walls. It seemed, even more than Mayu and the girls, I basked in the comfort of our home. After my wandering around the house repeatedly saying, 'Oh this is nice! This is *nice!*', cup of tea in hand, we walked across Sakai River down to Fuji Supermarket. The slowest shoppers in the store, getting in people's ways, we picked up some fried chicken, a sushi selection, some freshly made salads, ice cream, pastries, beer, and fresh juices. All mouthwatering stuff, much of it prepared daily on the premises. It was good to be back in the land where people demand food that tastes good.

It was now over two years since the earthquake, when we had had to make that journey across Sakai River to collect Maya from Kiddie Nursery, and a little under two years since Maya and I had bought ice cream together following the news of my diagnosis. How different we all seemed now. Mayu's MA had gone very well, and she would soon start teaching English at a couple of Japanese universities. As for Julia and Maya, they surprised David and our other English-speaking friends when they opened their mouths. Not so much because of what they said, but of how they said it – in a Birmingham accent.

While the accent eventually faded, Julia and Maya's ability to think critically flourished. As I've watched them grow up into young adults, their bicultural perspective continues to illuminate their understanding of the world. Not least, it's that ability to see a custom, a cultural practice, for what it is: a repeated, automatic action that people don't usually choose, but instead acquire unconsciously as part of growing up in a community. And they see that the custom isn't the only way, or sometimes even the best way, of doing things. Unlike people like Mayu and me who have had to clumsily learn these truths as adults through trial and error, the girls have seemingly acquired this understanding without effort. I won't say effortlessly, because that might imply such knowledge makes things easier. Despite the difference they can make, less-travelled paths are by definition less popular. Watching them grow, I've been reminded that knowing something that many others don't, can sometimes make for a lonely path.

The two of them had got into reading while in the UK, Maya enjoying the *Flat Stanley* books, and Julia becoming obsessed with *The Hunger Games*. From being someone who had no interest in nature, she now

32.1 Enjoying Enoshima soon after our return.

liked to climb trees and rabbited on endlessly about edible plants. Soon after we returned to Japan, we'd gone up to stay with Jackie and Hisako. The grandparents, with their detailed knowledge of flora in Hakone, were amused and pleased by this change in Julia.

One afternoon, they sent the two of them off to look for *shungiku*, a delicious edible chrysanthemum that grows in the nearby woods. As they returned home, laden with the plant, Maya turned round and noticed another native of Hakone, an enormous wild boar. Like several species in Japan (e.g. hornets, bears, snakes), these can be extremely dangerous animals. The boar was about ten metres behind the girls, approaching fast, her young pups in tow. Maya sprinted back home, shouting to Julia to run. Julia, realising the boar could get to her before she made it to the front door, dropped the *shungiku*, sprinted to a cherry tree at the edge of the garden and climbed up. She made it to safety as the boar angrily snorted its approach. After a good sniff round the base of the tree and eating some of the *shungiku*, the boar and her cubs wandered off, meaning that Julia could descend and run to the arms of her horrified grandmother, who'd watched this unfold from the living room window. So thank you Katniss Everdeen.

My personal readjustment to life in Japan was relatively more relaxed. The year in Birmingham hadn't just given me physical distance from the treatment, it had provided time for reflection. Time and space to better understand the relationship between space, time, and healing. The year meant I had a clearer perspective on how institutions, communities, and individuals contribute to healing. Rather than seeing two different systems, I now understood how specific practices and people create spaces for recovery.

And in that year I had become more physically robust. This embodied improvement meant I was becoming more confident about having a future, and more comfortable about reflecting on the past. In other words, I was developing a sense of the time that had parallels with my pre-cancer self. I say parallels because while my sense of time was relearning to project beyond the immediate, it was still irrevocably changed, as if I was wearing cancer-tinted spectacles. As time has progressed we've learnt to fit each other better. They remind me of our mortality, our shared vulnerability, and as such, reflect the values of my cancer-survivor Discourse. Perhaps like the bicultural path, my Discourse might have moments of lonely understanding, but also like the bicultural path, I was beginning to appreciate the depths of understanding cancer had brought. Nietzsche talked of the philosophical advantages his fickle health gave him over robust, boring types. I can't speak for others, but I find myself a much more reflective person since I had, no, in truth *because* I had, cancer. I would wish cancer on no one, especially myself, but I cannot say I regret having had it.

While I was learning how to wear these reflective spectacles in some degree of comfort, other things sat less comfortably. The day after we arrived back in the Orange House, I realised that something in the living room was making me nauseous. Looking around, my eyes hit on the reclining chair. This place where I'd felt increasingly enervated during and after the radiation, descending into silence and distance. It was still in excellent condition, so I carried it outside, leaving it with a note, saying, 'Free to a good home'. One of our neighours, an elderly man who lived down the hill towards Katase Primary School, cycled up, and confirmed that we really didn't want it. He then proceeded to carry it home on his shoulder while riding his bicycle.

'We're not in Bournville any more,' I said to myself, what with these pristine trains, wooden houses, great food, wild boars, and old people carrying furniture on bicycles. But rather than being strange, boars notwithstanding, these things felt familiar, reminders of our life here. Other reminders included the unrestrained reactions of my neighbours, friends, and colleagues to my health. 'Oh! You've put on weight! You're looking well!' was a common response to people seeing me, usually with a jolly glint in their eyes. I found comfort in the fact they were engaged witnesses of the past few years, of what our family had endured and survived. The palpable sense of injustice they had shown following my diagnosis had become palpable happiness upon our return. Their joy at my recovery wasn't about cultural norms but about human connections forged through crisis. These weren't 'Japanese' reactions but specific responses from people who had become part of our story, and I theirs. Spending the year in Birmingham had been the right choice for all of us, but being back in Katase I felt at home.

When I started out on my academic career, juggling teaching and doing a PhD, one of my senior colleagues said to me, 'If you want to be successful, say yes to everything.' I'd bought into this approach, and it had served me well. But I now had to be more discriminating in my choices if I was to practise self-compassion. I was still not as robust as I had been, and looking after my immune system by reducing stress has formed a big part of my cancer-survivor Discourse. Not long after returning to Todai, I was asked to take charge of a big project that was only indirectly linked to internationalisation. I said no, citing my health, and was surprised by how easily my rejection was accepted.

At work, I'd still be flying a lot, doing my teaching and research, but I was now better at making sure these were suited to the pace of my body. Mayu, David, and others were strong supports in this, and were quick to say when they felt I was taking on too much, admonishing me with, 'Remember San Francisco' and a stern stare. During my regular check-ups with Dr Nishi, too, the communication had changed from him coaxing me through the treatment, to us considering together the ways to deal with any challenges, such as fatigue. I now had more confidence in my cancer-survivor Discourse, and the boundaries with his Discourse, that of oncology specialist, seemed to have blurred. Together, with the help of others, we had calmed my unruly classroom, and we'd work on keeping it that way.

Another source of support, which I'd come across in my last month in Birmingham, was the book *The Compassionate Mind*, by the psychology professor Paul Gilbert. He outlines our three main emotional systems: the threat-focused self-preservation system; the incentive and resource-focused system; and the soothing, compassion-based system. The threat system, for instance, picks up on things that may threaten us, and provokes feelings of anxiety, anger, or disgust. As a result, we might fight, run away, or freeze. That feeling of being 'at home' is us operating from our compassion-based system. Steps to a happier life include learning (mindfully) to notice how much time we spend perceiving that things are threats, and boosting the soothing, contentment-focused side of our emotional make-up.

Easier said than done of course, particularly in the face of a threat like cancer. But I'd already learnt that things such as meditation, yoga, music, literature, and art can help us access the compassionate side of our minds when we feel under threat. As I've described in the previous pages of this book, I managed during my treatment to engage with these things, and they helped me survive well. High culture helped me endure the culture of cancer, as did things like mindfulness. Reading *The Compassionate Mind* provided a rigorous explanation of the value of such efforts, and a motivation to continue with them.

But rather than just saying something like 'mindfulness can give us a break from feeling bad', Gilbert's message is more active, and more hopeful. He states, 'the kinder and more compassionate we are with ourselves, the more we can develop the courage to tolerate difficult things'. Of all the things I'd learnt since the events of 2011, I think this counter-intuitive lesson that courage can be the product of kindness is among the most important. I had seen that tolerating, and perhaps accepting, such difficult things as the aftermath of an earthquake or cancer, if approached from a place of compassion and support, was possible. And the acceptance need not be passive, because the acceptance is of the paths or events of the past that have led us here and cannot be changed. In fact, I was appreciating that by operating from a more compassionate place, sustainable and considered action in the present becomes more achievable. Or at least, I might fail slightly better in my efforts.

As we settled back into Katase life, with the girls at school and Mayu and I working, we decided to take our time about the big decision of our future: to stay in Katase, or to move back to the UK. Moving to the UK would mean leaving the girls' doting grandparents, and our neigbours and friends. It would mean starting again, probably in a new city where we knew nobody. But at least now, we had a more informed position to decide from. We'd lost our rose-tinted spectacles about the UK, but we knew we could be happy there, too. And in the hopefully long run of our daughters' lives, we increasingly felt that the UK would be a better place for them to grow into being young women. We believed they'd have relatively more freedom to become themselves there, rather than being forced to either conform to or reject the tightly gendered constraints of Japanese society. And the truth is, these constraints were beginning to influence the girls' personalities in ways that didn't seem consistent with their natures. Yes, they'd have to fight their battles in the UK, as they would anywhere, but at least it looked like they'd have two parents in their corner.

This was a decision we'd mull over for a couple of years, before finally deciding to make the move to the UK in late 2015. We would be leaving so much we loved, so many friends and family. But we would not be losing them, not really saying goodbye. As a senior colleague from Todai said to me at my leaving party, 'Don't worry, you aren't really leaving. You'll always be a part of the university.' Katase feels the same, it will always be a part of us, our home. I'm reminded of the words of T.S. Eliot:

> We shall not cease from exploration
> And the end of all our exploring
> Will be to arrive where we started
> And know the place for the first time

To me, these words are about home, and perhaps the most important word is 'we'.

Postscript

I'm sitting in our house in Cardiff, Wales, our home since 2015. Having read this far, you'll know that 'our' and 'home' and 'our home' have very particular meanings in this book, 'situated meanings' in linguistics terminology. I recently asked both Julia and Maya what 'home' meant to them, and both replied, 'It's the people, isn't it', agreeing that the physical place itself isn't as important. Saying that, having lived in Cardiff as long as we lived in Fujisawa, they both see themselves as Japanese-Welsh. This hybrid identity is one in the making still, but one that can recount stories of earthquakes to Welsh friends, attend Welsh universities, and take Welsh cakes to their grandparents in Japan. And as I write this, I'm looking forward to us visiting those grandparents in Hakone in a few weeks, to welcome in 2025.

Cardiff has been a welcoming place for all of us, and Mayu and I are colleagues at Cardiff University. One of the joys of being an academic is a certain degree of freedom over what research you want to conduct. Mayu researches gender in British and Japanese popular music, whereas I've been moving into the area of cancer communication. I feel this is the most valuable work I've ever done. It allows me to apply many of the concepts I've spent years trying to figure out, such as Discourse, stereotyping, and culture, to an area of life that is so fraught with difficulty.

The shattering strain of cancer is best shared, and this book is an attempt to consider different perspectives that might facilitate such sharing. I've written from the perspective of a person with cancer, because that's what I know best, but like many of us I've also the experienced friends, loved ones, or acquaintances having cancer. And experienced the difficulties of talking to people with cancer, or to people who've lost loved ones. I hang my head when I remember some of the ham-fisted attempts I've made to communicate with people dealing with cancer, or dealing with the loss of their loved ones.

Sometimes there are no words that fit, and yet words are sometimes all we have. And for oncologists, nurses, and other healthcare professionals, words may be the only tool they have once the treatment has reached its conclusion. I recently ran a workshop on cancer and communication at the charity Tenovus Cancer Care, where we worked through some of these points and applied them to communicating with their 'clients' (people dealing with cancer, including patients and carers), as well as their colleagues and external partners. Pleasingly, they reported having some genuine 'light-bulb' moments, understanding better why misunderstandings happen with other teams, and also how an intercultural perspective offers new insights on the clients' experiences dealing with cancer.

In the workshop we worked through various concepts, such as discourse and Discourse. As I discuss in chapters 11 and 13, words combined with other words to make a text or talk is sometimes described as discourse. But discourse, to be genuinely meaningful, needs to be used by particular types of people doing particular types of things, often with other objects or tools or ways of dressing and acting, expressing particular values and views, and sometimes expertise, so that they are recognisable as being members of that 'type of people'. In other words, Discourse with a big D. The concept of Discourse runs through this book: while I've mainly focused on how 'the person with cancer' can be seen as a Discourse in itself, in the latter stages on cancer-survivorship Discourse I've also noted that oncologists might be seen as a separate Discourse. As, indeed, might cancer nurses, or carers of people with cancer. Communication between people with cancer and other people, such as oncologists, can be seen as intercultural because the people belong to different Discourses. That's one reason why cancer-communication is hard sometimes. The workshop participants said that seeing it as communication between different Discourses can help them better navigate its intercultural nature, and in future they would approach talking to others from this perspective.

I had my cancer treatment thirteen years ago, the same length of time I'd lived in Japan when I was diagnosed. I'm aware that much has changed in cancer care in that time, while some of the same tensions remain. In medicine more broadly, while the emerging area of personalised healthcare promises to eventually revolutionise treatment, there has been a recognisable move towards patient-centred care. Patient-centred care has been defined as 'taking into account the patient's desire for information, and for sharing decision-making and responding appropriately' (Stewart, 2001: 445).

The implication is that this has not historically been the case: the traditional biomedical model has tended to see, or rather to want to see, the patient as a passive body which the powerful medic fixes. In cancer care, the justification for such a change is seen in terms of outcomes, for instance engaging with lifestyles that will reduce risk, or improved communication and trust with oncologists (Epstein and Street, 2007). These are worthy aims, even if the emphasis on outcomes still seems somewhat instrumental in motivation. 'People are an end in themselves!', more than a few philosophers might cry. And to what extent can joint decision-making over cancer treatment be practically achievable or even desirable?

Herein lies the tension between people with cancer and the healthcare system, one that cancer charities work to address. Mishler (1984) discusses the different ways in which the prevailing biomedical model achieves dominance over patients whose understanding is based on the experiences and concerns of their daily lives (their 'lifeworlds'). The biomedical model finds expression as 'the voice of medicine' and the concerns of daily life are 'the voice of the lifeworld'. Whereas physicians are fluent in both voices, the patient can typically converse in only one. Mishler argues that because of this it is the physicians who have the responsibility for translating between these two voices 'to produce mutual understanding ... Physicians must translate patients' lifeworld statements into medical terms and medical statements of problems into patients' terms.' And patient-centred care cannot even begin without mutual understanding: how can a patient join in decision-making if they don't understand the medical evidence and the medical implications of any choices? Clearly, we can't.

These are some of the myriad challenges faced by clinical oncology teams, part of their Discourse of oncology, when hoping to engage patients in the treatment programme. How much does the person know? How much should I share with them? Are they in a sufficiently emotionally robust position to be able to understand what I'm saying, and then to make an informed decision about the various options? How long should I wait till they are emotionally stable enough to make an informed decision, or might their emotional state become worse in the coming weeks? What if they want to make a decision that will endanger their life? What if they decide to not have treatment?

In my case, I have a couple of good stories about the negative side of all this, told in earlier chapters. I say 'good' in terms of the story quality, not in terms of the reality. Had my oncologists listened to me about the chemotherapy, for instance, I would not have had a life-threatening reaction to the drugs. But I'm also aware that the oncologists were doing what they thought was best for me, based on the evidence they had. Were my case to happen today in many hospitals around the world, I'm not convinced the outcome would be different.

Which brings me to the topic of being a disagreeable patient, which I propose should be part of the Discourse of being a person with cancer. Before talking about what I mean, I'll briefly say something about the Discourse more broadly. Like any Discourse, this Discourse is multifaceted, and becoming membered in the Discourse (a club we'd rather not join) has certain pressures. In chapters 13 and 20 I discuss how, upon receiving a diagnosis, we are under considerable time pressure to learn the unwritten codes of our new reality. There's also the added problem of the chaos a diagnosis brings, for instance in terms of the emotional turmoil, but also the cognitive fatigue, along with financial, professional, and personal implications.

Using Kleinman and Benson's (2006) steps for culturally informed care on the part of clinicians as inspiration, I think the following steps are central in developing the Discourse of a cancer patient:

- Constructing your cancer metaphor, ideally as part of 'prehabilitation'
- Understanding your own health, and co-constructing your cancer narrative with close others and healthcare professionals
- Understanding the culture of oncology
- Pinpointing support mechanisms
- Learning how to support your immune system (mind the wacky stuff)
- Overall, increasing your cancer literacy

In different chapters, I've described how I, with the help of many others, went about this. For instance, in Chapter 14 I explain about the cancer metaphor I developed, and in subsequent chapters I talk about how it supported me. I also talk about the benefit of 'prehabilitation', and how

it enabled me to begin addressing all these areas. In the workshop I conducted at the cancer charity, the idea of patients developing their own
metaphor was received as both radical and potentially hugely empowering. For instance, one participant said of considering metaphors as
outlined here was, 'So useful. I will explore [promoting this with cli-
ents] as a prehabilitation option or part of self-advocacy.' For me, the
unruly-classroom metaphor meant I could find some equilibrium among
the waves of intrapersonal chaos that followed the diagnosis.

Throughout the treatment and subsequent healing process, I've been
learning about the culture of oncology. I'm currently collaborating with
healthcare professionals here at Cardiff University, and cancer charities,
so that we might help both patients with cancer and professionals in their
challenging roles. So what does all this have to do with being a disagreeable patient? Earlier in the book I express regret about not being more
forthright at times, for instance about the second dose of chemotherapy.
I think if patient-centred care is to be achieved, then this must allow for
disagreement between oncologists and patients. And allowances need to
be made for our different personalities, because some people will find
this much harder than others.

It's important here to distinguish between disagreement and conflict. In workplace decision-making processes, disagreement is often a
good thing, whereas conflict is often not. It's through disagreement, the
expression of diverging views and proposals, that an optimum solution
can be reached (Handford and Koester, 2024). Conflict, in contrast, usually involves damage to the relationship. If patients, oncologists (or anyone else) confuse disagreement with conflict, then the communication
ends up being conflictual. And as Koenig (2011) states, disagreement on
the part of patients is a form of agency, which in itself is a positive act. So
for patient-centred care to be patient-centred, there has to be an understanding of the benefits of disagreement on all sides. This also needs to
be part of the Discourse.

I had cancer and I am alive. My story is therefore one of the happy
cancer stories. Many years after a stage-4 diagnosis, I still have a fulfilling,
challenging job, a loving family, I'm still vain and I still play football. Like
all stories, mine is about a few people, especially me. I'm aware of the
danger here, in that I might be feeding into certain dominant, potentially harmful, narratives around cancer.

Yes, I had cancer and I am alive, but I could easily have done the same things that are recounted in this book and have died. The chemotherapy might have killed me, or it might not have (virtually) killed the cancer. I was given a 50/50 chance of survival – in another universe, I'm not here. I was lucky, and I did not rid myself of cancer. But there are many narratives around the 'bravery' of cancer patients that imply we survive because of our bravery, and that to survive we need to be brave; what does this imply about those who don't survive? As I mention at the beginning of this book, research shows that having a positive attitude has no relation with survival rates (though it can help with dealing with the new reality).

This dominant narrative around the brave individual also repudiates the morally justifiable choices of those who reject the social pressure to be optimistic, or others who do decide against having cancer treatment. A friend of mine was recently diagnosed with prostate cancer and asked me for advice. I advised him to resist the pressure to be brave, which comes from many angles and can constrain your chances to talk, to complain, to scream, to cry. I said instead he should just do whatever he felt he needed to do to get through this time: 'Fuck being brave.' He liked this very much. Deborah Steinberg talked about the right to be a 'bad patient'. For her, this involved rejecting treatment, with the obvious consequences, which in her mind was an affirmative choice. There were moments in my treatment when Mayu suggested I stop the radiation; this was born of love, of a desire for my suffering to end.

On a societal level, there is a danger that narratives like mine might inadvertently feed into the 'pernicious individualism' that Jackie Stacey has talked about. Here, the responsibility for cancer, and dealing with it, is strategically placed on the shoulder of the individual, rather than with society. Cancer is largely caused by environmental factors, such as the carcinogens in our air, water, and food. Society creates the environment in which we grow up and live, not the individual. As with smoking or climate change, blaming individuals for cancer serves the interests of the institutions responsible, and with great effect.

I note these points because I think it is important for everyone affected by cancer to consider them. Haruki Murakami wrote that you can tell the story of someone's life by the cancer they get. I don't think the parents in the children's cancer ward would agree. And even if we do draw a narrative line across some dots that lead to explaining a diagnosis, we should push against conflating those dots with personal responsibility for the cancer. We need to be very careful about the stories we tell around cancer.

And yet, we are story-making beings: stories construct our sense of self. Of the many books that have helped me understand cancer and other traumatic events that befall us, such as earthquakes, grief, or serious mental health issues, Arthur Frank's *The Wounded Storyteller* (2013) holds a special place in my heart. Stories are central to us at times of serious illness, for instance, because, like metaphors, they 'serve to repair the damage that illness has done' (p.53). Traumatic events throw us into chaos, and chaos is one of Frank's three types of illness narrative that I mention at the beginning of this book. The second is restitution stories, built on the idea of 'I was well yesterday, I'm sick today, but I'll be healthy again tomorrow.' These form the bulk of stories people and society tell, and like to tell, about illness. The third is the quest story, where the teller seeks to *use* the illness for some purpose, for instance benefiting others in a similar situation, or as a call to arms.

This book, while delving into chaos and restitution, is offered up primarily as a quest story. A case study of how intercultural communication can help make sense of the new reality a diagnosis creates, and how agency might emerge from such sense-making. But during the process of writing *Lump in my Throat*, perhaps the most important sentence I have read in any book is Frank's exhortation about chaos: 'The need to honor chaos stories is both moral and clinical' (p.109). While chaos may be hell for the person concerned, it can be deeply uncomfortable for others to hear about. The desire on the part of the person involved, their loved ones, and even healthcare professionals is understandably to get out of the chaos as soon as possible. But time is needed for this to happen. In one study with young women with metastasized breast cancer, they reported healthcare professionals' unwillingness to hear their negative emotions and found a culture of silencing in this context that led to the patients internalising the negative feelings. If we are othered by those responsible for caring for us, then how can we overcome the othering within ourselves, and how can we heal? This is why honouring chaos stories is indeed both moral and clinical.

In earlier chapters I've discussed Freud and Heidegger's notion of *unheimlichkeit* (unhomelikeness/the uncanny/the absurd), which is

I think another way of understanding chaos. Fredrik Svenaeus, who has written extensively on unhomelikeness and illness, argues that it is incumbent on healthcare professionals to help the sick person return to some sense of homelikeness. The point is that it is not just the body that needs 'fixing'; healing needs to consider this otherness in the embodied mind. During illness, our body threatens us, because of the unhomelike nature it has taken on. Svenaeus states, 'It is the mission of health care professionals to try to understand such unhomelike being-in-the-world and bring it back to homelikeness again, or, at least, closer to home.' I'd add that friends and loved ones can also build the path that lets us find our way closer to home.

Home resides in their compassion, and their love.

Figure Acknowledgements

Hiroshi Yamaguchi 3.2; Shigeo Takahara 6.2; Haruyoshi Yamaguchi / Bloomberg / Getty Images 8.1; Maurice Joosten 11.1a; Justin Wateridge 11.1b; 701 Studios 11.1c; Maya Handford 11.1d; Jennifer Hayden 16.1; skynesher / E+ / Getty Images 16.2; copyright for the Cabinet of Dr Caligari resides with Murnau-Stiftung 30.3; Philippe Lissac /GODONG / The Image Bank Unreleased / Getty Images N.1, N.2; all others, author's collection.

Acknowledgements

This book has been eight years in the making and has gone through many iterations during that time. Several individuals have been involved in its creation, most prominently my wife Mayu Handford and my friend David Peace. Both coaxed me into writing it in the first place, have kept actively interested in the project, and have been honest but encouraging critics of these versions. 'You could do better' was a common message they each communicated, often nonverbally through a shrug or a silence, over the years and iterations. The debt I owe them both can never be repaid, and is evident in the book. I owe a similar debt to Maurice Joosten, who again commented on earlier drafts, penned a chapter (reproduced in full on the Cambridge University Press website), and who, like Mayu and David, features prominently in the story of keeping me alive.

Other friends who have also spent hours upon hours of their time reading earlier drafts and providing constructive criticism include Srikant Sarangi, Justin Wateridge, Graham Webb, Terry Pritchard, Geraldine Mark, Hannah O'Mahoney, Richard Gwyn, Hamish Macaskill, Simon Gibbs, Maria Handford, and Alison Wray. An additional thank you is for Hannah O'Mahoney, who allowed me to conduct a workshop with her colleagues at the charity Tenovus Cancer Care on the key ideas from the book. Clare Hudson, Producer of *The Idea*, (BBC Radio Wales) invited me to appear on her show; this involved part of a lecture I gave at Cardiff University on cancer and communication, and a follow-up interview with the journalist Catrin Nye. Sophy Roberts, a friend of a friend, was again extremely generous in commenting on an earlier draft. Her book *The Lost Pianos of Siberia* made me realise how literary, personal, and engaging travel writing can be. I could write pages explaining how each of the individuals listed here helped to improve the text, but for brevity's sake I will assume that each person knows how much they helped, and will hear from me again. While my name is on the front cover, and any errors or issues are my responsibility, the value of this book lies very much with these people. My daughters Julia and Maya have also provided feedback, as well as a few tears at the memories recounted here.

Becky Taylor, the editor at Cambridge University Press, has been wonderfully encouraging since I first suggested the idea for the book and throughout the whole process. Her colleague Izzie Collins, who came to the project during the final stages, has also provided invaluable support. Indeed, the enthusiasm and professionalism of all those I've dealt with at 'The Press' has been brilliant. It was my close colleague Dawn Knight who suggested to Becky over dinner that I'd be a good person to write a trade book, so thank you, Dawn! Several other colleagues at Cardiff, particularly from the Centre for Language and Communication Research, have been really supportive with the book, such as Alison Wray.

I must express special gratitude towards the eight (!) anonymous reviewers Cambridge University Press hired for evaluating the book proposal and several example chapters, and the two reviewers who commented on the complete draft. Again, their feedback was very encouraging, perceptive, and useful. Also of use were the comments provided by Caroline Oakley at *Up Close Editing*, which pushed me to enrich the narrative of earlier drafts by developing the themes of the book. Although not directly connected with this book, I must also thank my University of Nottingham professors Mike McCarthy, John McRae, and the late Ron Carter for teaching me the importance of writing clearly, and so much more.

I'd also like to thank others who have read specific chapters, such as April-Louise Pennant who validated my comments on race and provided suggestions for the chapter on hair and intersectionality. Elena Semino has been very generous with sharing her Lancaster University team's work on developing cancer metaphors, and with her time. And thank you to all those who have given me permission to use their real names.

Looking at the list of people above, I notice that they all really believed that this book could make a difference to people dealing with cancer, personally or professionally. I am humbled by this selfless support and would not have had the guts to write this book in this way without them. By 'in this way' I mean I've tried to weave together aspects of literary memoir, popular science book, self-help guide, travel book, and critical academic text, often drawing on the texts they've directed me to read. The bulk of these texts are listed at the back of the book. I need to give a special mention to Jim Gee, whose concept of Discourse with a big 'D' has influenced me so much. Jim has also been a generous mentor over the years, particularly when I was recovering from the cancer treatment and asking for feedback on the manuscript. Along with Jim's works, two other books deserve special mention. My colleague and running/football mate Martin Willis recommended I read *The Wounded Storyteller* by Arthur Frank, which along with Oliver Sacks' *The Man Who Mistook his Wife for a Hat*, showed me the value in being brave with the pen when writing about health.

Notes

As I explain in the Introduction, this Notes section will provide background to some of the points raised in the main text and will also list the various sources on which I've drawn. There are several works that have been central to the ideas I've developed here, and which I cite in various chapters. I've grouped them thematically below, although there is inevitable overlap.

Medical anthropology/sociology
Frank, A. (2013). *The Wounded Storyteller: Body, Illness, and Ethics* (2nd edition). Chicago: Chicago University Press.
Jain, L. (2013). *Malignant: How Cancer Becomes Us.* Berkeley: California University Press.
Jain, L., & Stacey, J. (2015). On writing about illness: A dialogue with Jain and Stacey on cancer, STS, and cultural studies. *Catalyst: Feminism, Theory, Technoscience,* 1(1): 1–29.
Kleinman, A. (1980). *Patients and Healers on the Context of Culture: An Exploration of the Borderland between Anthropology, Medicine, and Psychiatry.* Berkeley: University of California Press.
Mishler, E. (1984). *The Discourse of Medicine: Dialectics of Medical Interviews.* New Jersey: Ablex Publishing.
Roter, D., & Hall, J. (2006). *Doctors Talking with Patients/Patients Talking with Doctors: Improving Communication in Medical Visits.* Westport: Praeger.
Stacey, J. (1997). *Teratologies: A Cultural Study of Cancer.* London: Routledge.

Linguistics/Intercultural Communication
Gee, J. P. (2015). *Social Linguistics and Literacies: Ideologies in Discourses* (5th edition). Abingdon: Routledge.
Piller, I. (2011). *Intercultural Communication: A Critical Introduction.* Edinburgh: Edinburgh University Press.

Scollon, R., Scollon, S., & Jones, R. (2012). *Intercultural Communication: A Discourse Approach.* Chichester: Wiley Blackwell.

Cancer memoir/biography
Hitchens. C. (2012). *Mortality.* London: Atlantic Books.
Kalanithi, P. (2016). *When Breath Becomes Air: What Makes Life Living in the Face of Death.* New York: Vintage Press.
Lorde, A. (1980). *The Cancer Journals.* London: Penguin.

Critical Theory/Philosophy
Hall, S. (2025). 'The spectacle of the other', in S. Hall, S. Nixon, & J. Evans (eds.), *Representation: Cultural Representations and Signifying Practices* (3rd edition). London: Sage.
Sontag, S. (1978). *Illness as Metaphor.* New York: Vintage Books.
Svenaeus, F. (2011). Illness as unhomelike being-in-the-world: Heidegger and the phenomenology of medicine. *Medical Health Care and Philosophy,* 14: 333–343.

Japanese society
Befu, H. (2001). *Hegemony of Homogeneity: An Anthropological Analysis of Nihonjinron.* Melbourne: Trans Pacific Press.
Sugimoto, Y. (2021). *An Introduction to Japanese Society* (4th edition). Cambridge: Cambridge University Press.

References to other cited sources are given in the relevant chapter notes below.

PREFACE

Resilience is in fact a word that I first really noticed around the time of the Fukushima triple disaster of 2011, initially in the phrase termed 'resilience engineering'. Following the devastation of the earthquake, tsunami, and nuclear meltdown, my engineering colleagues at the University of Tokyo were heavily invested in promoting and applying this concept as Japan strove to rebuild both better infrastructure and structures. The early chapters of this book explore this time. When used about people, 'resilience' is often applied to an individual. But I think this point can be qualified. Resilience may be better understood as a function of people's social networks, rather than their personality (Ungar, 2013). I had family, friends, and colleagues who enabled me to be resilient during the cancer ordeal, and who still do. Without such relationships, I am not sure I'd be here writing this book.

On quest narratives, it's worth quoting Frank's (2013: xv, reference above) own description of his experience with cancer, and how he also began to find a way out of the chaos:

> My period of chemotherapy was bordering on chaos when my understanding of what I was going through began to shift. A sequence of experiences brought me out of an obsession with my own pain and vulnerability and gave me a sense that I was participating in something shared. Time spent being ill ceased to be time taken away from my life. Instead, how I lived with illness became the measure of how well I could craft a life, whether I was well or healthy. This attitude is the basis of understanding one's story as a quest narrative. Illness remains a nightmare in many ways, but it also becomes a possibility, especially for a more intimate level of connection with others.

This quote chimes with much of my own experiences with cancer, recounted in later chapters, and the way it opened up new ways of seeing life. The notion and relevance of quest stories are explored in the Postscript chapter.

This is also a good time to talk briefly about the approach I take in this book, or in academic terms the methodology. In the preceding paragraph I briefly mention how my personal experiences opened up new ways of understanding life. While some of these new ways are highly personal, my cancer experience also enabled me to understand society, and to reflect on the links between individuals (dealing with cancer) and society. In other words, the relationship between the micro (self) and the macro (society), between personal agency and sociocultural practices. Frank calls this type of approach 'automythology', and notes how the wounded body of the storyteller is 'a pivot point between microcosm and macrocosm' (2013: 126). The approach is also termed autoethnography, with 'auto' referring to self, 'ethno' referring to the sociocultural, and 'graphy' referring to the combination of and reflection on the two as research.

Autoethnography is tricky because, as Duncan (2004) notes, it can easily become overly emotional and self-indulgent: it needs to draw on sources beyond the personal, and interrogating the theoretical through the personal is hard. In writing and rewriting *Lump in my Throat*, I have attempted to address these concerns, for example by interrogating the theoretical concept of culture through my personal experiences and actions. Reflecting on and learning from my attempts to navigate the professional practices of the healthcare systems is one such example.

A final point on the methodology concerns data – specifically, the data I used to write the book. In terms of 'primary' data collected by me, I have used my medical records and other relevant documents, along with diary notes from the time, informal interviews and conversations with relevant individuals, emails (both from the time and subsequently), and even the odd recording of interactions. Photographs, some reproduced in the main text, have proved an important type of data. They are date-stamped and provide empirical evidence of half-forgotten contexts. The book also makes plentiful use of secondary data, for instance published reports and articles, which are typically cited in this Notes section. In terms of academic ethics, informed consent was granted by all identifiable individuals, and they kindly gave me written permission to use their real names. Where it was not possible to contact certain people (for instance, because they had passed away), names and identifying features have been changed to ensure anonymity. As this work is in English, I've followed the convention of putting Japanese given names first (e.g. Shigeo) and family name last (e.g. Takahara).

The Margot Duncan reference is:

Duncan, M. (2004). Autoethnography: Critical appreciation of an emerging art. *International Journal of Qualitative Methods*, 3(4), Article 3. Retrieved 30/05/2025 from http://www.ualberta.ca/~iiqm/backissues/3_4/html/duncan.html

The Michael Ungar reference is:

Ungar, M. (2013). Resilience, trauma, context, and culture. *Trauma, Violence & Abuse*, 14(3): 255–266. doi.org/10.1177/1524838013487805

INTRODUCTION

The reference for Brian Street's work on culture as a verb is:

Street, B. (1993). Culture is a verb: anthropological aspects of language and cultural process, in D. Graddol, L. Thompson, & M. Byram (eds.), *Language and Culture*. Clevedon: British Association of Applied Linguistics.

Mainstream academic (and folk) understandings of intercultural com-munication (ICC) typically equate it with inter-national communication. In this mainstream approach, ICC is typically between members of dif-ferent nations. Different nations have different cultures, these cultures determine to some degree people's behaviours, and therefore commu-nication between these different cultures (that is, nations) is inevitably a challenge. Problems in ICC occur, and that's because the gaps between cultures are so big. 'Japan is so exotic!' for instance. But often we don't know what the differences are. In this mainstream orientation, it is this lack of knowledge that is the big problem. More education about cultural *differences* is therefore the solution.

The approach to ICC used in *Lump in My Throat* is different. Here, ICC involves interactions between people where at least one party *per-ceives* some aspect of the other's identity as different, and as relevant to understanding that person. This perceived difference might be nation-ality, race, gender, profession, basketball team etc. Crucially, the person sees this difference as a way of explaining and evaluating the behav-iour of the other person. And usually power plays a role, with one side of the interaction having less of it than the other. As a cancer patient in an oncology ward, you tend to have a lot less power than the med-ical staff. As a migrant, you may have less access to social goods than the citizens of the place, and possibly other 'disadvantages'. But some migrants are privileged, too, having considerable status or wealth, so we can't assume one label means the same thing. But perhaps the most important aspect of this 'critical' ICC orientation concerns stereotypes and 'the other'. I've found the work of the cultural theorist Stuart Hall particularly enlightening here, and have referenced one source above. Whereas the mainstream approach to ICC says not knowing enough (about cultural differences) is the biggest issue, the critical orientation argues that people in fact 'know' too much. (A wonderful demonstra-tion of this is the popular TED talk by Hans Rosling, where he says the problem we face is not ignorance, it's preconceived ideas. It's a quick mention, but it's clearly the motivation for his work www.ted.com/talks/ hans_rosling_the_best_stats_you_ve_ever_seen?subtitle=en).

In any communication, you assign an identity to me, and I assign an identity to myself (and vice versa). Successful ICC occurs when the assigned identities match, unsuccessful ICC occurs typically where they do not match. For instance, from a critical ICC perspective, rather than lack of knowledge of other cultures being the biggest cause of problems in ICC, it is the overabundance of stereotypes and preconceived ideas that veil our sight. Because of both academic research and personal experience, I am convinced of the value of the critical perspective, and the seductive yet dangerous pitfalls of the mainstream approach.

I have not given a strict definition of culture in this chapter. Following Wittgenstein, I think definitions are rather over-rated, and culture is recognised as one of the most difficult words in English to define. So, again following Wittgenstein, we might talk of 'culture' in terms of its family resemblances, along with what it isn't (as applied in this book). I've already noted the difference between mainstream academic and critical approaches to intercultural communication, and at the heart of this distinction sits a different understanding of what culture is.

In the critical approach, the 'culture as verb' makes a lot of sense, because it captures the idea that culture is not something fixed, inherent in people (part of their 'essence', to which they belong), but instead is something that is performed over time, a series of practices. And because culture is something that is done in and forms society, it is done by people who have different access to social goods, different levels of power. The 'way we do things round here' quote is important in that it shows what 'our' culture is and is not: us, not them; in our place, not somewhere else. Culture is intimately tied to identity, and many of our cultural identities are defined by what they are not. The critical perspective on culture therefore strongly rejects the notion of cultural essence, or essentialism, which underlies the mainstream approach, as essentialism has been shown to deepen inequalities and prejudice. It is very interested in the way things such as stereotypes, which result from essentialist ways of thinking like, 'they're just different from us, deep down … they can never become proper members of our community', influence communication and other types of behaviour. As such, culture is something that needs explaining, rather than something that explains peoples' behaviour. I'll be returning to these themes throughout the book.

As a stronger example of othering, I've seen UK-based colleagues in education dismiss the abilities and potential of students from Asia, because they are from 'collectivist' cultures, and therefore 'aren't critical or creative' and 'will never be able to think for themselves'.

There's interesting research exploring this very phenomenon in universities, where Japanese students in Australia are deemed passive by their Australian lecturers, even though they participate just as actively as the other students: Nakane, I. (2002). Silence in the multicultural classroom: perceptions and performance in Australian university classrooms. *Inter-Cultural Studies*, 2, 1728.

There is a lot of research exploring the damage that stereotypes, racism, and ethnocentrism cause in health contexts, for example Nazroo, J. (2004). Race/ethnic inequalities in health: Moving beyond confusion to focus on fundamental causes. *Oxford Open Economics*, 3(1): i563–i576.

In the final paragraph of the Introduction I mention increasing agency while you have cancer. Agency might be defined as the amount of freedom a person in society has to act as they wish. Alternatively, we might say it's all about power: how much power does a person have (to do things, and be free from other things), and how does society constrain a person? Understanding this relationship between agency and power in society is the primary motivation for critical approaches in the social sciences, for instance critical intercultural communication. This includes examining how those who don't have power are often institutionally subjugated or maligned, for instance through being negatively stereotyped in the media, and how those who do have it maintain and use it to their own benefit.

CHAPTER 1

The Louise Glück poem is contained in Glück, L. (1996). *Meadowlands.* New York City: Ecco.

CHAPTER 2

As with many health-related concerns, the NHS site provides a good description about HPV, and vaccinations on its website: www.nhs.uk/conditions/vaccinations/hpv-human-papillomavirus-vaccine/

CHAPTER 3

The quote from Jane Didion is Didion, J. (2005). *The Year of Magical Thinking.* London: Fourth Estate. The Herman Ooms quote is cited in the article 'Ghosts of the Tsunami' by Richard Lloyd Parry in the *London Review of Books*: Parry, R. L. (2014). 'Ghosts of the Tsunami'. *London Review of Books*, 36(4). www.lrb.co.uk/the-paper/v36/n03/richard-lloyd-parry/ghosts-of-the-tsunami. The Tolstoy quote is from Tolstoy, L. (1878/2016). *Anna Karenina*, translated Rosamund Bartlett. Oxford: Oxford World Classics.

CHAPTER 4

The earthquake was magnitude 9.1 at its epicentre, and the biggest earthquake to hit Japan in its recorded history. Japan gets around 10 per cent of the world's earthquakes, despite accounting for only 1 per cent of the world's landmass. This means that in a year, Japan suffers between 2,000 and 5,000 earthquakes across the archipelago. Japan sits on four of the world's eight major tectonic plates, and when these shift then Japan shakes to varying degrees. On that day, 11 March, some survivors in Fukushima said it was akin to being inside a cocktail shaker. In total there were more than 1,000 aftershocks after the earthquake, many of which were over 6.0 or even 7.0 on the Richter scale. Even ten years afterwards, a 7.1 aftershock occurred. I don't remember how many aftershocks hit on 11 March 2011, but there were many, at least three big ones within forty minutes of the main quake.

More than 18,000 people died as a direct result of the earthquake, although nearly all these souls were lost in the ensuing tsunami. As in many parts of Japan beyond the Tokyo and Osaka-Kyoto metropolitan areas, the ratio of elderly people affected by the Fukushima tragedy was very high. This may explain the fact that 57 per cent of those who died were sixty-five years old or above. Children accounted for about 4 per cent of lives lost. More than 700 children. As became apparent afterwards, only 50 per cent of schools in the area had the required evacuation plans. Richard Lloyd Parry's book, *Ghosts of the Tsunami* (2017, London: Jonathan Cape) explores with great understanding and compassion the events and the aftermath.

Roland Kelts' article in *The New Yorker*, *Japan's Radioactive Nightmare*, three years after the disaster, is one of many available online articles discussing the issues around the lack of information/disinformation: Kelts. R. (2014, 11 March. *Japan's radioactive nightmare*. The New Yorker. www.newyorker.com/culture/culture-desk/japans-radioactive-nightmare.)

As a researcher of communication, perhaps I shouldn't have been surprised by the media reporting. A lot of excellent research has been done on the way the 'reporting' of news is inherently ideological and skewed, and that's before we enter the realms of fake news. Events and participants are always represented; in other words, meaning is produced, it is not simply found; and it is always partial, in both senses of the word. For instance, one study comparing media coverage of Fukushima in Germany, France, the UK, and Switzerland found that the news aligned with the particular nation's stance on nuclear power. Germany and Switzerland foregrounded the nuclear issue in reporting on the triple disaster and related it to domestic nuclear power plants, whereas the UK and French press focused more on the tsunami and 'rarely related the nuclear catastrophe in Japan to domestic nuclear programs'. Such reporting reflected the relatively anti-nuclear stance of Germany and Switzerland, and the contrasting stance in the UK and France. Still, a bit like a dentist having emergency root canal treatment, at the time I was too busy experiencing this partiality to be interested in analysing it.

The study comparing media coverage of Fukushima in Germany, France, the UK, and Switzerland is: Kepplinger, H., & Lemke, R. (2016). Instrumentalizing Fukushima: Comparing media coverage of Fukushima in Germany, France, the United Kingdom, and Switzerland, *Political Communication*, 33(3): 351–373. For more general work on representation and the media, see the Stuart Hall-edited collection, referenced at the beginning of this section.

CHAPTER 5

The concept of 'in-groups' and 'out-groups' somewhat parallels the Japanese *uchi–soto* distinction discussed in the main text, and has been extensively studied in Social Identity Theory, developed by social psychologists Henri Tajfel and John Turner. Their research reveals how humans naturally favour their in-groups, perceiving more nuance and humanity within them, while often viewing out-groups as homogeneous and sometimes threatening. The wiki page is a clear introduction and has many key references: en.wikipedia.org/wiki/Social_identity_theory. For further reading on the *flyjin* phenomenon:

Cadwell, P. (2019). Foreign residents' experiences of the Flyjin phenomenon in the 2011 Great East Japan Earthquake. In S. Bouterey & L. Marceau (eds.), *Crisis and Disaster in Japan and New Zealand.* Singapore: Palgrave-Macmillan. link.springer.com/chapter/10.1007/978-981-13-0244-2_5.

The prime minister of the time, Naoto Kan, has discussed how close Japan came to a huge disaster, and how 'helpless' he felt in the face of the disaster: McCurry, J. (2012, 29 May). *Fukushima inquiry: I felt helpless, says former PM.* The Guardian. www.theguardian.com/world/2012/may/29/fukushima-inquiry-naoto-kan.

The work of the British Embassy at this time is discussed here:

Oppenheim, R., & Franklin, K. (2016). The aftermath of the Fukushima Daiichi Accident: A perspective from the British Embassy in Tokyo. *Clinical Oncology,* (28)4: 272–274 www.clinicaloncologyonline.net/article/S0936-6555(16)00008-X/fulltext.

This '2011 Tohoko earthquake and tsunami' wiki link provides more background on the devastation caused: en.wikipedia.org/wiki/2011_T%C5%8Dhoku_earthquake_and_tsunami#Cultural_impact.

The Japanese sociologist Yoshio Sugimoto (2021: 251, reference above) has this to say about the triple disaster:

> The Fukushima tragedy was man-made at every step. Although the earthquake itself was unavoidable, much of the resulting human tragedy could have been prevented if Japanese decision-makers had taken a different path before, during, and after 11th of March 2011. In particular, the focusing nuclear explosion and its ensuing disaster revealed collusion at the top level of the country, involving the nuclear power industry, the national bureaucracy, and the three-way power bloc. Most mainstream mass media, as well as nuclear science academia, were also enmeshed in the complicated web of mutual collaboration and complicity.

This web is widely called 'the nuclear village', and demonstrates the danger of *uchi*-type relationships operating without official oversight.

I'm aware that I give a somewhat simplistic representation of the concept of *kawaii* here. For a more in-depth analysis that considers how *kawaii* can also be subversive in Japanese society, see Slade, T. (2018). Cute fashion: The social strategies and aesthetics of kawaii, in T. Slade

& A. Freedman (eds.), *Introducing Japanese Popular Culture*. Abingdon: Routledge, pp. 402–423.

The John Agard poem 'Half-Caste' is in Agard, J. (2004). *Half-Caste and Other Poems*. London: Hodder Children's Books.

CHAPTER 6

The term *gaijin*, while literally meaning 'outside person' or foreigner, is usually used of non-Asian non-Japanese people, particularly those of White or Black ethnicity.

Although the stereotypical image of an 'international couple' in Japan is indeed a white man with an ethnically Japanese woman, statistically speaking there are more than double the number of Japanese men married to non-Japanese women, typically from other Asian countries. See: 'International Marriage in Japan: Trends in Nationality of Spouses': www.nippon.com/en/features/h00174/.

The quote from Yoshio Sugimoto is from Sugimoto (2021, cited above).

CHAPTER 7

The sociologist Yoshio Sugimoto (2021, cited above) argues that modern Japan, with its predominance of urban nuclear families and urban life-styles, is no longer collectivist, if it ever was.

CHAPTER 8

The Tomonori Kino poem is cited here: 'Celebrating Spring amid Devastation in Tokyo.' NPR. 4 April 2011. www.npr.org/2011/04/04/135106109/celebrating-rebirth-amid-devastation-in-tokyo. It is cited in a slightly different translation in *A Hundred Verses from Old Japan* (1909), translated by William N Porter: see sacred-texts.com/shi/hvj/hvj034.htm.

Of the other threats and problems caused by the disaster, the economic impact has been massive. The number of destroyed buildings is estimated at around 138,000, almost half a million people were evacuated, and radiation remains so high in certain areas that the destroyed towns will not be rebuilt. Whole communities have been permanently wiped from the map.

Agriculture, forestry, and fishing are three badly affected industries, and the total cost to the economy may be as high as $1 trillion.

The disaster on 11 March unleashed a mental-health crisis for those directly affected, and the burden of this fell on women (see below for references). The negative impact on the jobs women were more likely to do, and damage to their social networks, are some of the reasons. Another study found that men directly affected by the disaster become involved with more risk-taking, with gambling and drinking increasing. Once again, women in homes with men gambling and drinking more, along with increased instances of domestic abuse, added to the mental health epidemic. There are also societal parallels between 11 March and COVID-19. A recent *Lancet* article stated the increase in suicides among Japanese women and children had risen because of the COVID crisis, with women's jobs being disproportionately affected, and again because of domestic abuse.

While these studies highlight the varied damage caused to different groups, there was other research that found positives in the gloom, as I mention in the main text. Another study examined the mental health and well-being of Japanese residents who were not directly affected by the disaster. It found that among young people the disaster led to an increase in 'prosocial behaviours', such as making donations and volunteering, and an increased appreciation of everyday life.

There was plenty of global reporting on the retired engineers re-entering the plant, for instance: Buerk, R. (2011, 31 May). *Japan pensioners volunteer to tackle nuclear crisis.* BBC. www.bbc.co.uk/news/world-asia-pacific-13598607. There is a good deal of research on the greater diversity within than between groups, for instance: Deater-Deckard, K., et al. (2018). Within- and between-person and group variance in behavior and beliefs in cross-cultural longitudinal data. *Journal of Adolescence,* 62: 207–217. pubmed.ncbi.nlm.nih.gov/28662856/.

For further information on the impacts of the disaster see this Brookings.edu link: www.brookings.edu/blog/up-front/2013/03/11/earthquake-tsunami-meltdown-the-triple-disasters-impact-on-japan-impact-on-the-world/.

This article explores the mental health issues following the disaster:

Yokoyama, Y., Otsuka, K., Kawakami, N., Kobayashi, S., Ogawa, A., Tannno K., et al. (2014). Mental health and related factors after the Great East Japan

Earthquake and tsunami. *PLoS ONE* 9(7): e102497. doi.org/10.1371/journal
.pone.0102497.

This article explains the risks, such as men's alcohol consumption:

Hanaoka, C., Shigeoka, H., & Watanabe, Y. (2015). Do risk preferences change?
Evidence from panel data before and after the Great East Japan Earthquake.
National Bureau of Economic Research Working Paper Series. www.nber.org/papers/
w21400.

This is *The Lancet* article on Covid and women's suicide rates in Japan:

Yoshioka, E., et al. (2022). Impact of the COVID-19 pandemic on suicide rates in
Japan through December 2021: An interrupted time series analysis. *The Lancet
Regional Health – Western Pacific.* 24: 100480

These are the cited studies on prosocial behaviours and young people,
and trust:

Uchida, Y., et al. (2014). Changes in hedonic and eudaimonic well-being after
a severe nationwide disaster: The case of the Great East Japan Earthquake.
Journal of Happiness Studies. 15: 207–221. link.springer.com/article/10.1007/
s10902-013-9463-6.

Yamamura, E., et al. (2015). Trust and happiness: Comparative study before
and after the Great East Japan Earthquake. *Social Indicators Research*, 123: 919–
935. www.researchgate.net/publication/282795656_Trust_and_Happiness_
Comparative_Study_Before_and_After_the_Great_East_Japan_Earthquake.

Circular reasoning has been termed 'analytic stereotyping' by my colleague Srikant Sarangi, for instance in his highly influential article:

Sarangi, S. (1994). Intercultural or not? Beyond celebration of cultural differences in miscommunication analysis. *Pragmatics*, 4(3): 409–427.

CHAPTER 9

Along with refusing the promotion, another first in the faculty was my
taking paternity leave.

The Befu quote (2001: 67, reference above), which describes
the dominant cultural identity discourse known as *nihonjinron*, is
more than twenty years old. Sugimoto (2021: 30–31, reference above)
argues that things have not changed much in the succeeding twenty
years:

Nihonjinron continues to flourish even at the beginning of the twenty-first century... Though somewhat timeworn and outdated, the monocultural Nihonjinron model of Japan has continued to influence the popular and academic debate over the characteristics of Japanese society. This is partly because this model contributes to the identity formation of the Japanese and serves as a kind of civil religion, and partly because it forms the basis for Japan's cultural nationalism.

The situation for mixed-race children in Japan is complex. This wiki link on the term *Hāfu* is a clear introduction: en.wikipedia.org/wiki/Hāfu. This CNN article shed some light on the reality many face:

Jozuka, E., & Jones, V. (2020, 23 September). *Japanese Hafu stars are celebrated. But some mixed-race people say they feel like foreigners in their own country.* CNN. edition.cnn.com/2020/09/22/asia/japan-mixed-roots-hafu-dst-hnk-intl/index.html.

This book is primarily set in Japan, hence the stronger focus on all aspects of life there. As I discuss in Chapter 31, my daughters have also experienced issues because of their ethnicity in the UK, as indeed has Mayu. It would be possible to write another book just on this, but that would be a different book. As one other example, when we moved to Birmingham, the next-door neighbours were a mother and her two young boys. The mother would acknowledge me, but would refuse to speak to Mayu, and her two sons would sometimes peek through the fence dividing our homes and make slanted-eye faces at the girls.

For further information on Japanese demographics, see: www.worl dometers.info/world-population/japan-population/.

On my parents' marriage and divorce: it is a vivid example of the non-essentialist nature of national identity and how cultural differences may lead to conflict. They divorced partly because of immense cultural differences between them that emerged in the early 1970s, as a consequence of the Troubles and their personal involvement there. But before the violence erupted in Northern Ireland, these cultural differences did not exist. It was the changes in Ulster that led to the conflict between them, not innate identities.

The conversation with the professor at Oxford brought home the opening sentence of the hugely influential book *The Nature of Prejudice,* about humanity having 'gained notable mastery over energy, matter, and inanimate matter generally, and are rapidly learning to control physical suffering and premature death. But, by contrast, we appear to be living in the Stone Age as far as our handling of human relations is concerned.' Thankfully, through personal experiences, teaching students, and also my work with people in companies, I knew that prejudice could be confronted and even reduced. Indeed, classrooms and training rooms provide one of the few platforms for discussing and reflecting on prejudice in a considered manner. But like cancer, the earlier you find it the better.

The *Nature of Prejudice* quote is from page xiii of Allport, G. (1954). *The Nature of Prejudice*. London: Addison-Wesley.

CHAPTER 10

Japan's poor gender equality is well documented and not going in an encouraging direction. In 2024, for instance, Japan came 118 out of 146 countries in the gender equality rankings – a fall of 38 places compared to 2006. See the World Economic Forum *Global Gender Gap Report 2024*: World Economic Forum. (2024, 11 June). www.weforum.org/publications/global-gender-gap-report-2024/.

This BBC article reports on the rigging of women's results in Japanese medical schools: BBC. (2018). *Japan medical schools 'rigged women's results'*. https://www.bbc.co.uk/news/world-asia-46568975.

It's worth mentioning the Birmingham accent, as it's another example of how othering can operate in society, and how I'd internalised this. As a professional linguist, I sincerely believe that all accents are equal. There is nothing inherently 'better' about one accent than another; but in society, some accents are seen as less prestigious than others, and the stereotypes around accent can have real-world effects, like job prospects. The local Birmingham accent being a case in point. So while I objectively know that no accent can indicate someone's intelligence or morality, and we need to combat the stereotypes, I hate to admit I did wonder how I'd feel if Julia and Maya ended up bringing back Brummie accents to Japan with them. Linguists at Queen Mary's University have done fascinating, important work on this area: Sharma, D. et al. (n.d.). *Talking proper: Could accent bias harm your job prospects?* Retrieved 8 November 2025 from www.qmul.ac.uk/sllf/research/featured-research/could-accent-bias-harm-your-job-prospects.

CHAPTER 11

The book Hiro and I wrote: Tanaka, H., & Handford, M. (2008). *Sanka Suru: Eigo no Meeting (Discursive Strategies in Business Meetings)*. Tokyo: Cosmopier.

From a young age, I've been intrigued by how people say things to each other that seem acceptable or not. This is a big reason why I decided, while an undergraduate, to become an English-language teacher and moved to Japan in 1994. Like many people who acquire English as a first language around my age, I never learnt the explicit grammar of the English language while at school. It wasn't until I began to teach it that I came to know what the present perfect continuous tense was, or the difference between an adverb and an adjective. The embarrassment of having students who know more than you can be highly motivating.

In the multibillion-dollar industry that is (English) language teaching, classroom materials are typically based around the sentence: how do you make a correct sentence, what type of sentence-level errors do (Japanese) students typically make, that kind of thing. But the longer I taught English, the more I became aware that so much of what we might term correct, or rather appropriate, usage does not occur at the level of the single sentence. Focusing on a single, grammatically correct sentence as a way to understand communication was like trying to understand the richness of the natural world by analysing geometrical shapes.

William Blake's famous image of Sir Isaac Newton ignoring the beauty, the fecundity of nature when attempting to measure it (Figure N1) springs to mind, a parallel focus on simple form when there is so much variety and beauty beyond. An aside: somewhat incongruously in my

N1 William Blake's critique of Isaac Newton's approach to the natural world.

N2 Sir Isaac Newton outside the British Library.

opinion, an imposing bronze statue of this image sits outside The British Library in central London (Figure N2). It's like a sentence being taken out of context, and now meaning virtually the opposite of what it was intended to mean (another problem with sentence-level focus). I think Blake would not be impressed.

Returning to the sentence/meaning issue: a language student might be able to say, 'I have been studying English hard for six years', demonstrating both correct use of the present perfect continuous tense and of the irregular adverb 'hard'. But they also need to know when, how, and who to say it to, in other words, building the sentence into a conversation that seems to flow naturally. Focusing only on sentence-level grammar did not help students with these important aspects of communication.

I decided to do an MA in English Language partly because of this frustration. I didn't know it then, but I was in search of discourse. There are many definitions of discourse, but the one I first came across was, 'language beyond the sentence'. 'Beyond the sentence' is nicely vague, covering both the way a single sign on a wall, saying 'No Smoking', is meaningful, and also how a string of questions and answers in a shop encounter or conversation between friends is meaningful.

Not long into my MA, in 2000, I realised that discourse as meaning beyond the sentence was useful, but it still left many of my questions unanswered. I was now in the linguistic rabbit warren that is explaining meaning in context. I could see how sentences formed paragraphs in writing, and how speaker turns combined to form a conversation, but this level of discourse didn't explain how constrained so much communication is. It is indeed possible to say anything in theory, but analysis of authentic communication shows that we often say the same things again and again. The linguist Patrick Hanks, riffing on T. S. Eliot, states,

'Humanity cannot bear too much creativity', and it's very true. (The phrase is a reference to T. S. Eliot's line in his poem 'Burnt Norton' that 'humankind cannot bear very much reality'. See Eliot. T. S. (1943). *Four Quartets*. New York: Harcourt, Brace and Co.) If you step outside what's usual, people might not like it, or you, very much. But it also depends on who 'you' are – some people can say more, and have more freedom to say more, than others. Neither grammar nor discourse 'beyond the sentence' could explain all this.

The late Ron Carter, my professor and mentor at Nottingham, suggested I look at the concept of Discourse with a big 'D', to help me answer some of these questions. Ah! That's it!' I beamed, as I read the accessible yet brilliant work of James Paul Gee. Discourse with a big 'D' concerns the 'who' aspects of communication, and how meaning is made in relation to the 'who'. Yes, language beyond the sentence that forms texts and conversations is important, but it only gains meaning when used by particular types of people doing particular, recognisable things. I'll return to Discourse in a minute (if you keep reading this Notes section).

The reference to Patrick Hanks' book is Hanks, P. (2013). *Lexical Analysis: Norms and Expectations*. London: MIT Press.

Some of the most rigorous and insightful work on cultural differences and conflict has been done by Eero Vaara and his colleagues. See for example:

Vaara, E., Sarala, R., Stahl, G., & Björkman, I. (2012). The impact of organizational and national cultural differences on social conflict and knowledge transfer in international acquisitions. *Journal of Management Studies*, 49(1): 1–27.

The reference to my book on business meetings is Handford, M. (2010). *The Language of Business Meetings*. Cambridge: Cambridge University Press.

The reference to my work on Japanese engineers is Handford, M. (2020). Training 'international engineers' in Japan: discourse, Discourse and stereotypes, in L. Mullany (ed.), *Professional Communication: Consultancy, Advocacy, Activism*. London: Palgrave.

Jim Gee has published widely on his concept of Discourse with big D. I've added one reference at the beginning of this section (Gee, 2015), and he has a great webpage with access to blogs, publications etc: jamespaulgee.com.

The photographs showing different Discourses (sculptor, hikers, alt rock fans, and powerlifter) allow for some comparisons and reflections. Clearly the different Discourses use different tools – whereas the sculptor uses particular materials, the hikers may use sticks to help with walking, appropriate shoes and clothes. A closer look at the hikers' clothes in the photos show some differences: whereas my three friends are wearing walking shorts and sports tops more typical of UK-based hiking, I am dressed in linen trousers and a linen shirt. This is because in Japan I like to go hillwalking in such attire, it's cooling and protects my pale skin from sunburn, and in Japan nobody comments. But my three friends thought my choice of clothing worthy of much comment and cracked many jokes. I also remember several other hikers staring at my attire as we walked past them. This shows how doing something unusual in a Discourse can provoke comment, or in some cases censure or even ejection from the Discourse. The following year, when we walked again, I was careful to dress in a more 'appropriate' outfit, and no comments were made.

The photos also demonstrate how, in certain Discourses, language may not be the most important aspect. In powerlifting competitions, the ability to lift heavier weights is the key aspect. The same is true of being a sculptor, and even hikers and alternative music fans are not required to produce language. But they are required to know the 'rules of the game', the conventions that both reflect and constitute the values and beliefs of the Discourse in question.

In terms of addressing national stereotypes, the argument Hiro and I tried to engage the trainees with went something like this: Yes, our brains want to make sentences like 'Japanese people are like X', but beyond some statistically testable generalisations, such as 'Japanese people on average live a long time', how confident can we be about such statements? We often hear things like 'Japanese people are the most polite nation in the world', both from Japanese and non-Japanese. To say some nation is more polite than another, there would need to be two things that don't exist: an international standard of politeness, and an objective way of measuring politeness. With height, or weight, or age, we have such standards and measures, but not with things like politeness. The way politeness works in one culture is different to another, so what's polite in one place may not have the same meaning in another, or what's expected in one place may not be expected in another. For instance, in the UK it's fairly common for people to hold a door open for strangers who are walking behind you in a shopping centre. In Japan I noticed there is no such expectation.

But that doesn't stop us developing stereotypes about things like politeness. I still inwardly tut when the stranger in front of me doesn't hold the door open for me in Tokyo. I then mentally beat myself up a bit, knowing that I'm unfairly judging them by inappropriate norms. It would be like frowning at guests in my UK home who don't take their shoes off upon entering our home (yes, I've done that, too). Some people say, 'But stereotyping is natural, we all do it.' In reply, defecating in the woods and sleeping in trees are also 'natural', but I'd rather use a high-tech Japanese toilet with built-in bidet, and sleep on Egyptian cotton sheets, thank you very much.

CHAPTER 12

The poem that stands as an epigraph to the chapter is written by me. The novel by Mori Ogai is Ogai, M. (1913/2013). *The Wild Geese*. Translated by Sandford Goldstein and Kingo Ochiai. North Clarendon, VT: Tuttle Publishing. The Melanie lyric is from her song 'I Don't Eat Animals' on the live album *Leftover Wine* (Buddah, 1970). Melanie (Safka) (1947–2024) was an American singer-songwriter.

Mayu's type of reflexology is known as Sokushindo, and is originally from Taiwan. The website medical.net has a report on reflexology helping ease migraines: Robertson, S. (n.d.). Can reflexology help ease migraines? Retrieved 8 November 20205 from www.news-medical.net/health/Can-Reflexology-Help-Ease-Migraines.aspx.

Cancer Research UK evaluates the efficacy of reflexology, along with other alternative medicines: Cancer Research UK. (n.d.). *Reflexology and cancer*. Retrieved 8 November 2025 from www.can cerresearchuk.org/about-cancer/cancer-in-general/treatment/complementary-alternative-therapies/individual-therapies/reflexology.

One study in the journal *Cancer* on acupuncture and dry mouth is Meng, Z. et al. (2012). Randomized controlled trial of acupuncture for prevention of radiation-induced xerostomia among patients with nasopharyngeal carcinoma. *Cancer*. 118: 3337–3344. doi.org/10.1002/cncr.26550.

On the power of the placebo effect, see *Harvard Medical Review*: Harvard Medical Review. (2024, 22 July). *The power of the placebo effect.* www.health .harvard.edu/mental-health/the-power-of-the-placebo-effect.

The Mukherjee quote is from page 6 of Mukherjee, S. (2011). *The Emperor of All Maladies: A Biography of Cancer.* London: Fourth Estate. The reference to Mickey's Mouse's brooms refers to the 1940 Walt Disney musical animation film *Fantasia.* In a section set to 'The Sorcerer's Apprentice' by Paul Dukas, Mickey Mouse is the apprentice magician whose spell backfires – the cleaning implement he magicked into being floods the workshop and then when Mickey breaks it to try to end the mayhem it multiplies into an army of uncontrollable brooms.

The Fredrik Svenaeus quote, page 333, is from Svenaeus, F (2011), cited above.

Jackie Stacey (1997), cited above, has a lot of interesting things to say about types of alternative medicine, along with some of the charlatans operating in this area.

I had thought my thought about the shoes was original, but in *The Wounded Storyteller* I see Arthur Frank (2013, cited above) reports another cancer patient saying the same thing.

CHAPTER 13

The different ways in which time can be perceived include future-oriented (goal-oriented and liking planning), past-oriented (tending towards nostalgia and maintaining the status quo), and present-oriented. While people may have individual and group tendencies towards one orientation, changes in context can lead to changes in orientation. This article on temporal consciousness provides a clear introduction to these concepts: Stanford Encyclopedia of Philosophy. (2010/2023). *Temporal consciousness.* https://plato.stanford.edu/entries/consciousness-temporal/

For more on topics like time and culture, see Scollon, Scollon, & Jones (2012), cited above.

The reference to the past being a different country alludes to the first line of British writer L. P. Hartley's novel *The Go-Between*: 'The past is a foreign country: they do things differently there.' Hartley, L. P. (1953). *The Go-Between.* London: Hamish Hamilton. The quotation from

Kalanithi (2016) on statistics is from page 135. The subject–object quote is from page 141. The topic of how we organise the various actors and what they do in sentences, 'transitivity', and illness is a fascinating one. For one application of transitivity to cancer, see Karimi, N. et al. (2018). Advanced cancer patients' construction of self during oncology consultations: a transitivity concordance analysis. *Functional Linguistics*, 5:6. link .springer.com/article/10.1186/s40554-018-0057-9.

The quote about the grammar of cancer is on page 4 of the Jain & Stacey (2015) article cited above.

CHAPTER 14

The quote about illness being constructed is from Richard Gwyn (2002). *Communicating through Illness*. London: Sage. The full quote (page 6) further develops this idea:

> Illness is constructed, reproduced and perpetuated through language. We get to know about our own illnesses through the language of doctors and nurses, friends and relatives, and we often recycle the words picked up from our consultations in the doctor's surgery into conversation, sprinkling our stories of sickness with epithets that give the impression of a grander knowledge of medical science. When we open the newspapers or switch on the television or radio, we encounter an increasing variety of articles and programmes offering information, advice and warnings about every conceivable dimension of health and care of the body.

Dr Hannah O'Mahoney from Tenovus Cancer Care for brought the term 'prehabilitation' to my attention. These are some useful links: Macmillan Cancer Support. (n.d.). *Prehabilitation videos for people living with cancer.* Retrieved 8 November 2025 from https://www.macmillan.org.uk/cancer-information-and-support/stories-and-media/videos/prehabilitation-videos Durrand, J., et al. (2019). Prehabilitation. *Clinical Medicine*, 19(6):458–464. www.ncbi.nlm.nih.gov/pmc/articles/PMC6899232/. Richards, M. (2024, 20 August). *Hospital gets patients ready for ops with workouts.* BBC. www.bbc.co.uk/news/articles/cz73l97zr9no. The William Blake poem 'Auguries of Innocence' can be found in *The Complete Poems*, edited by Alicia Ostriker, 1977. London: Penguin.

CHAPTER 15

Dr Arthur Barky's book is Barsky, A. J. (1988). *Worried Sick: Our Troubled Quest for Wellness*. New York City: Little, Brown. The George Orwell quote is from chapter 3 of Orwell, G. (1961). *Down and Out in London and Paris*. New York City: Harcourt Brace Jovanovich.

The references to Hitchens (2012), Stacey (1997, quote page 63) are from the works cited at the beginning of this section. The reference to F. Scott Fitzgerald is to his article 'The Crack-Up': Fitzgerald, F. S. (1936). 'The Crack-Up'. *Esquire*, 1 February. classic.esquire.com/article/share/97a6b0a8-ba1c-4b7b-aa64-0d08dd9fb952

Erving Goffman conducted much of the early groundbreaking work on frames, for example Goffman, E. (1974). *Frame Analysis: An Essay on the Organization of Experience*. Cambridge, MA: Harvard University Press.

I think it's worth saying a bit more about frames. Frames are sets of expectations that we use to interpret reality. Frames affect the way we see the world at that point in time, and the meaning of what is said: is the interaction framed humorously, for example? Each frame will lead us to notice, and to ignore, different things, and to attribute particular values to them. In frame theory, it is not possible to interact with people or things outside of a frame: we inevitably frame everything. Michael Agar, in his very accessible book on the relationship between language and culture (Agar, M. *Language Shock: Understanding the Culture of Conversation*, published by HarperCollins), says that 'Frames take language and culture and make them inseparable' (1994: 132)

Like Discourse, frames shape how we act, think, and communicate. But while Discourse describes the broader social identities we inhabit (doctor, patient, teacher), frames help explain how we interpret and navigate those identities moment by moment. As a cancer patient, I was learning not just the practices of a new Discourse – the medical terminology, the hospital routines, the expected behaviours – but also how to frame my experience within that Discourse. Understanding these different frames helped me navigate the medical Discourse more effectively, just as understanding cultural frames helps in intercultural communication. Arthur Frank (2013, page 53) argues that stories 'serve to repair the damage that illness has done'. This is because stories 'do not simply describe the self: they are the self's medium of being'. This shows the importance of making the right stories.

CHAPTER 16

Like so many others before me, I found reading Susan Sontag's *Illness as Metaphor* (1978, cited above) a truly enlightening experience. In it, she argues persuasively that the reality of cancer is often shrouded in euphemisms and metaphors, such as 'passed away after a long illness' or the patient being 'invaded' with cancer. Sontag's argument is that you need to face up honestly and rationally to what cancer is, and what it is to you.

According to Sontag, the typical metaphors used in descriptions of cancer are taken from the language of warfare: 'cancer cells do not simply multiply; they are "invasive". ('Malignant tumours invade even when they grow very slowly', as one textbook puts it.) Cancer cells "colonize" from the original tumour to far sites of the body … Rarely are the body's "defences" vigorous enough to obliterate a tumour that has established its own blood supply …' (p. 64). She goes on to say that cancer treatment also employs such metaphors, with its aims to "kill" the cancer cells, and in the United States there was even a "War on Cancer", again a metaphorical usage. At the time of the COVID-19 pandemic there were similar debates in the media on politicians' language use.

Sontag is highly critical of such use of metaphorical language, arguing that it encourages social stigmatizing of people with cancer, and also gives the disease an aura of fear that can petrify those dealing with the disease. She therefore argues that rejecting metaphorical language use, and confronting the disease in literal terms, is the best way of dealing with the disease and liberating sufferers. I agree with her point that the war metaphors used about cancer can be potentially dangerous and debilitating. Saying that, some people do prefer to frame their cancer as a battle, and that works for them. Moreover, I don't agree that this means all metaphors should be rejected (and I don't believe we can do that anyway, as I explain below).

In the quotation at the beginning of Chapter 16, it is a little ironic that Sontag argues that the best way to deal with illness is by purifying our thought of metaphorical thinking, when 'purifying thought' is itself a metaphor. The quote is also an elegant example of a powerfully developed metaphor (illness and health as dual citizenship). Indeed, every clause in the quote contains some metaphorical language, for instance 'the night-side of life ... a more onerous citizenship ... dual citizenship ... the kingdom of the well ... the good passport', and so on.

I raise this point not to criticize Sontag but to emphasise that metaphorical language or thinking should not be rejected out of hand – and nor should we try to do this. It can be profoundly useful for the listener (or reader) or the speaker: a well-formed metaphor can enable new insights, as professional communication shows (see Handford, M., and Koester, A. (2024). *Language and Creativity at Work*. Abingdon: Routledge). The Sontag quote helps us understand the massive change in perspective that sickness brings. For me, it both comforts and encourages resolve.

The reference to the metaphor book is George Lakoff and Mark Johnson's *Metaphors We Live By* (1980, Chicago: Chicago University Press).

As I briefly mention in the main text, I think Lakoff and Johnson's main point is that metaphor is much more typical in everyday language use, such as when friends are chatting or politicians arguing or businesspeople negotiating, than is typically assumed to be the case. The second point is that the very way we think, the way our mind works, uses metaphor. They call this 'conceptual metaphor', in contrast with metaphors we see in everyday language, which are called 'linguistic metaphor'. Linguistic metaphors are instances of underlying conceptual metaphor. For example, the expression 'they blew their top' is a linguistic metaphor, but one which reflects the underlying conceptual metaphor ANGER AS A HOT LIQUID IN A CONTAINER. The expression 'he flipped his lid' is also an instance of this. Lakoff and Johnson argue that we make sense of the world, of our feelings, our relationships, and so on through such conceptual metaphors. Without metaphors, it is hard or even impossible for us to make sense of many aspects of our lives.

The reference to my colleague Lisa El Rafaie's work on visual cancer narratives is El Rafaie, E. (2019). *Visual Metaphor and Embodiment in Graphic Illness Narratives*. Oxford: Oxford University Press. The reference to Jennifer Hayden's graphic illness narrative is Hayden, J. (2015). *The Story of My Tits*. Neptune, NJ: Top Shelf Productions.

I recently came across two other instances of making your own cancer metaphor. I was watching a BBC Storyville programme on Lance Armstrong, and part of it concerned how he dealt with his stage-4 cancer condition. It had spread from his testicle to his lungs and brain, and he underwent a very long period of daily chemotherapy treatments, along with post-chemotherapy surgeries. In talking about his experience, he said that he imagined he was in a competition with his cancer. He said that he put the daily chemo doses on a board, with each dose a point for him against the cancer. And this way he could imagine himself beating the cancer. For a competitive athlete, this makes perfect sense: Armstrong drew on what he knew, and how he sees himself, and framed the relationship with cancer in those terms.

The reference for the Lance Armstrong programme is Holmes, A. (dir.). (2016). *The Lance Armstrong Story – Stop at Nothing.* BBC Storyville. See www.bbc.co.uk/programmes/b048wq0z.

The second example is by Ibram X. Kendi, author of the bestselling *How to Be an Antiracist.* In this book, he talks about how he got cancer not long after he came to the realisation that racism is not caused by ignorance but by self-interest. What he means is that powerful policy-makers make racist policies because of self-interest, and then they create racist ideas to justify their self-serving policies. These racist ideas then justify the inequitable effects of the policies, which cause further hate and ignorance. This line of reasoning aligns with the counterintuitive, profoundly enlightening argument that race is the child of racism, and not vice versa.

Kendi, arriving at this realisation about the way racism is justified around the time he was diagnosed, started to see cancer in terms of this realisation. He could deny the existence of the cancer, as people do with racism, and this would be the easier option. But it could not lead to heal-ing; for that, we need admission, and confession. And instead of focusing on the self-limiting possibilities of cancer and its treatment, he focused on the joy he would feel if he could survive.

The full reference is Kendi, I.X. (2019). *How to Be an Antiracist.* London: The Bodley Head.

Lancaster University's cancer-metaphor menu can be found online: www.lancaster.ac.uk/news/articles/2014/battle-metaphors-for-cancer-can-be-harmful/.

The line by Arthur Rimbaud is cited here: Vogue Portugal. (2022, 14 April). 'Car je est un autre.' www.vogue.pt/english-version-fashion-sto ry-arthur-rimbaud-quote-issue.

These references concern the relationship between mental attitude and cancer survival:

Chow, E., Tsao, M., & Harth, T. (2004). Does psychosocial intervention improve survival in cancer? A meta-analysis. *Palliative Medicine*, 18(1): 25–31. pubmed .ncbi.nlm.nih.gov/14982204/.

Coyne, J. C., & Tennen, H. (2010). Positive psychology in cancer care: Bad science, exaggerated claims, and unproven medicine. *Annals of Behavioral Medicine: A Publication of the Society of Behavioral Medicine*, 39(1): 16–26. doi.org/10.1007/ s12160-009-9154-z.

Hauser, D., & Schwarz, N. (2015). The war on prevention: Bellicose cancer metaphors hurt (some) prevention intentions. *Personality and Social Psychology Bulletin*, 41(1): 66–77. pubmed.ncbi.nlm.nih.gov/25352114/.

Graves, K. D. (2003). Social cognitive theory and cancer patients' quality of life: A meta-analysis of psychosocial intervention components. *Health Psychology*, 22(2): 210–219. doi.org/10.1037/0278-6133.22.2.210.

The BBC has a useful page on macrobiotic food: Lienard, S. (2024, 9 January). What is the macrobiotic diet? BBC goodFOOD. www.bbcgood food.com/howto/guide/what-macrobiotic-diet.

The quote about Tommy the tumour is from Stephens, J., & Thorne, S. (2022). When cancer is the self: An interpretive description of the experience of identity by hematology cancer patients. *Cancer Nursing*, 45(2): E504–E513. pubmed.ncbi.nlm.nih.gov/34352803/.

CHAPTER 17

The quote is from David Peace's *Patient X*: Peace, D. (2019). *Patient X*. London: Faber and Faber. The Carol Ann Duffy poem is in her collection *Selling Manhattan*: Duffy, C. A. (1987). *Selling Manhattan*. London: Anvil Press.

The figures about green spaces in cities are from: World Cities Culture Forum: Percentage of green space (parks and gardens). www.treehug ger.com/global-cities-most-and-least-public-green-space-4868715#:~:tex t=With%20a%20paltry%206.7%20percent,and%20Tokyo%20(7.5%20 percent).

The culture shock model is from Oberg, W. (1963). Cross-cultural perspectives on management principles. *Academy of Management Journal*, 6: 129–143.

CHAPTER 18

As with any type of cultural comparison, the tendency when considering health is to focus on differences. But as the renowned medical anthropologist Arthur Kleinman argues (1980: 24, cited above): 'The single most important concept for cross-cultural studies of medicine is a radical appreciation that in all societies, healthcare activities are more or less interrelated.' And it seems that healthcare systems across much of the world share far more than they differ. The Sanshiro reference is to *Sanshiro*, by Natsume Soseki: Soseki, N. (1908/1977). *Sanshiro*, translated by J. Rubin. Seattle: University of Washington Press.

CHAPTER 19

The term 'intersectionality' was introduced by the Black American legal scholar Kimberlé Crenshaw as a way of explaining how multiple identities, such as race, gender, and class, simultaneously operate to marginalise certain groups (and by implication advantage others). When US society considers 'women' it tends to be white women; for 'Black', it is Black men. This, Crenshaw shows, can erase the concerns and opportunities for Black women.

I can't hope to give a sense of the breadth and societal explanatory value of this concept, so I'll just say a little about how it might relate to the intercultural. Exploring how intersectionality can be aligned with a critical intercultural approach has received some attention, given the shared interest in power. As Dreama Moon (2013: 41) states, 'By attending to notions of intersectionality scholars are more likely to produce knowledge that is specific and local, rather than abstract and overly generalised. In addition, we are more likely to be able to observe how positions of power and privilege may play out in intercultural interactions. In this way, identification can be seen as both voluntary and imposed, both embraced and struggled over and with, both rejected and claimed.'

Intersectionality, and the way we perceive each other's intersectional identities, can I think have relevance for patient-doctor interactions. Eliot Mishler, in *The Discourse of Medicine* (1984), argued that medical interactions involve two types of 'voice': the voice of medicine, and that of the voice of the 'lifeworld' – our everyday way of communicating, which we acquire from childhood. Doctors can use both voices, being members of both the medical profession and of society in general, whereas patients are typically only fluent in the voice of the lifeworld. So doctors need to be able to 'translate' back and forth when talking to patients: what do the patient's lifeworld ways of communicating tell us about the illness, and how can the relevant medical information be communicated in a comprehensible way? These 'voices' have strong parallels with the notion of Discourse discussed in earlier chapters, being much more than just language.

When these different 'voices' (or Discourses) come into interaction, I think we can categorise it as a type of intercultural communication. In later chapters I'll reflect more on this useful distinction, but here I'd like to suggest that problems can arise, depending on how we see the person we're talking to.

I noted in the chapter how Black doctors can be othered when the patient doesn't approve of what they're hearing, their Blackness being made more relevant than their professional identity. But similarly, doctors may make aspects of the patient's intersectional bundle of identities relevant when, in reality, they aren't so relevant. In particular, they may see aspects of their different lifeworlds as explaining 'challenging' behaviour. A doctor might think, 'She's acting aggressively because she's a working-class woman', when in fact she's deeply threatened by the diagnosis, the implications for her work status, or perhaps someone crashed into her car on the way to the hospital. We can hope that through awareness of our tendency to stereotype differences, better communication and better health outcomes can eventually be achieved. Kleinman and Benson (2006) propose that the Hippocratic oath, saying 'Avoid harm', which hangs above many doctor's doors, should be replaced by 'Avoid harm by stereotyping'. Perhaps we should all have that over our door.

The full reference to this paper is Kleinman, A., and Benson, P. (2006). Anthropology in the clinic: The problem of cultural competency and how to fix it. *PLoS medicine*, 3(10): e294. journals.plos.org/plosmed icine/article?id=10.1371/journal.pmed.0030294.

The reference to the widely cited Crenshaw paper is: Crenshaw, K. (1989). Demarginalizing the intersection of race and sex: A Black feminist critique of antidiscrimination doctrine, feminist theory, and antiracist politics. *University of Chicago Legal Forum*, 8: 139–167.

There's also a more recent Ted Talk by Kimberlé Crenshaw, titled 'The Urgency of Intersectionality': www.ted.com/talks/kimberle_crenshaw_the_urgency_of_intersectionality?subtitle=en.

The Moon reference is: Moon, D. (2013). 'Cultural reflections on culture and critical intercultural communication', in T. Nakayama and R. Halualani (eds.), *The Handbook of Critical Intercultural Communication*. Oxford: Wiley-Blackwell.

The title of April-Louise Pennant's book is *Babygirl, you've got this! Experiences of Black girls and women in the English educational experience* (London: Bloomsbury, 2024). April-Louise kindly commented on a draft of this chapter, and guided me to the following articles on the complex relationship between hair and Black women's intersectional identities:

Norwood, C. (2017). Decolonizing my hair, unshackling my curls: An autoethnography on what makes my natural hair journey a Black feminist statement. *International Feminist Journal of Politics*, 20(1): 69–84. doi.org/10.1080/1461674 2.2017.1369890.

Teteh, D. K., et al. (2017). *My crown and glory*: Community, identity, culture, and Black women's concerns of hair product-related breast cancer risk. *Cogent Arts & Humanities*, 4(1). www.tandfonline.com/doi/full/10.1080/23311983.2017 .1345297.

Joseph-Salisbury, R., & Connelly, L. (2018). 'If your hair is relaxed, white people are relaxed. If your hair is nappy, they're not happy': Black hair as a site of 'post-racial' social control in English schools. *Social Sciences*, 7(11): 219. www .mdpi.com/2076-0760/7/11/219.

On the fear of hair-loss, and racial disparities, see Williams, D. R., & Mohammed, S. A. (2009). Discrimination and racial disparities in health: Evidence and needed research. *Journal of Behavioral Medicine*, 32(1): 20–47. pubmed.ncbi.nlm.nih.gov/19030981/.

The quote from Lorde 1980 (cited at beginning of this section) is from p. 48.

On the barriers sexual minority women may face, see Kelly-Brown, J., et al. (2022). Intersectionality in cancer care: A systematic review of current research and future directions. *Psycho-Oncology* 31(5): 705–716. doi .org/10.1002/pon.5890.

CHAPTER 20

One irony in interdisciplinary education concerns what people learn and what they will need in the future. It's increasingly accepted that critical thinking, communication, collaboration, and creativity (the '4Cs') are the key skills that workers will need in the twenty-first century, whatever their job. Google, for instance, did a massive data-crunch on employee records, and found that even in their highest-of-tech industry, these '4Cs' were among the most important attributes of successful employees, well above IT skills, for instance. See Strauss, V. (2017, 20 December). 'The surprising thing Google learned about its employees – and what it means for today's students.' The Washington Post. www.washingtonpost.com/news/answer-sheet/wp/2017/12/20/the-surprising-thing-google-learned-about-its-employees-and-what-it-means-for-todays-students/

And these are exactly the skills that Arts, Humanities, and Social Sciences degrees inculcate in their students. Unfortunately, many policy-makers and even university leaders choose to ignore this, with their attacks on these disciplines, departments being closed, and the mere lip-service they pay to genuinely interdisciplinary research.

CHAPTER 23

The quote about the resistance of patients is from page 1112 of Koenig, C. (2011). Patient resistance as agency in treatment decisions. *Social Science and Medicine*, 7: 1105–1114.

Along with somewhat reduced saliva production and neck cramps, cognitive fatigue is a lasting side-effect of my illness and treatment. In 2017, after having moved back to the UK for work, I had to take some months off because my overloaded brain refused to process information. I've since learnt to manage it better, through a regime of regular aerobic and anaerobic exercise, daily mindfulness practice, acupuncture, diet, ginseng and turmeric, strategic napping, and aiming for quality of work over quantity. Thankfully my employer, Cardiff University, has been supportive of my situation. For research on the long-term effects of IMRT, see Kiang, A., et al. (2016). Long-term disease-specific and cognitive quality of life after intensity-modulated radiation therapy: A cross-sectional survey of nasopharyngeal carcinoma survivors. *Radiation Oncology*, 11: 127. ro-journal.biomedcentral.com/articles/10.1186/s13014-016-0704-9.

A report on the link between cognitive function and post-cancer reality is Meadows, M. (n.d.). *Cognitive function after cancer and cancer-related treatment, UpToDate,* Wolters Kluwer. Retrieved 11 November 2025 from www.uptodate.com/contents/cognitive-function-after-cancer-and-can cer-treatment.

On reducing treatments because of toxicity, see Haitham, M., & Blanchard, P. (2018). Treatment de-escalation for HPV-driven oropharyngeal cancer: Where do we stand? *Clinical and Translational Radiation Oncology*, 8: 4–11.

CHAPTER 25

For information on IMRT, see: www.mayoclinic.org/tests-procedures/ intensity-modulated-radiation-therapy/about/pac-20385147. Freud wrote about *unheimlichkeit* in his 1919 essay 'The Uncanny': Freud, S. (1919). 'Das Unheimliche'. *Imago, 5*(56): 297–324. See www.freud.org .uk/2019/09/18/the-uncanny/.

CHAPTER 26

For Jonathan Swift's 'The Benefit of Farting' see archive.org/details/ bim_eighteenth-century_the-benefit-of-farting-e_puff-indorst-fart-in-ha_1727. Reference: Swift, J., and Fart in hando Puff-indorst. (1744). *The Benefit of Farting Explain'd: Or the Fundament-all Cause of the Distempers Incident to the Fair-sex: … Wrote in Spanish, by Don Fartinando Puff-indorst, … and Translated into English, … By Obadiah Fizzle, … To Which Are Added, I. The Wonderful Wonder of Wonders:* … R. Thomas. The reference to St. Augustine is from *City of God*, Book xiv, 24, (2003), published by Penguin. Reference: Augustine of Hippo. (2003). *City of God.* Translated by H. Bettenson. London: Penguin.

Like me, Jackie Stacey explored a lot of alternative options during her cancer, as I noted above. But as reported in her book *Teratologies* (1997, cited above), she had some negative experiences which she partly attributes to being a gay woman. She also powerfully discusses the likes of Louise Hay and other self-help gurus who argue that diseases like cancer are a manifestation of negative thinking. She gives them impressive short shrift.

On business mergers and culture: there's a lot of research showing that, while cultural differences are often used as an excuse for why things have gone wrong in international business (including mergers), the problems are often more to do with poor management of the process, a lack of clear goals or due diligence, or stereotypes about 'the other'. But by blaming the failure on 'culture differences', responsibility for the real causes can be ignored. One such piece of research is Långstedt, J. (2018). Culture, an excuse? – A critical analysis of essentialist assumptions in cross-cultural management research and practice. *International Journal of Cross Cultural Management*, 18(3), 293–308. mnacommunity.com/insights/why-mergers-and-acquisitions-often-fail/.

Le Pétomane translates as 'The Fart-Maniac', who was a famed professional flatulist: en.wikipedia.org/wiki/Le_P%C3%A9tomane.

It seems these woodblock images may have had a political message, in that they were created at a time when Japan was coming under increasing pressure to open its borders to Western countries and their influence. The farting may perhaps have represented views towards the outsiders, or possibly towards the Japanese who were supporting such changes, see allthatsinteresting.com/he-gassen.

On the medicinal value of loquat see Liu Y. et al. (2016). Biological Activities of Extracts from Loquat (Eriobotrya japonica Lindl.): A Review. *International Journal of Molecular Sciences*, 17(12):1983. pmc.ncbi.nlm.nih.gov/articles/PMC5187783/.

CHAPTER 27

For the poem by Li Po (also known as Li Bai), see www.poetryfoundation.org/poems/48711/zazen-on-ching-ting-mountain. The quote from the Monty Python film is from *The Meaning of Life* (1983), directed by Terry Jones, Universal Studios. The Angela Carter essay is 'Sugar Daddy', see Carter, A. (1995). 'Sugar Daddy'. *The Granta Book of the Family*. London: Granta Publications. granta.com/sugar-daddy/.

CHAPTER 28

The point about using medical terminology as a 'mechanism of resistance' is from Waskul, D., & van der Riet, P. (2002). The Abject Embodiment of Cancer Patients: Dignity, Selfhood, and the Grotesque Body Author(s): *Symbolic Interaction*, 25(4): 487–513. The full quote, reproduced here, is from p.496:

> When patients adopt the discourse of medicine they may do so not simply because it is the only language they have to describe what is happening to them but also because this way of talking positions the self more distantly and more powerfully over an increasingly abject and out of control body. Their language represents a mechanism of resistance against the implication that the self and the out of control abject body are one and the same.

Clearly, the degree to which cancer patients will feel their body as an abject, out of control entity will depend on the type of cancer, the treatment regime, the individual's personality, and their personal circumstances.

The references to Christopher Hitchens are from *Mortality* (2012), cited above. The quotation is from page 41. The Dylan Thomas poem can be found in Wain, J (ed.). (1980). *The Oxford Anthology of English Poetry: Blake to Heaney.* Oxford: Oxford University Press.

The feelings about suffering from this time bring to mind W. H. Auden's poem 'Musée de Beaux Arts':

> *About suffering they were never wrong,*
> *The old Masters: how well they understood*
> *Its human position: how it takes place*
> *While someone else is eating or opening a window or just walking dully along*

In the final part of the poem, Auden talks about Icarus plunging into the sea, having flown too near the sun, an event hardly noticed by others getting on with their lives. (This poem can be found in Auden, W. H. (1938/2010). 'Musée des Beaux Arts' from E. Mendelson (ed.), *Selected Poems.* London: Faber and Faber.) During the final weeks of treatment, my own mundane reality involved considering whether each subsequent dose of radiation was doing more harm than good. Was I flying too close to the limits of radiotherapy, itself a kind of mad sun? There was no way of knowing. Medical science predicts well for groups, not so well for the individual.

CHAPTER 29

My father and I agreed about very little, but one thing we had in common was a strong dislike of Rupert Brooke's poetry. Our reasons were different, though. As an ex-soldier who'd seen active duty, he detested the blithe glorification of dying for one's country. For me, it is more the way Brooke essentialises national identity – in other words he makes it fixed, inherently different from others, and in his case better. Brooke's most famous poem 'A Soldier' – captures both these aspects:

> *If I should die, think only this of me:*
> *That there's some corner of a foreign field*
> *That is for ever England. There shall be*
> *In that rich earth a richer dust concealed*
> *A dust whom England bore, shaped, made aware,*
> (and so on and so on…)

(Source for the poem is Brooke, R. (2013). *Collected Poems*. Cambridge: Oleander Press.) Had he been an academic, I suspect Brooke would have loved the dominant approach to intercultural communication. Because our national identity is fundamental to who we are (the argument goes), we may travel abroad, but it is always abroad; our essential core remains our national identity. This is because nationality forms the essence, the core, of our selves. We therefore share far more with people from the same country, and with whom we speak the same language, than we do with people from abroad. Yes, we may have other aspects of our identity, like having a profession, but that's always inflected by our nationality. So I'm a *British* linguist first and foremost. Geert Hofstede, the highly influential academic associated with this approach, said that national culture differences are 'a nuisance at best, often a disaster' (www.geert-hofstede.com/). This is because culture (he argues) is at its core national, and national cultures are *inherently* different, to varying degrees. One of Geert Hofstede's most influential works is Hofstede, G. (2001). *Culture's Consequences: Comparing Values, Behaviors, Institutions and Organizations Across Nations*, 2nd edition. Thousand Oaks, CA: Sage Publications.

This is seductive stuff, because it aligns with the stereotypes and banal nationalism we've encountered since birth. And if you browse any books on cross-cultural business, or intercultural communication, you'll find no shortage that rely on this approach. But as my time following the Fukushima earthquake had shown me, our relationship with a place is not necessarily fixed, nor is it determined by being born there. Belonging is a different thing, and we belong to many Discourses. A starkly different war poem, 'The Man He Killed' by Thomas Hardy, where a British soldier reflects on having shot a man for whom, in peacetime, he would have bought a drink in the pub, poignantly captures how contextually dependent our identities are. The poem can be found in Hardy, T. (1975). *Chosen Poems of Thomas Hardy*. London: Macmillan Education Ltd.

On the two times that surround our lives, Nabokov makes a related point in the opening page of his memoir, *Speak, Memory*:

> The cradle rocks above an abyss, and common sense tells us that our existence is but a brief crack of light between two eternities of darkness. Although the two are identical twins, man, as a rule, views the prenatal abyss with more calm than the one he is heading for.

The full reference is Nabokov, V. (2016). *Speak, Memory. An Autobiography Revisited.* London: Penguin Modern Classics, although the first edition was published in 1951.

The Lochlann Jain and Paul Kalanithi references are from the sources cited at the beginning of this section: Jain (2013) and Kalanithi (2016). The Jain quote is from page 220 of *Malignant.*

CHAPTER 30

The Gordon quote is from page 290 of Gordon, D. (1990). Embodying illness, embodying cancer. *Culture, Medicine and Psychiatry,* 14(2):275–297. pubmed.ncbi.nlm.nih.gov/2401153/.

On the different terms around survivorship and the implications for mental health, Park and Zlateva (p.430) say the following:

> Survivor identity appears most common and most associated with active involvement and better psychological well-being, but other identifications are also common and simultaneously held. Adoption of specific cancer

identities is likely to impact interactions with health care providers, including those in general internal medicine, and health behavior changes.

The whole article is worth reading because of the nuanced and sometimes unexpected implications of adopting these different terms.

Park, C., & Zlateva, I. (2009). Self-identity after cancer: 'survivor', 'victim', 'patient', and 'person with cancer'. *Journal of General Internal Medicine*, 2(2): 430–435. doi: 10.1007/s11606-009-0993-x

The Gumperz reference is from Gumperz, J. J. (1996). The linguistic and cultural relativity of conversational inference. In J. J. Gumperz & S. C. Levinson (eds.), *Rethinking Linguistic Relativity*, 374–406. Cambridge: Cambridge University Press.

The quote from Paul McCartney and John Lennon is from the Beatles' song 'Getting Better' from their album *Sgt Pepper's Lonely Heart Clubs Band* (1967).

CHAPTER 31

Since this time, the NHS has adopted IMRT.

The report on the event I presented at is available here: lshubwales .com/blogs/cross-sector-collaboration-unlocking-power-data-and-digi tal-technologies-cancer-care.

The benefits of acupuncture for xerostomia is clinically demonstrated. See Johnstone, P., et al. (2002). Acupuncture for xerostomia: clinical update. *Cancer*, 94(4):1151–1156.

The person responsible for developing this type of treatment is Dr Niemtzow, the father of 'Battlefield Acupuncture': see Moore, M., Complementary and Alternative Medicine: A Profile on Dr Richard C. Niemtzow: www.jba.af.mil/News/Features/Display/Article/460993/ complementary-and-alternative-medicine-a-profile-on-dr-richard-c-niemtzow/.

Julia's experiences brought to mind the distinction between overt and covert racism, and their relationship. What the boy said to Julia was clearly an overt, single instance of a racist act. The school's reaction, I would argue, is an instance of covert or institutional racism, because it was more difficult to pinpoint as racist (allowing much deniability), but in reality it acts to reinforce racism within the school, and is therefore far more serious and damaging than the single slur.

On the links between a personal cancer diagnosis and racism, Ibram X Kendi's *How to Be an Antiracist* (2019), Chapter 18, has some very insightful things to say (full reference above).

CHAPTER 32

The reference to Nietzsche is from: Nietzsche, F. (1974). *The Gay Science*, translated by Walter Kaufmann. New York: Vintage Books.

The T.S. Eliot quote is from Eliot, T. S. (1943). *Four Quartets*. New York: Harcourt.

The Paul Gilbert reference is Gilbert, P. (2010). *The Compassionate Mind*. London: Robinson.

Gilbert's arguments about increasing empathy and compassion have particular relevance for the relationship between anything we perceive as 'other', and how we might reduce such a threat (if we wish to). They explain the cause, and possible solution to, the anxiety around intercultural interactions of any kind that I discuss in this book, for instance with foreigners, healthcare professionals, the self, cancer, and so on.

The reference to *Flat Stanley* is to the series of books written by Jeff Brown and published by Egmont books. *The Hunger Games* reference is to the series of books written by Suzanne Collins, published by Scholastic Ltd.

POSTSCRIPT

These are the cited works in this final chapter:

Epstein, R., & Street, R., (2007). *Patient-Centered Communication in Cancer Care: Promoting Healing and Reducing Suffering*. NIH Publication No. 07-6225. Bethesda, MD: National Cancer Institute.

Handford and Koester (2024) – reference above.

Kahraman-Erkus, O., et al. (2024). 'My body is a cage': A qualitative investigation into the self-discrepancy experiences of young women with metastatic cancer. *Chronic Illness*, 20(1):117–134.

The Haruki Murakami reference is from his story 'Blind Willow, Sleeping Woman' in Murakami, H. (2006). Blind Willow, Sleeping Woman: Twenty-four Stories. Translated by P. Gabriel and J. Rubin. New York City: Alfred A Knopf.

Kleinman, A., and Benson, P. (2006) – cited above.

Koenig (2011) – reference above.

Mishler (1984) – reference above. The quotation is from page 172.

Stacey (1997) reference above.

Steinberg, D. L. (2015). The bad patient: Estranged subjects of the cancer culture. *Body & Society*, 21(3): 115–143. doi.org/10.1177/1357034X15586240.

Stewart, M. (2001). Towards a global definition of patient-centred care: The patient should be the judge of patient-centred care. *BMJ: British Medical Journal*, 322(7284): 444–45. JSTOR: www.jstor.org/stable/25466260.

Svenaeus (2011) – reference above. The quotation is from page 336.

The quote from the workshop mentions self-advocacy, a term I haven't used in this book, but which arguably the book is centrally concerned with. Many cancer charities support their clients in this endeavour towards greater self-empowerment, and this is a useful paper on the topic: Hagan, T. L., & Donovan, H. S. (2013). Self-advocacy and cancer: a concept analysis. *Journal of Advanced Nursing*, 69(10): 2348–2359. doi .org/10.1111/jan.12084.

The full reference for Sophy Roberts' book is Roberts, S. (2020). *The Lost Pianos of Siberia.* New York City: Doubleday. The reference for Oliver Sack's book is Sacks, O. (2022) *The Man who Mistook His Wife for a Hat.* London: Picador.

Index

For EU product safety concerns, contact us at Calle de José Abascal, 56–1°,
28003 Madrid, Spain or eugpsr@cambridge.org.